THE UNKNOWN MAN

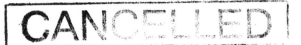
A suspicious death at Somerton Beach

An unknown man on a beach to die.
A rejected admirer or expendable spy?
The mystery potion supplied by another or thee.
'he answers known only to you, or a few, but not me.

Gerald (Gerry) Feltus
2010

First published in Australia in 2010 by
Gerald Michael Feltus
PO Box 112 Greenacres SA 5086
Reprinted 2011, updated 2017

Author: Gerald (Gerry) Michael Feltus

Editing: Bernard (Bernie) O'Neil MA, MPHA
PO Box 2, Klemzig SA 5087

Design: Rhys Sandery
SeeSaw Advertising Pty Ltd
Level 1, 187 Rundle Street, Adelaide SA 5000

Cover: Ashton Stepney and Rhys Sandery

National Library of Australia Cataloguing-in-Publication entry
Feltus, Gerald Michael
The Unknown Man - (A suspicious death at Somerton Park)

ISBN 978-0-646-54476-2

Copies are available online from: www.theunknownman.com
Site menu: Home Page – About the Book – About the Author – Sales –
Contact (E-mail: theauthor@theunknownman.com to contact author, to provide information, make comments or to submit requests for additional details)

Subjects: Case studies – Identification – Death – Causes – Anonymous persons–
Missing persons – Poison – Codes – Somerton Beach – Adelaide – South Australia.

Dewey Number: 614.1

DEDICATION

This book is dedicated to the members of the South Australian, national and international law enforcement agencies, other official organisations, the media and the public who directly or indirectly over time have contributed greatly to the very frustrating investigation into the identity of *The Unknown Man*. Despite their commendable efforts, most of the participants have died without his identity being established.

ACKNOWLEDGMENTS

I thank greatly those people with a genuine interest in *The Unknown Man* who by their many questions encouraged me to write the story. I acknowledge the help of many people and organisations in researching and producing this book, particularly the sources of information and valued assistance of:

ABC-TV archivists who located a copy of 'Inside Story' for me years ago.
Libraries throughout Australia that provided publications with information from newspapers and newspaper cuttings and other similar sources for information that gave a timeframe for relevant events.
The Advertiser and The Sunday Mail in Adelaide for supplying photographs.
Len Brown who provided information on the original police investigation.
The family of Alfred Boxall for information about their father.
Dr Kenneth Brown for producing the dental record.
Dr Ross James for his assessment of the cause of death and assisting with the correct terminology for some complex words.
Bernie O'Neil for his patience and exceptional editing skills in the production of this book.
Rhys Sandery, Melanie Brook and all the friendly staff of SeeSaw Advertising for their designing and the final structuring of the book.
Tony Elliott for many meaningful discussions.
Margaret Williams for proofreading and contributing to the structure of the story.
My daughter, Jacqueline, for structuring the final draft presentation and to her husband Michael for scanning and reproducing material.
My daughter Karin and partner Stephen for online structuring.
My granddaughter, Ashton, for her assistance with the photographs and illustrations.
My wife Lesley, and other grandchildren for their assistance and patience as I pursued '*The Unknown Man*'.

Gerald (Gerry) Feltus APM
October 2010

Link Chart

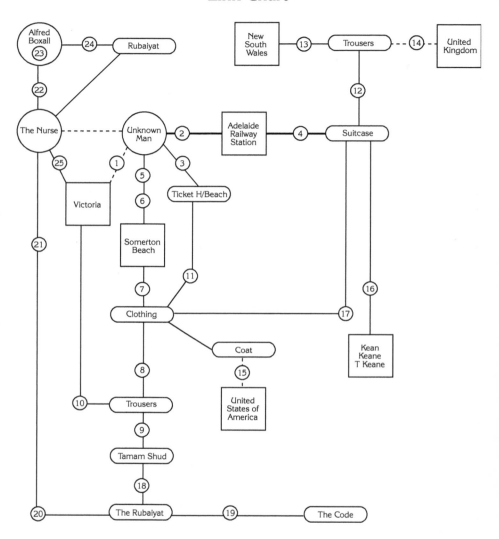

THE UNKNOWN MAN

Legend to chart

1. On Tuesday 30 November 1948, '*The Unknown Man*' presumably arrived per rail from Melbourne, Victoria.
2. '*The Unknown Man*' arrived at the Adelaide Railway Station.
3. A one way train ticket to Henley Beach was purchased.
4. The suitcase and contents were booked into the Railway Station Cloak Room.
5. On the same day a bus ticket to Glenelg was purchased.
6. During the morning of 1 December, 1949, the body of '*The Unknown Man*' was located on the foreshore of Somerton Beach.
7. The clothing worn by the deceased was searched.
8. An examination of the trousers revealed the name of the manufacturer and a specific item.
9. A torn piece of paper with the words 'Tamam Shud' was located in the fob pocket on the interior of the waist band of his trousers. It was rolled in a tight circular shape.
10. Inquiries revealed that the trousers were manufactured in Victoria.
11. The unused train ticket to Henley Beach was located in the clothing.
12. The suitcase was located in the unclaimed section of the Adelaide Railway Station Cloak Room. A similar pair of trousers was located in the suitcase.
13. Inquiries revealed that the trousers were manufactured in Sydney, New South Wales.
14. Laundry or dry cleaning identification marks on a pocket of the trousers were checked throughout Australia without a result. They were suspected of being marks similar to those used in the United Kingdom.
15. A coat the deceased was wearing is believed to have been manufactured in the United States of America because of a particular style of stitching.
16. Other items in the suitcase had the name tags removed except three items that had the names Kean, Keane and T. Keane written on them.
17. A comparison of the clothing worn by the deceased and items in the suitcase identified them to the deceased.
18. The torn piece of paper with the words 'Tamam Shud' was identified to a copy of the Rubaiyat that was found after it has been tossed into a vehicle in Glenelg.
19. Written on the back cover of the Rubaiyat were five lists of letters which were believed to be a 'code'.
20. A telephone number also written on the rear cover of the Rubaiyat was identified to a nurse living at Glenelg.
21. The nurse stated that when she was nursing at the Royal North Shore Hospital in Sydney, she met an Army Lieutenant named Alf Boxall in the Clifton Gardens Hotel.
22. The nurse stated she later gave a copy of the Rubaiyat to Alf Boxall at the hotel.
23. Boxall was interviewed and agreed he had received a Rubaiyat from the nurse.
24. He took police to his home and produced the Rubaiyat that the nurse had inscribed.
25. After moving from Sydney the nursed lived in Melbourne and later moved to Adelaide.

CONTENTS

LIST OF ILLUSTRATIONS, MAPS AND DIAGRAMS

PREFACE

On the last day of Spring 1948 a stranger at the Adelaide Railway Station purchased a train ticket to Henley Beach and booked his suitcase into the Cloak Room. Then after purchasing a bus ticket he arrived at the seaside suburb of Glenelg. In the early evening a man was seen lying against the seawall on the foreshore of nearby Somerton Beach.

On 1 December, the first day of Summer, the body of a well-dressed man was found in the same position that the person had been seen the previous evening. His trousers were manufactured in Victoria. In the fob pocket there was a tightly rolled piece of torn paper bearing the words 'Tamam Shud'. All name tags had been removed from the clothing. His expensive coat had a specific style of stitching that was indicative of it having been manufactured in America. The unused train ticket and the used bus ticket were in his clothes. The Cloak Room receipt was not in his possession, nor was any identification or money.

An autopsy determined that the cause of death was an unidentified poison that had dissipated from his body. The suitcase in the Cloak Room contained items confirming it was the deceased's. The clothing in it had also had the name tags removed, except for three items with Kean, Keane and T Keane written on them in Indian ink. A pair of trousers was manufactured in Sydney but laundry marks on the pocket lining indicated a possible link to the United Kingdom.

It was established that the piece of paper with the words 'Tamam Shud' had been torn from a copy of the Rubaiyat of Omar Khayyam. Publicity surrounding this sensational death eventually caused the actual copy of the Rubaiyat to be found discarded in the back of an unlocked vehicle at Glenelg. A list of five columns of letters written on the back of the book led to claims of this being a 'code'. Also on the book was a telephone number that was traced to a woman living in Glenelg, near where the man's body had been located. The woman had been a nurse in Sydney where she apparently completed four years training before moving to Melbourne and then Adelaide.

When interviewed by the police the nurse said she had given a copy of the Rubaiyat to an Army lieutenant, who she nominated, at the Clifton Gardens Hotel in Sydney, during the Second World War. Inquiries in Sydney located the lieutenant and he produced the copy of the Rubaiyat that had been given to him by the nurse. So, who was the mysterious man who had been linked to the nurse by her telephone number in the back of his Rubaiyat?

His body was preserved in formalin. But, despite efforts nationally and internationally, he was never identified. A cast was made of his bust before he was buried in West Terrace Cemetery, Adelaide. A group of businessmen did not want him to be buried as a pauper so they contributed to a proper burial service and a headstone.

To this day the man has not been identified, the 'code' has not been deciphered and the mysterious circumstances remain unexplained. All that remains is a plaster cast of his bust and a grave with a headstone that identifies him as 'The Unknown Man'.

INTRODUCTION

I was born at Streaky Bay on the West Coast of South Australia in 1943, and grew up in a farming environment about 55 km inland from the coast. I was the second eldest in a family of six boys and one girl.

I can recall blackout curtains over windows during the Second World War, and I remember not comprehending why this was so. How or why a Japanese aircraft would pick out and bomb a dimly lit kerosene lamp shining through the window of a lonely farmhouse in the scrub defied the reasoning of a child. Large formations of Australian aircraft were often observed flying west, and vice versa. Newspapers were rarely seen in our area. If you were lucky, on a clear night a 6 volt battery 'wireless' with a connection to an earth wire and a very long aerial would sometimes produce a crackling broadcast of happenings in the world.

I recall my mother frantically shouting at us to chase animals away from the Oleander bushes should they venture too close. She always said that Oleanders were very poisonous and the animals would die if they ate them.

The rationing of almost everything during the war was maintained after that conflict ended: many items were in very limited supply or were sometimes unprocurable. 'Whitewash' was mixed in large quantities and the house was painted a vivid white. A great number of displaced persons and other migrants arrived in Australia after the war. Some of the men from the Baltic countries (referred to as 'Balts') were working on neighbouring farms. These men commonly walked many miles through rough scrub to attend 7.30 a.m. Sunday church service at the Chandada Hall. On cold, wet and windy days local families would often convey them home to their places of employment.

While *The Unknown Man* was contemplating his journey to South Australia, I was observing acts of nature that would cause me to distinctly remember 1948. There was a very severe drought with no cereal crops of note on the farm, not a blade of grass anywhere, and most of the animals slowly dying of starvation. I was with my father as he drove around the 8000 acre (3240 ha) farm, through the masses of bush, trying to locate and assist the starving stock.

I have vivid memories of being with him on one occasion when we came upon a nice black cow, lying on her side with every bone showing through her skin. He tried for some considerable time to roll her upright, and eventually placed a dish with a small amount of oats near her mouth. She was obviously too far gone and could not lift her head without assistance. I watched as she rolled onto her side. I saw my father walk to the old Rugby Buckboard and return with his .22 rifle. He loaded the rifle and shot her in the head. I was horrified, not because he had shot her but because the cow belonged to Auntie Isobel. I did not think you were allowed to shoot other people's cows! I could walk through those thousands of acres of dense scrub today and find the exact spot where the cow died.

I received my initial schooling at Chandada Primary School which was about 8 km in a direct line from the farmhouse, through some open ground, mallee scrub and neighbouring paddocks. The single schoolroom under the control of one teacher contained about 30 children from Grade I to Grade VII. I completed Grade VII at the age of 12 years. The nearest high schools were at Streaky Bay and Port Lincoln, which meant my parents would have to find somewhere for me to board there. Instead they decided that along with my older brother and other boys from the district I would attend Sacred Heart College at Somerton Park as a boarder. I attended this Catholic college in 1956.

The expense for the family meant that, unfortunately, I finished my schooling at the age of 13. In that year the first of the atomic tests at Maralinga, in the western desert region of

South Australia, commenced.

One of the strict requirements of the college was that each boarder had to have his name clearly marked in Indian ink on every item of clothing. Each week dirty clothes had to be handed to the laundry, and specific items of the uniform went to another section for dry cleaning. If a name could not be marked directly on an item, mothers would make a name tag and sew it on.

Boarding was quite an adventure for this young lad. So too was travelling between the college and home during school holidays. Sometimes at the end of a school term the group of West Coast country boys would catch the double-decker bus to the Adelaide Railway Station, where we secured our suitcases in the Cloak Room. Later that evening we would catch the train to Outer Harbour where we would board the MV Minnipa and sail overnight to Port Lincoln.

Arriving just after daybreak we would wander around the streets of Port Lincoln, calling on friends or relatives to pass the time. Then late in the afternoon we would board a train, and arrive in the early hours of the following morning at Poochera Railway Station, where our parents would be waiting. The process was reversed when we returned to school. Most return trips were made by the Birdseye Bus Service.

During the warmer months a daily ritual after school was for the boarders to walk the short distance along Whyte Street to Somerton Beach where Sacred Heart College had a change room. There you would don your bathers, have a swim, shower off the salty water and walk back to the boarding house. On Sundays during the winter months the boarders would be organised into a walking group, and we would all walk to that change room from where we would sometimes walk along the beach south to Brighton or north to Glenelg.

On the very first walk we went towards Glenelg. A short distance along the beach, the group stopped near a set of steps that connected the Esplanade to the sandy foreshore. An older boarder then told us the story of how many years before the body of a murdered man was found there, and that it was quite a mystery because no-one knew who he was. Thereafter, whenever we walked that route, we stopped there and asked many questions, but not many answers were forthcoming.

Almost a decade later, in 1964, I joined the South Australian Police Force. I then read the many feature articles that appeared periodically in the local newspapers about *The Unknown Man*. Often as part of my uniform police duties, I was allocated the dreaded Patrol 6. In addition to normal patrol duties, Patrol 6 had the specific task, during the hours when the City Morgue was unattended, of collecting its keys, meeting the ambulance delivering a body there, placing the corpse in the refrigeration unit and attending to the documentation. Not an altogether pleasant task at any time, the worst time for this duty was on night shift because a corpse always seemed to arrive just before the allocated meal break.

Early in my career I met the then retired Lionel Leane and some people who had been attached to Coronial Investigations. After joining the Criminal Investigation Branch (CIB) I met Len Brown, Errol Canney, Charlie Hopkins, Kevin Moran and Ron Thomas. Brown was the Officer-in-Charge when I was attached to the Breaking Squad.

Late in 1975 the South Australian Police went through a period of de-centralisation with structural changes that impacted on the CIB. The Homicide, Motor and Breaking Squads were all disbanded and some of their members were transferred to the Major Crime Squad (MCS). This new squad comprised three teams of nine investigators. Detective Sergeant Ron Thomas and I were attached to the same team.

Along with the selected personnel, a number of old and current unsolved homicide files were transferred to the squad. The Somerton Beach file on *The Unknown Man* was one of these. Although the incident was never classified as a murder, the case was monitored, particularly because feature articles continually appearing in the media generated responses from the public that needed attention and action. Ron Thomas was a very capable and respected investigator who had worked for many years in the Homicide Squad. He, along with Kevin Moran, had been involved previously in this case and so it was logical that he inherited it in the MCS. I thought highly of Ron and it was interesting to observe him turning a deaf ear to the friendly ribbing he received from others about wasting time on an old file that no-one really cared about. Whenever time permitted he devoted special attention to the file, and I was privy to interesting discussions on the subject with him.

I transferred out of the MCS in May 1979 and Ron eventually retired from the Police Force. Interest in the Somerton Beach file also stopped, and it began to gather dust among other old files. In October 1992, after postings within various sections of the CIB, I returned to the MCS (now named the Major Crime Task Force) as a Senior Sergeant in charge of an investigative team. Around the turn of the century we compiled a list of all the old homicide files, and they were allocated to various team members to maintain a watching brief. One of the listed files I inherited was the Somerton Beach file.

Despite numerous searches, however, the file itself could not be located. Then in about 2002 a small portion of the file was found. The absence of the file was probably caused by the many changes of offices and buildings over the years. A few more documents were later located in boxes in storage areas. Due to a heavy workload and other priorities I could not justify giving much attention to the case. The files did not contain any information of a concrete nature. With my interest piqued I decided to devote some of my spare time to creating a file that showed some semblance of order.

A number of conspiracy theorists often raise questions based on the extent or lack of material contained within the old Somerton Beach file. It is impossible for me to define what a 1948 police investigation file might contain. The folders I eventually located were in no semblance of order and contained dozens of letters from members of the public relating to missing persons, some copies of interstate investigations, old newspaper cuttings (some with no source or date) and several miscellaneous documents. During my follow up inquiries I was able to obtain a copy of the coronial investigation, some duplicated copies of statements, duplicated newspaper cuttings (also with source and date missing) and other miscellaneous documents. My sources included retired police officers and other interested parties. I have been unable to locate or obtain any record of several exhibits known to have existed. I have not been able to locate notes relevant to the autopsy or the current status of specimens that were taken. In sections of this book I have made specific reference to particular exhibits and culling procedures. From my observation the Somerton Beach file is comparable to, if not better than, other old files from the same era, I do not support the theory that material has been deliberately removed from the file for any perfidious purpose.

'Spare time', what's that? Weeks spent researching in libraries throughout the country, locating and speaking with retired police officers and attempting to obtain information from other relevant departments. The more information I obtained, the more the mystery of the event deepened. Unanswered questions led to further unanswered questions, as did even the answered questions. Where does one stop? I had outlaid large sums of money on interstate travel, accommodation and purchasing documents. This did not take into account the hundreds of hours devoted to researching subjects and locating and speaking with people who could assist me. As I neared retirement age, I was in no way satisfied with what I had achieved in this matter. I retired from the Police Force in November 2004, firmly believing that this would provide the ideal opportunity to complete my project.

How wrong I was! After some work projects for interstate government agencies, each of about 6 months' duration, in 2005–09, my attention to the project was falling well behind. I was also being hampered by dozens of people who have maintained or developed a genuine interest in the mystery, and others who had journalistic interests, making contact with me about the subject. I answered hundreds of questions from people on various matters, many of them repetitiously covering the same subjects. I could not believe there were so many people interested in train times, the structure of a pasty, Kensitas cigarettes, the clothing worn by the deceased on a hot day; and what eventually happened to some of the people nominated in the media as missing persons. I have had lengthy discussions with people who have raised logical reasoning and others who firmly believe their own analysis. At no time have I attempted to dissuade people from their own opinions.

Some people have demanded to know, and believed they have a right to know, the identity of the nurse in the story. They could not accept that it is a sensitive subject and if that information was revealed it could have a serious impact on family members. During my conversation with the nurse she told me she had not discussed with her family that she was in fact implicated in the initial investigation into the death of *The Unknown Man*. Although I was fully aware of the identities and whereabouts of her family, I respected her wishes and I did not approach them. Since her death I have made personal contact with the family and a very friendly discussion ensued resulting in a wealth of information being exchanged. Expressions of dismay were voiced by the family at recent serious and unfounded allegations. Therefore, to protect their children and grandchildren they wish to remain anonymous. They are happy with the details I have included in this book and with my approach to the subject. Thus, the nurse will remain Teresa Johnson.

Contained within the old Somerton Beach file are a large number of personal letters from people who believed that *The Unknown Man* may have been related or known to them. I have used the details from a mere selection of these letters to show the extent of the response generated by the continuous publicity on the subject. If the names and details were revealed in the media or other public sources they have been included in this book. If not, the names and some sensitive material have been excluded.

I have obligingly answered all queries to letters, emails and telephone calls to the best of my ability. I have gone out of my way to assist people, correct their information and sometimes point them in the right direction. I only once had to terminate a telephone conversation with a gentleman interstate who contacted me under the guise that he was an expert in the field of codes, and believed he had solved it. I answered dozens of his unrelated questions and eventually asked him if he was going to share his findings. He said he would not, and demanded that I write down everything I knew about the matters and send it to him. I advised him that I did not think he was who he purported to be. I doubted his reasons for contacting me, because of the specific questions he was asking. I believe he was in some way associated with the media.

Apart from a few callers who were either very rude or completely lacking in people skills, most people had a genuine interest in the subject and I found it a pleasure discussing matters with them. I also received inquiries from people compiling family histories who were attempting to find missing links. When the description of *The Unknown Man* was relayed to them they quickly removed him from their chain.

Although the time-consuming discussions often put my own effort on the 'back burner', I realised there was a need to compile a record of the facts known to me to assist the large number of people interested in the subject. I have developed my own opinions on the issues and events but I have deliberately limited my specific views. It is sometimes better for readers interested in the subject to develop their own opinions and not be influenced by others.

It would have been far easier for me to write a flowery mystery novel encompassing the known details, the war years, and themes of spies and lost loves, but I chose not to do so. I have structured the information in a factual way to present *The Unknown Man* mystery to readers wanting answers or to those wanting to conjure up their own stories. Some time ago I decided that this story must have a cut-off point otherwise there would be a need to update the information continually. So I end the story with 'A Final Twist' in December 1959. But the appendices provide additional information and updates on various subjects to assist the inquisitive reader.

I make no claim to be an expert in any field except those areas of expertise gained through my own experiences. In some respects you have to place yourself in the shoes of *The Unknown Man* to comprehend factors during the period. Having been born prior to 1948 certainly helped me to understand and appreciate the environment and conditions of those times.

Tamam Shud, you will soon realise, means 'the end'. As this mystery will have no end, I search for a Persian word or term that means ad infinitum.

Meanwhile, form your own opinions!

AUTHOR'S NOTE

Shortly after joining the Criminal Investigation Branch of the South Australian Police Department I had the privilege to work with Senior Detective Tom Ferguson. I took note of a number of things he mentioned that should always be applied in police duties, and he particularly impressed up me to; "Never make a promise you cannot keep, and never betray a confidence." I am fully aware of the legal exceptions and the political implications associated with these rules. Without giving complicated examples it should not be hard to comprehend the reasons why certain promises must be kept and the confidentiality of witnesses and information must be protected.

In about 2002 I inherited a 'cold case' relating to the death of a male person found on the foreshore of Somerton Beach on the first of December, 1948. During the course of my investigations into the circumstances of this matter, I identified a female person, who as a result of my on-going inquiries, and my conversations with her was obviously a major witness. She had been identified as a nurse by occupation in numerous media articles, but her identity was never revealed in any police reports, media reports or the eventual Coroners' investigation.

Because the man was never identified and the circumstances surrounding his death were very mysterious, the story captured the attention of people throughout Australia and other parts of the world. Media promoted the story on a yearly basis continuously produced further input into the investigation and increased public interest in the mystery. In one media release I did make a casual statement that I may write a book on the subject when I retired.

Sometime after I retired I received a large number of communications from people who requested that I write a book on the subject. I then commenced to write a transcript on the subject of my involvement in the investigation containing information that I was at liberty to produce.

I was advised by the nurse that she had married and her children, other family and friends were not aware of her association in the matter being investigated. Taking into consideration the rules I have mentioned in paragraph one, as a police officer I could not reveal her identity or supply any information that would possibly assist in revealing her identity in my book. I never mentioned her correct name or that of her husband, family members, any address, telephone number or other relevant information. I was aware that during my investigations I had left a trail to the Royal North Shore Hospital in Sydney, and if someone followed that trail to a specific file the identity of the nurse would be revealed. I know that Derek Abbot followed that trail.

I self-published my book titled 'The Unknown Man' in the latter part of 2010, and released it to cater for what I expected to be a niche market. In the book I referred to the nurse as Teresa and Tessie Powell, her husband as Prestige Johnson, and their son I named Leslie. In 2007 Derek Abbot placed the death notice of the nurse, containing the identities of all her immediate family on his web site. Family became aware of the post and when angry members made contact with Abbot he quickly removed the notice. Unfortunately the damage had been done and the information was noted by large numbers of people who had an interest in the subject. From that time the family identities appeared in numerous web sites. It was soon apparent that if a new web site was created, it was open slather for known web surfers to gain access and competitively be the first to provide personal details relevant to the family.

Many readers commented it was obvious that my profession restricted me from providing the considerable information I possessed, when some members of the public could contribute specific information that was bordering on libel. I do agree that I may have erred on the side of caution in respect to a number of subjects.

Because the specific family details have appeared on numerous web sites and most forms of the media, I am now satisfied I am at liberty to provide their correct details.

The nurse was Jessie (later Jessica) Ellen Harkness, born in Marrickville, New South Wales, on 18 February 1921. Her husband was Prosper McTaggard Thomson, born in Charters Towers, Queensland, on 26 October 1912. They had a son Robin McMahon Thomson, born in Adelaide, on 11 July 1947, and a daughter Katherine Helena Thomson, born in Adelaide, on 7 September 1950.

I am not at liberty to identify the gentleman who located the copy of the Rubaiyat that was linked to The Unknown Man, in his motor vehicle.

FOREWORD

Two people have described my shoes. One said, 'They are practically new, and very clean. They looked as though they had been polished that morning or later'. The other said, 'They looked as though they had just been polished'. I cared for my shoes.

I have been described as a man who was aged in his 40s. If this is correct I was born early in the 20th century as I died late in 1948. To comprehend the complexities surrounding my unusual death, I must take you for a walk in my shoes through a sequence that requires me to include certain facts and events. Within my story I will identify some of the players and provide you with the known parts they played. There are many pieces of the puzzle that I cannot tell you now, although I believe at the time of my death there was sufficient information to complete the jigsaw.

World turmoil and conflict in the 1940s combined with the mysterious circumstances surrounding my death brought 'spy' and 'affair of the heart' theories to the fore. So there was little wonder that numerous 'arm chair detectives' and would be novelists became interested in me: their deductions could easily rival the scripts from *The spy who came in from the cold* or *Message in a bottle*.

Some say I died by my own hand and others say I was murdered. That is for you to decide.

To appreciate the many events that took place during my lifetime, you can take a walk in my shoes – as *The unknown man* briefly outlines some of those happenings.

I was a real person – a son, a brother?, a husband?, an admirer?, a loner?, a migrant?, an employee? Unfortunately all attempts to give me back my name have failed. It is now many years since my diabolical death, and my only wish is to be identified and then to rest in peace. Help me if you can!

The Unknown Man

CHAPTER 1

EVENTS 1904–48

T he following sequence of events is selected to provide an understanding of the environment that prevailed during the life of *The Unknown Man*. The sequence will also capture events that encompass the activities of individuals who figured in his life.

The Russians are coming

In 1904 there were concerns in Australia that Britain would become involved in the escalating conflict between Russia and Japan. Japan blamed the intentions of Russia in Manchuria and Korea for the conflict. Russia's Baltic fleet set sail for their Manchurian base at Vladivostok. As a result Japan eventually declared war on Russia.

Australian volunteers and nurses offered their services to Japan in the conflict with Russia but Japan did not accept the offers.

To defend itself against a possible invasion from Russia in the 19th century fortifications had been built along the Australian coastline. Two of these were Fort Largs and Fort Glanville in seaside suburbs of Adelaide. With their mounted heavy guns pointing out to sea, and kilometres of linking tunnels and bunkers they were ready to repel any Russian ship should one venture into our sovereign waters. The fortifications were never needed.

In what has been described as one the greatest naval battles of all time Japanese warships destroyed Russia's Baltic fleet in 1905. Of the 38 ships in the fleet all but three were sunk, disabled or captured. The Japanese Army defeated the Russian Army based in Manchuria and the Asian intentions of Russia could not be realised.

American President Theodore Roosevelt helped to mediate a peace treaty which was signed by Russia and Japan on 5 September 1905. Under the terms of the agreement Russia evacuated all troops from Manchuria and recognised the exclusive rights of Japan in Korea, and they guaranteed not to intervene there.

The Russians are not coming

So the Russians were not coming, but for years to come, new and old world leaders continued to play the simple old daisy flower game to form alliances. As each leader plucked a single daisy petal and let it fall he knew who he was referring to as he recited, 'He loves me, he loves me not. He loves me, he loves me not'.

Australians at war

Australians have participated in conflicts in countries far from home, including the Sudanese and Boer Wars and the Boxer Rebellion. In the First World War many Australian soldiers died and their remains lie in the fields of many countries. Australians were heavily committed in Europe, Gallipoli and major actions throughout the Middle East.

In that era Australians were very isolated and in most cases the only form of entertainment was provided within their own social groups. People learnt to play musical instruments, and dances and concerts were arranged whenever possible. If you could carry a tune singing was a popular pastime but, if not, recitals were just as popular. Poetry appealed to many people, and poems were read, learnt and shared.

A book of poems – The Rubaiyat

It was probably as a result of their involvement in the Middle East that Australian soldiers were introduced to the book of verse known as The Rubaiyat of Omar Kayyam. Omar Kayyam was a Persian poet, among other things, who was born in 1048 at Naishapur, in the northeast of modern-day Iran. The Rubaiyat was translated into English by Edward Fitzgerald: his first pamphlet version became available in the late 1850s. His translations eventually became one of the reading public's most popular books. Returning soldiers introduced this book to Australia, and it may have been one of the most widely read and discussed books of that time.

War with Nazi Germany
In the evening of Sunday 3 September 1939 the Prime Minister of Australia, Robert Menzies, announced to the nation, 'It is my melancholy duty to inform you officially that, in consequence of a persistence by Germany in her invasion of Poland, Great Britain has declared war upon her, and that, as a result Australia is also at war'.

In a very short space of time there was national security legislation, the press was censored, enemy aliens were interned and the militia called for volunteers. Conscription was introduced and in an ironic twist the most popular song was 'Over the Rainbow'.

The year 1940 brought doom and gloom: on Thursday 18 July all men aged 20 to 24 in the year ending 30 June 1941 were called up for military service.

Diplomatic relations with Japan
The first diplomatic relations between Australia and Japan were established and the appointment resulted in the Prime Minister saying, 'This step will do much to cement and extend the cordial relations that have so long existed between Australia and Japan. The appointment will be widely welcomed, both in Australia and Japan'.

The war with Germany and Italy
Australian personnel attached to the Army, Air Force and Navy were fully engaged in the war in Europe and North Africa and as a result a large number of German and Italian prisoners of war were transported to internment camps in Australia.

On Saturday 14 December 1940 a new militia call-up was announced that widowers with no children and all unmarried men between the ages of 19 and 33 years by 30 June 1940 were required to enlist in January 1941.

Although early 1941 saw a swift and telling victory over the Italian Army in North Africa it was not long before the German Army was pushing the allies out of Greece. General Rommel now moved into North Africa and Crete was evacuated by the Allies. Things were not looking all that good on the war front, and the situation was not helped by the confirmation that the HMAS Sydney had been sunk off the coast of Western Australia by the German raider Kormoran, which had been posing as a Dutch freighter. The Sydney's complement of 645 personnel all perished. Also, the HMAS Waterhen and HMAS Parramatta were both sunk in the Mediterranean.

Japanese aggression in Asia
Japan was still taking aggressive action in Asia. Meanwhile, Sydney Harbour became a hive of activity when the US Pacific Fleet of six warships arrived on a goodwill visit. The world's largest passenger ship, the Queen Elizabeth, and many other troop carriers arrived, and conveyed Australian troops to the Middle East, Malaya and Singapore.

War with Japan
Then came the dreaded 'Toro, Toro, Toro', and on 7 December 1941, Japanese bombers caused havoc to the US Pacific Fleet at Pearl Harbour, with the result that the USA entered the war. Australia was also in peril and the intentions of Japan were obvious. Nazi Germany, being allied with Japan, also declared war on the USA. England and some of its imperial members had no alternative but to declare war on Japan.

The Johnson family

At this point I mention the Johnson family. The father was born in England and had family connections to Liverpool and Glasgow, Scotland. He moved to Australia where his family were born and raised in the mining and cattle country of Central Queensland. The Johnsons later moved to Sydney and obtained employment there. In the middle of 1936 Prestige, the second son, who was living at Blacktown, a suburb of Sydney, moved to Melbourne where he married and lived in Mentone.

On 29 December 1941, Prestige, then aged 29 and still living at Mentone, enlisted in the Australian Army. In taking this action he joined two other brothers who had previously enlisted in the Armed Forces in Sydney.

Alfred Boxall

For some considerable time Alfred Boxall had been troubled by what was happening throughout the world. With the war raging in Europe and now Pearl Harbour, things were not good. He was 35 years of age, married with one child and living with his family in the comfortable Sydney seaside suburb of Maroubra, not far from the ocean. He loved the sea; in fact, he was almost surrounded by it. A short distance to the south was Botany Bay and to the north was Port Jackson. In from the ocean, through the narrow turbulent heads, was the famous Sydney Harbour.

Sydney was a bustling city, with a fantastic harbour. He enjoyed his work as a motor mechanic at Randwick. It was only a short distance from home and after work and on the weekends he could visit beautiful beaches. He always looked forward to having a beer and a chat with mates but in recent years the talk always came back to the war. Many mates were now fighting overseas: it seemed that everyone had friends and relatives involved. Many reports were coming back about tragedies and losses and the feeling with each passing day was that things would get worse before they got better.

Although it was not often mentioned, a feeling of guilt was always at the back of many minds. All those mates fighting overseas, and here were able-bodied men enjoying themselves. Alfred was no exception. Sure he was exempted and, yes, he could volunteer, but he had obligations and the decisions were weighing heavily on his mind. He was also aware that Sydney's General Post Office Clock was being dismantled and placed in storage in anticipation of air raids.

Alfred was no stranger to war. He had been born in London in 1906 and so had lived through the First World War. He had had first-hand experiences of war and he knew the impact it had on people's lives. People known to his family and friends had been killed in the war, and the impact on survivors could only be imagined by those not involved.

From England he had migrated to Australia with his family. Many relatives and friends were left behind, some never to be seen again as Australia was on the other side of the world.

Australia was good to him. He acquired a wife and family, a home, a good job and many friends. He was looking forward to a comfortable future. He was a proud Australian but like most migrants his place of birth was still home.

With England again engaged in a terrible war, he realised that Australia was the target of a frightening foe sweeping down through Asia.

Alfred Boxall enlists

In early 1942 the Japanese were literally sweeping through South East Asia. They were on Australia's back door when they bombed towns in Papua New Guinea. Despite Alfred's previous discussions about joining the Australian Army, the current climate made the decision for him.

With the blessings of his family and friends Alfred arrived at Paddington in the morning of 12 January 1942 to enlist in the Australian Military Forces. Alfred, who was 5'7" (170 cm) tall with grey eyes, dark brown hair, a dark complexion and scattered linear scars over the outer surface of his left arm, was marched to the General Details Depot. He was taken 'on strength' and sent for training near the New South Wales town of Cowra.

Japan attacks Australia

Singapore fell to the Japanese in 1942 and 15 000 Australian troops were made prisoners of war. Australian soil was no longer safe and in February 1942, Japanese planes operating from aircraft carriers in the Timor Sea bombed Darwin. Eight ships were sunk and about 240 people were killed. This was the first of many bombing raids on Darwin. It has been said that more Japanese aircraft were used in the initial raid on Darwin than in the bombing of Pearl Harbour.

The Philippines had also been captured, causing General Douglas MacArthur, Supreme Commander of the Allied Forces in the South-West Pacific, to establish his campaign headquarters in Australia.

Boxall attached to the North Australia Observation Unit

Alfred was an astute, mature and very capable tradesman. He commanded the respect of other trainees and his potential was noticed. On 23 June 1942 he was transferred to the North Australia Observation Unit (NAOU). Australia was now in dire straits. The Japanese were in Timor, and after landing on the Papuan coast they had advanced along the Kokoda Trail towards Port Moresby.

In 1942 three Japanese midget submarines entered Sydney Harbour and sank a ferry boat and some naval personnel had been killed. Apparently their target was the American cruiser Chicago. A week later a Japanese submarine surfaced off Bondi and shelled the eastern suburbs of Sydney. On the same night another submarine surfaced further north and shelled Newcastle.

Alfred was posted to the Northern Territory where, apart from normal intelligence duties on the mainland, he was required to carry out special operations under the direct orders of GOC Warforce. His duties included small craft operations in the Timor Sea and servicing observation outposts on the northern coastline. These operations were carried out by Captain David Herbert, his brother Sergeant Xavier Herbert (the author of the novels Poor Fellow My Country and Capricornia) and Alfred. Captain Herbert was attached to the Australian Water Transport Company and his brother was attached to the NAOU. Both brothers were born in Western Australia and had enlisted in Sydney.

In June 1943 Alfred was transferred to the Australian Water Transport Company but remained with the NAOU until September. He returned to Sydney knowing the serious situation in the north. He was very pleased to be reunited with his family and friends.

A large number of ships had been lost and a Japanese reconnaissance aircraft had even flown over Sydney. This brought back the many vivid memories Alfred had from his posting along the northern coast where he had seen Japanese aircraft flying overhead, and had witnessed the impact of their bombing and strafing runs.

Apart from the bombings of Darwin and nine towns in Western Australia, the Northern Territory and Queensland were targets of the Japanese. It was also during this period that the Australian hospital ship Centaur was sunk by a Japanese submarine off the Queensland coast, resulting in the loss 268 lives. These events made Alfred realise that no part of Australia was immune to their reach. Indeed, it appeared that the Japanese were poised to invade Australia.

Australian women were now being conscripted.

The nurse – Teresa Powell

Teresa Powell, who was to play a major part in the mysterious events that surrounded *The Unknown Man*, was living in Sydney. Tess, Tessie or Tina (as she sometimes preferred to be called) was a trainee nurse at the Royal North Shore Hospital at Gove Hill in the suburb of St Leonards. Born at Marrickville in early 1921, she was the third child in the Powell family. Her father had been born in England but had moved to Australia where he met and married his Sydney wife in Fremantle, Western Australia. They lived in what Tessie would describe as a large house in Sydney. Members of her family had also enlisted in the Armed Forces.

Tessie commenced her nursing career at the Royal North Shore Hospital in 1942. She lived in a nearby suburb a short distance from the Clifton Gardens Hotel. The hospital did not receive war casualties but it was prepared for civilian casualties. Many staff served in the Middle East, the evacuation of Greece, Tobruk and France, where one staff member lost her life. Many were recalled when Japan entered the war. They were sent to New Guinea, where they cared for the wounded on the Kokoda Trail. There was an element of great sadness when one staff member was posted as missing and never found, while being evacuated from Malaysia. Another unfortunate nurse was captured and taken prisoner by the Japanese in Rabual. With other nurses she suffered deprivation, hunger, illness and humiliation for 3 years until she was rescued.

The tide begins to turn

The Australian 9th Division returned home after success in the North Africa campaign and approximately 178 000 American servicemen were now based in Australia. Successful sea battles were beginning to hamper the supply to Japanese forces in Asia and the Pacific and the tide appeared to be turning in the battle for Papua New Guinea.

Prestige Johnson discharged from the Army

In September 1943 Prestige Johnson was discharged from the Army, after a lengthy sickness.

Boxall promoted to lieutenant

In December 1943 the experience of Alfred was recognised and he was promoted to lieutenant. He was immediately seconded as an instructor in the Water Transport Wing. He enjoyed this role and his qualifications allowed him to also pass on to others the knowledge he had gained from his firsthand experiences. He was also fortunate because his posting allowed him to be near his family when his daughter Lesley was born in June 1944.

Notable events – 1944

1944 was notable for the bushfires that ravaged the country for months: at least 60 people were killed and there were very large losses of stock and property.

On behalf of the Allies the South Australian Government carried out an extensive search for uranium, one of the major components of the atomic bomb. Some minor deposits of low-grade uranium were mined at Mount Painter in the Flinders Ranges in remote South Australia. Apart from deposits in Canada, Czechoslovakia and the Belgian Congo, this was then the only known source of uranium in the world.

Japanese forces were suffering serious setbacks to the north of the country and it appeared that their momentum was being contained. In Europe the massive landing of Allied forces on the beaches of Normandy in France in June would be remembered as D-Day.

A diversion was created when the husband of the 'Pyjama Girl' was sentenced for her murder. His conviction brought to an end one of the great murder mysteries in Australian history. For 10 years her body had lain unidentified in a formalin bath in Sydney. She was simply known as the 'Pyjama Girl' after her body dressed in embroidered pyjamas had been found stuffed into a concrete drain at Albury on the New South Wales–Victoria border. She had suffered a shotgun wound to the head and her battered and bruised body had been set alight. Thousands of people viewed the body and many people claimed to know her identity. The continuing investigation led to the discovery of hundreds of missing women. One case went to court in an attempt to prove that the body was that of a woman named Anna Morgan. Police eventually presented the body in a different manner. After building up the face, dressing the hair and applying makeup, the body was quickly identified as Linda Agostini. The evidence of identification came from a dentist who suggested she was Englishwoman Linda Platt, who had come to Australia in 1927.

In this year Oswald Avery and his colleagues in New York solved a great biological puzzle. They discovered that genes, those hereditary units which determine the characteristics of all living things, are made from deoxyribonucleic acid or DNA for short. The mystery of the nature of the genetic material had been solved but it would be many years before hereditary instructions in DNA were encoded to determine how it was passed from parent to offspring.

Drinks at the Clifton Gardens Hotel

Alfred Boxall was enjoying a drink with a couple of mates when he first heard about the Cowra breakout. He listened with interest because Cowra was where he had done his training, and he was familiar with the area and the 50-acre (20 ha) prisoner-of-war camp. More than 1000 Japanese prisoners of war had attempted to escape. Sentries fired on the group as they broke through the wire and 353 prisoners were killed. Four Australian guards had been killed and many others wounded. Of the 378 Japanese who made good their escape, 25 died in the ensuing search and the others were all captured and returned to the camp. As the drinking group took in the news they were saddened by the death of the guards but there was no sympathy for the large number of Japanese prisoners who were killed or injured. At this time many stories were filtering through of terrible atrocities being committed on Australian prisoners-of-war in Burma and other places.

During this time Alfred was based at the Army complex on the northern shore of Sydney Harbour. The Clifton Gardens Hotel was nearby and it was not uncommon to have a drink with mates and discuss current events, and how the war was progressing. It was not a hive of activity but many servicemen patronised the hotel because it was within walking distance, and a comfortable location to enjoy a drink with good company. The staff were pleasant, and an added advantage was that by knowing them on a personal basis you could sometimes stay on after the 6 o'clock closing time and finish your drink, or sneak in another quick one.

Although the law said hotels could not sell liquor after 6 p.m. it would be a brave publican not to show a little flexibility to all those servicemen. No-one wanted to start a riot and the police were inclined to turn a blind eye. Providing there was no trouble, everyone was happy. Most of the patrons had heard the story about the disturbance in Brisbane where at least six servicemen and a number of civilians were shot, one fatally.

During the war most items were rationed but you could obtain a beer if it was available and if you could afford it. Alfred was a reasonably frugal person but he did enjoy a drink and he sometimes met new people, including service personnel and sometimes nurses from a nearby hospital. Someone always knew someone who was either a patient at the nearby hospital or knew some of the staff.

The Clifton Gardens Hotel was like one big happy family and provided an opportunity to forget for a short time the depressing side of life. Alfred enjoyed the privilege of being so well known at the hotel that he could knock on the back door after closing time, and he and his mates would be supplied with a few quick drinks. Other people also had this privilege. Some abused it, but the majority did the 'right thing'. If Alfred was asked to describe these occasions he would no doubt say, 'You would sneak down the stony stairs, around the little bay and into the pub. You might have a couple of 'snorts' [drinks] and so forth, and away'.

The Allies' island-hopping campaign against the Japanese was successful in reclaiming conquered territory, and General MacArthur fulfilled his promise of 'I will return' when he eventually stepped ashore in the Philippines. Alfred also wanted to return, to the sea that is. He had had enough of his current posting as an instructor, and he wanted to be where the action was, and he knew this action was in the seas north of Australia. His commanding officer knew his views. They had discussed it often. The answer was always the same, 'Yes, but not right now. We need you to train these inexperienced personnel. Be patient Alfred, you will be transferred back to active service soon.' But Alfred needed to be wanted and he needed to be in active service at the end.

Alfred was patient. Hell, he was experienced, he was capable and he knew the area where it was all happening. Sure, he could tell people he had been involved in active service but the intimate details he could never discuss. Some of his mates knew some of the details, but to discuss even general army matters with strangers in particular was not the accepted thing. Some of his mates may have mentioned matters to strangers, but Alfred would never be drawn into the conversation when it related to intelligence. It was hard at

times, and it was sometimes obvious in conversations that someone may have said something out of place. There is an aura of mystery and intrigue about the subject of intelligence, and Alfred often found it difficult to gauge whether or not people were seeking restricted information or just contributing to a friendly and general conversation. He would never deliberately offend anyone and if the subject of intelligence was ever raised he was more than capable of steering the conversation to another topic. He was a good communicator, and with a couple of beers under his belt he could generate and maintain interesting conversations on any number of topics.

Boxall meets the nurse

It was during one of his visits to the Clifton Gardens Hotel that Alfred first met Tessie. He was having a quiet drink when Joy, the girlfriend of a fellow officer from Queensland, introduced him to her. She appeared to be a rather shy girl and said she was a nurse at the

THE UNKNOWN MAN

Royal North Shore Hospital. During the ongoing conversations Alfred learnt that her correct name was Teresa Powell but she preferred to be called either Tessie or Tina. She said her father was born in England, and this enabled Alfred to expand on the subject of his own background. The conversation flowed in a friendly manner. Yes, he was married, and he was the proud father of two children, and his second child, a daughter named Lesley had been born recently. He discussed where he lived at Maroubra, and she told him about her family.

Alfred was impressed. Although a little quiet and reserved at first, it was soon obvious that she was an intelligent person. Her knowledge of numerous topics was quite amazing, and when the Rubaiyat entered the conversation she could discuss it with the best of them, and described it as a book of love poems. He had enjoyed her company. There was a certain aura of mystery about her, and he did note that at one stage she said she was born at Marrickville. Alfred hoped that they would meet again. Indeed, there had been sufficient details revealed in their conversations for that to happen.

In 1945 everyone was predicting the end of the war in Europe. In the Pacific theatre of war, however, badly mauled pockets of Japanese forces were still firmly entrenched throughout Asia. Japan was intending to fight to the bitter end: large losses of life were occurring, and many more deaths and casualties were expected. Alfred finally received notice that he would be returning to active service after being appointed Engineer of Craft in the Australia Small Ship Company.

The Rubaiyat gift

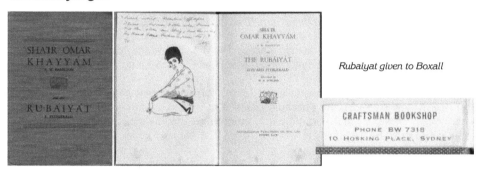

Rubaiyat given to Boxall

Tessie also heard of this appointment through friends, and shortly after they met by chance at the hotel. It was to be a parting drink before Alfred embarked on active service. It could also have been their final meeting. It was there that Tessie presented Alfred with a copy of the Rubaiyat. He read the neat writing she had inscribed inside the cover:

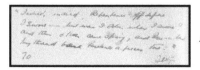

Indeed, indeed. Repentance oft before
I swore – but was I sober when I swore?
And then and then came Spring, and Rose-in-hand
My thread-bare Penitence apieces tore.
It was signed 'JEstyn'.

Alfred knew it was verse LXX of the Rubaiyat of Omar Khayyam. As they parted only they knew the significance of the inscription.

Prior to going on service Alfred gave the copy of the Rubaiyat to his wife.

On many a quiet evening he would gaze out over the lonely and isolated seas and think of his family and friends. He would also sometimes ponder over the passage 'was I sober when I swore?'.

Splitting the atom

As early as 1907 Albert Einstein reasoned that atoms, the basic unit of all matter, were held together by forces that if released could produce enormous amounts of energy. For 30 years scientists agreed that the ability to harness this energy lay far into the future.

Just before the Second World War, German scientists succeeded in splitting the atom for the first time. Most Western scientists remained sceptical about the potential until they read the Maud Report in 1941, in which a group of British scientists argued that it was possible to construct 'an effective uranium bomb' containing 11 kg of active material, that would detonate an explosion equivalent to 1 828 884 kg of TNT. The information in this report resulted in the formation of the top secret Manhattan Project in America.

Japan had also been enriching uranium for research into the possibility of producing a 'super bomb'. The Japanese Army and Navy both supplied money to support research on Japan's A-bomb: at one stage the military leaders considered scrapping a battleship to supply steel to the project team. One can only speculate as to the outcome of the war if either Germany or Japan had been successful in manufacturing an atomic bomb.

Communists in Australia

In 1940 the Australian communist movement was not supportive of the country's partici-pation in the war against Germany. At that time the Soviet Union was a neutral country, and had agreements with Germany in respect to its expansion and war on neighbouring countries. The Communist Party was banned as an illegal organisation by the Australian Government. The ban in June 1940 was lifted late in 1941 after the Soviet Union entered the war against Germany and the Party changed its view and supported Australia's war effort and gave an undertaking that it would co-operate in preventing industrial stoppages and absenteeism.

In April 1943 hundreds of Australian and American servicemen were being employed at loading wharves around Sydney because of a strike by wharf labourers. Perishable goods were held up by the strike. It was quoted by an observer that the servicemen loaded 50% more cargo than the 'wharfies'.

Uranium in Australia

Uranium ore was discovered in Australia in 1906 at Radium Hill in northeast South Aus-tralia. In 1910 additional deposits were found at Mount Painter in the Flinders Ranges and these were worked in the Second World War. The construction of a road to the mine was made through very difficult terrain, and teams of camels were used to carry supplies. Very soon 259 km^2 around Mount Painter were surveyed to locate other uranium sources. Experienced miners were released from wartime duties and university geology students were used to assist in examining likely sources. In a short time mining commenced and ore was being transported to the nearest railway.

The Manhattan Project

Although surrounded by secrecy the Manhattan Project was infiltrated by Soviet agents from the very beginning. Klaus Fuchs, a brilliant refugee German scientist, started working on the bomb in England and later joined the project team in Los Alamos, America. Fuchs was a Communist and he kept the Soviets informed of all developments in the project. In June 1945, within a month of Germany's surrender, he handed to his Soviet contact all documentation relevant to the A-bomb.

On 16 July 1945 the first experimental atom bomb was tested in the desert of New Mexico. President Truman was informed of the success of the test on the eve of the Potsdam Conference. The conference was where it was eventually agreed to divide Germany into four zones of occupation: Soviet, American, British and French. The city of Berlin deep inside the Soviet Sector was also divided into four zones of occupation. Road, rail and air corridors were established to service the isolated Berlin.

Vyacheslav Molotov, who was at the Potsdam Conference with Josef Stalin, the Soviet leader, said:

> Truman decided to surprise us at Potsdam ... He took Stalin and me aside and – informed us they had a secret weapon of a wholly new type, an extraordinary weapon ... it's difficult to say what he was thinking, but seemed to me he wanted to throw us into consternation. Stalin, however, reacted to this quite calmly, and Truman decided he hadn't understood. The words 'atomic bomb' hadn't been spoken, but we immediately guessed what was meant.

Within days Stalin ordered Molotov to speed up the Soviet's bomb project.

The atom bomb and Japan – the Second World War ends
The war in Europe had ended in May 1945, and in June the League of Nations was replaced by the United Nations as an organisation dedicated to maintaining world stability and peace.

On 5 July a bombshell hit Australia – Prime Minister John Curtin died suddenly.

On 6 August the first atomic bomb was dropped on Hiroshima and on 9 August, a second atomic bomb of a different type, a plutonium bomb, was detonated over Nagasaki. On 10 August the emperor of Japan announced his intention to surrender and the war was over.

Communist influence in the unions
In 1945 there were ongoing concerns within the Australian Labor Party in New South Wales about the communist influence in the union movement. Then in June 1946 the Australian Labor Party severed ties with the Communist Party of Australia. A statement was released which in part read, 'We declare the Communist Party is a danger to Australian democracy and a permanent foe of the Australian Labor Party'. By this time communists had gained strong positions of influence within Trades and Labour Councils in the country.

Woomera Rocket Range
Britain looked upon the vast unpopulated deserts of Australia as ideal locations to carry out full-scale atomic weapons experiments. In November 1946 the Australian Government announced the establishment of an experimental rocket range facility in South Australia. The first range would be constructed in three stages of 480, 1760 and 4800 km in length and 320 km wide. Some people raised concerns for the welfare of Aboriginal people living within the test range but these were largely ignored. The selected site was named Woomera after an Aboriginal word meaning 'spear thrower'.

Immigration to Australia
In November 1946 Arthur Calwell, the federal Minister for Immigration, announced to Parliament that free and assisted passage schemes would be adopted to bring more migrants

from Britain and continental Europe to Australia. He said, 'There was a time just four years ago when Australia faced its gravest peril. Armies recruited from the teeming millions of Japan threatened to overrun our cities and broad hinterland. They were so many. We were so few'.

The migration program was hampered by shipping shortages. The maximum capacity that could be spared for migrants was well below that required to transport the 30 000 people the government had intended to receive. Caldwell said, 'The days of our isolation are over. We live in an age when the earth's surface seems to be contracting under the influence of scientific discoveries. The call to all Australians is to realise that without adequate numbers this wide brown land may not be held in another clash of arms'.

The nurse moves to Melbourne
In 1946 Tessie Powell terminated her employment as a nurse in Sydney and moved to Mentone, a suburb of Melbourne, to live with her parents who had moved to Victoria. Later that year she realised she was expecting a child. Sometime in the first half of 1947 she then moved to a suburb in Adelaide, South Australia. In the middle of the year she gave birth to a baby boy named Leslie. After the birth she moved to near Somerton Beach.

Boxall continues his service
Alfred Boxall remained in the military and served in Cairns, Port Moresby, Bougainville, Rabaul and the Solomon Islands. On 29 December 1946 he was appointed First Engineer and continued Water Transport duties in Brisbane, Ambon and Darwin. Apart from small amounts of normal leave he returned home to Sydney on 15 January 1948 from his last Water Transport duty. On 12 April 1948 he was discharged from No. 13 Small Ships Company.

Alfred returned to his previous employment at Randwick. By the end of the war 993 000 Australians had enlisted in the Armed Forces. There were 95 746 casualties, including 28 753 deaths. During the war about 550 000 men and women – about 1 in 12 of the population – served outside Australia. At one stage more than 52 000 women were in the women's services, and more than 160 000 men and women were engaged in munitions production.

Sir Mark Oliphant
Sir Mark Oliphant was born in Adelaide in 1901. During the Second World War he worked on radar and atomic energy in Britain and the United States of America. After the war he was appointed the director of the Research School of Physical Sciences in the Institute of Advanced Studies at the Australian National University in Canberra. He later returned to South Australia as its Governor from 1971 to 1976.

In January 1947 the nuclear scientist visited the Mount Painter area with South Australia's Premier Tom Playford. Oliphant said, 'Some hundreds of thousands of tons of ore exist from which qualities of uranium approaching a thousand tons might be obtained'. The potential to establish a nuclear industry to produce atomic energy and weapons in Australia was then more than a possibility.

Post-war years
The dancing in the streets throughout the world that greeted the end of the war soon gave way to the realities of the situation. Countries were in ruin and the lost souls of displaced people wandered the streets and towns.

The Soviet Union was emerging as a super power and had built up a momentum that continued to grow. They had sacrificed plenty, they had debts to settle and someone had to pay. Yes, America had 'the bomb', but America was 'over there' and this was the heart of Europe. The Russian Bear was demanding vast reparations worth billions of US dollars from Germany, and factories and machinery were being dismantled and transported back to the United Soviet Socialist Republic (USSR).

France had demanded reparations from Germany at the end of the First World War and this had devastated the German economy and assisted in the rise of Nazism. The Americans and the British were against the policy of reparations and instead wanted to revive Germany and develop a prosperous Europe. The French, who were still haunted by an ancient rivalry, were very fearful of a German recovery. The question of national security caused the Americans to focus upon the USSR and they were frustrated by French obstructionism. The British wanted to go slow and saw themselves as an intermediary between the French and the Americans.

Secretary of State Marshall in a broadcast to the American people said, 'We cannot look forward to a reunified Germany at this time. We must do our best in the area where our influence can be felt'.

The USSR meanwhile could sit back and pull the strings. The Russians claimed the Western powers snubbed the Allied Control Council by holding a secret meeting in London to discuss Germany's future. They had well-established spies who passed this information on.

In 1948 a communist coup seized power in Czechoslovakia. On 20 March 1948 the Soviet delegation walked out of an Allied Control Council meeting, effectively ending the Council. The North Atlantic Treaty Organisation was formed and signatories agreed to keep troops in Germany for a period of 50 years.

Deep within the Soviet controlled area of East Germany the Allied sectors of West Berlin were isolated from the West. With one hand clutching the divided island city of Berlin the USSR flexed its muscles and tested the resolve of the opposition, and they offered the other hand in an arm wrestle challenge. The invitation was open to all comers and would be known as 'The Cold War Challenge' for many years to come.

It was in this climate that more migrants began to arrive in Australia. A free passage scheme was offered to British and American servicemen who had served in Australia during the war. Assisted passage was offered to others in order to meet a target of 70 000 migrants each year.

Several hundred thousand people registered for migration. Many of them were registered for up to 18 months, and were prepared to travel under any conditions.

Displaced persons from the Baltic States were among the first of the new migrants to arrive under the auspices of the International Refugee Organisation. Some of these migrants would be employed at the Woomera Rocket Range.

During this period some people engaged in the shipping trade would jump ship upon reaching an Australian port and disappear into the population. There is no doubt that other people of questionable character and background entered the country as legitimate migrants using fabricated identification.

The Atomic Age and spies
Between 1946 and 1948 the USA detonated 23 nuclear devices at Bikini Atoll in the Marshall Islands in the Pacific Ocean. In 1949 a radioactive cloud was detected drifting east across the Pacific to America and Canada, and west across the North Atlantic. The USSR had entered the Atomic Age after they exploded a nuclear device in Kazakhstan. Mines in Czechoslovakia were the source of the uranium ore. Western nations were shocked because they did not believe that the USSR was so far advanced in knowledge and materials

to produce a nuclear device.

In a world of spies and espionage the East and the West continued their arm wrestle. The USSR had established a successful spy network throughout the world, and exercised strict control over its own people.

The USA and Britain would be reeling for years due to the damage caused by traitors in their midst, and the knowledge that they harboured many communist sympathizers. Western nations had very open policies and borders while the USSR had the 'Iron Curtain' to control its people and to prevent infiltration into its spy network. With mass migration to the West, and very few westerners willing or able to sneak into the USSR, the future advantage of espionage was weighted heavily in favour of the communists.

Australia enters the Atomic Age

Australia was no exception to the spy world. An Aboriginal word 'maralinga' meaning thunder was given to a site being developed in South Australia west of Woomera. The 'thunder' would be heard when British–Australian nuclear tests took place here in the 1950s.

The Communist Party in Australia was a fickle organisation. It hampered Australian efforts against Germany early in the war, but immediately Russia was invaded they were more than supportive of the Allied effort.

With the end of the war this minority group reverted to its original social and political agitation. Backed by communist leaders in the union movement a strike by coal miners in 1949 brought the coal industry to a standstill. The strike had been part of a growing level of Australia-wide industrial action. One newspaper argued, 'The lesson, for the nation and the world to see, is this: communists can be beaten wherever they show themselves if the people will only stand up and fight them'.

A Royal Commission would eventually be appointed to investigate the activities of the Communist Party in Australia.

Spies in Australia

The Soviet Government claimed that 20 000 displaced persons migrating to Australia were doomed to 'slave labour' conditions. With the influx of migrants from many nations, and little hope of screening them effectively, infiltration by communist spies was established easily. There were communist spies and supporters in Australia and certain activities in South Australia were a focus of their attention. The Commonwealth Investigation Service became the Australian Security Intelligence Organisation in 1949 and joined the international intelligence networks in 'Spy on Spy', a game that had no rules.

Was *the Unknown Man* a spy associated with that game?

CHAPTER 2

A STRANGER ARRIVES IN ADELAIDE

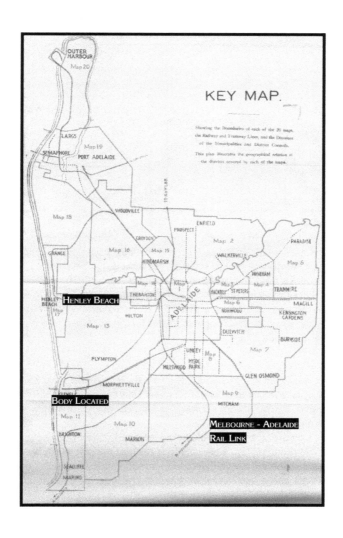

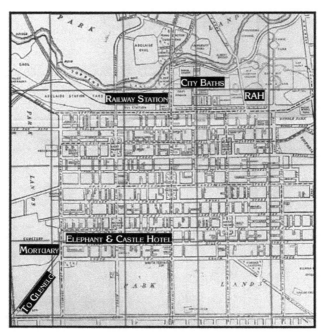

Trains in Australia

Trains were one way to travel in Australia. When a transcontinental line was completed in 1917 the east coast was finally linked to Perth on the west coast. Never mind that in travelling from Brisbane to Perth you had to change trains six times because of the varying track gauges or that it took six days to travel across Australia. In contrast, the standard gauge journey between Melbourne and Adelaide was pure luxury – take a seat in the early evening, an overnight journey, arriving around 9.15 a.m., no changing of trains and just short stops at the many railway stations along the route. Taking all things into consideration, it was quite a pleasant journey.

Post-war years

Although the post-war years would eventually show signs of a booming economy and employment was slowly becoming available, there was little people could spend their money on. All across the country there were shortages of almost every consumer item, including things as basic as a pair of socks.

In 1948 petrol, butter and tea were still being rationed, although meat, sugar and clothing had come off the rationing list. Beer was in very short supply: when Shirley Strickland became the first Australian female athlete to win a medal at the London Olympics, her victory was celebrated with a cup of tea! In that year the legendary cricketer Don Bradman retired from Test matches.

International political developments included the assassination of Mahatma Gandhi in India, the state of Israel being formed, the ongoing blockade of Berlin by the Soviet Union (a Royal Australian Air Force contingent joined the airlift operation), Czechoslovakia was now behind the 'Iron Curtain' after a coup d'état, the communist State of North Korea was proclaimed, and the communist army of Mao Tse-tung was sweeping all before it in China.

THE UNKNOWN MAN

A Railways ticket seller

Douglas George Townsend was very tired as he reached out to kill his enemy, the alarm clock, after it had been ringing loudly in his ears for some time. If only there was some way you could close your ears and make the annoying noise go away, and allow him to sleep a little longer, he thought. He knew how tempting it would be to sleep on, and that was why he placed his alarm clock some distance from his bed. To reach it meant sitting up and that in itself woke him sufficiently to realise he was about to start a new day.

It was still quite dark outside, as you would expect when you have to start work at 6.15 a.m. After studying most of the night it was hard to get ready for work. He was a bright young man and as he thought of his future profession the tiredness left his body. As a student it was good to have a part-time job: the money was most welcome even though it was not a lot. Today was Tuesday and that was also good. Sleep in tomorrow and maybe a treat – a trip to the beach with his mates would be a welcome diversion.

It would be warm today, as it had been for the past week. So it should be, as it was 30 November 1948 – tomorrow would be the first day of summer. As was usual he caught the train at the Emerson Crossing Station in the southwest and journeyed to the Adelaide Railway Station.

Townsend as usual was early for work: with his heavy schedule of study and work he had grown into a very organised person. He was employed at the Adelaide Railway Station as a ticket clerk on a temporary basis. Today he was selling tickets for the Port Adelaide and North Line routes, from one of the booths fronting onto the footpath at the southern side of the Station. If it was anything like yesterday it would not be too busy, but for the Railways Department there was a lot of paperwork and everything was accounted for.

Another Railways man at work

Ralph Craig was also a railway man. He had started with the South Australian Railways in 1923 and he was going to stay with them until he retired. He had started as a packer and now he was a Porter in the Cloak Room at the Adelaide Railway Station. The Cloak Room was at the rear of the station. It was a very busy place as it provided a service to many people from all walks of life who could leave their suitcases, parcels, bicycles and goods there for a period of time.

As most people travelled by public transport, if you needed somewhere to leave items in Adelaide, the Cloak Room was the logical place. Craig was grateful he had a steady job with the Railways, and he enjoyed working in the Cloak Room, accounting for the shelves of property. At times maintaining the detailed records of all the time and date stamped tickets he sold was not achieved without a few headaches.

Craig, like Townsend, commenced work early on 30 November. When he finished his busy work day the previous day there was still a lot of property that needed shifting and rearranging. He wanted to get it finished before the rush started.

It was a job where you recognised regular customers such as those who deposited their bicycle in the morning and collected them in the afternoon when they returned from work. New customers would usually tell you why they were depositing property. Craig could often look at a customer and predict what they would say: 'I am down from the country', 'I have just arrived from interstate', 'I am catching a train out tonight' or 'I'm looking for some-where to stay'. He often felt sorry for some of his customers as they scraped together the few pennies to pay the fee, and he handed them their half of the ticket with the date and time stamped on it. They would need that portion to redeem their property, and it had to match the portion retained in the office. The fee was a daily rate and if it was not collected within the correct period an additional fee was added.

He could almost pick those who would not return, and those who would return in a few days with a hard luck story, but no money to redeem their property. He could not return the property without payment and so such items were later placed on a shelf with other unclaimed property, where it remained for the time specified by regulations and then was sold. There were already several items on the unclaimed shelf and Craig checked the records and placed a few more items alongside them.

The trains run on time

'The trains always run on time', all loyal railwaymen will boast proudly.
On this day the Melbourne Express was true to the motto as it pulled into Adelaide Railway Station at 9.15 a.m. Similarly, the Broken Hill Express pulled into the station on time at 9.17 a.m.

The Adelaide Railway Station was a busy place and the many newspaper sellers were trying to catch the attention of the commuters. 'Read all about it. Thousands of political refugees flee Hungary', cried one seller trying to capture attention with an international topic. 'Get your newspaper here. Holden, Australia's own car on sale now', yelled the opposition introducing an item of local interest.

A stranger arrives

It was in this hustle and bustle that the neatly dressed, well-built stranger took his brown suitcase from the overhead rack in his carriage, and stepped onto the platform. He joined the throng of passengers in walking towards the exit gate. Perhaps he wondered where he might find somewhere to wash and clean up. After sitting all night on the swaying and rocking train he had not slept much, and he certainly needed somewhere steady to get his 'cut throat' razor out for a shave.

The barrier porters

John, a Barrier Porter, did not enjoy this time of the day. He did not like the labels of being overzealous and too strict. He had lost half his foot in a work-related accident with the Railways many years before, and because of this disability he had been given a job punching tickets as passengers entered the platform.

On the other side of the gate his workmate Joe had also stopped smiling as he observed the large throng of departing passengers. Joe had lost a couple of fingers, and he was very grateful when the Railways gave him a job as a Barrier Porter.

Many times John and Joe had discussed how people walked with deliberate intentions to the gate, but as soon as they exited a lot of them stopped, milled around and some appeared quite confused. Why could they not just walk a further 20 m and then stop? This was when you had to be alert because other people were trying to enter the platform to catch other trains.

No-one was allowed on the platform without getting their ticket punched, and it was sometimes quite difficult to ensure this was done. There was also the odd sneak who tried to slip in through the crowd, and on to the platform without a ticket. John and Joe had both been reprimanded recently for allowing people to get on trains without tickets. But they were aware of all the tricks. Of course there were measures in place to catch the cheats, but still they tried.

What the sneaks did not know was that an inspector got on the train at the first station and asked for all tickets to be produced. John and Joe had a good system of checking, and they both firmly believed that no-one got past them without having a ticket, and that they had punched it. They often had to explain that the people who did get on the trains without a ticket had probably either jumped a fence somewhere or got off one train and on to another without leaving the platform. They were both satisfied that no-one slipped through their gate, and they accepted the reputation of being over officious.

A visitor to Adelaide

The stranger to Adelaide who arrived that morning did not mill around the exit gate but looked for someone who was not in a rush to assist him. He knew only a little about Adelaide. It was a cloudy morning but he knew that the temperature would rise. Besides, he needed a shave and somewhere to freshen up.

He did not wish to book into a hotel or boarding house at this stage, and thought that maybe there was somewhere suitable within the Railway Station. He approached a Railways employee and asked if there were facilities at the station, but was advised that apart from toilets, no other provisions existed in the building.

A walk to the City Baths

The Railways employee obligingly suggested that he should walk around the corner to the City Baths where facilities were available, and maybe take a swim at the same time. He liked the suggestion and walked out the front of the Railway Station to North Terrace. Following the directions he had been given, the stranger walked past the impressive Parliament House, turned left into King William Road and a short distance on the left was the entrance to the City Baths.

'You name it, we have it – swim, sauna, lockers, showers, toilets, towels, whatever', said the friendly receptionist. It sounded like a good deal for a few pence, and it suited the needs of the stranger. He felt refreshed when he left the building. Clean shaven, fingernails cleaned and neatly dressed in polished shoes, fresh shirt, tie, jumper and a sports coat he was quiet proud of his appearance. For a man almost 50 years of age he was in good shape: at 5'11" (180 cm) tall with broad shoulders and hazel eyes, he could easily pass for someone in their early 40s despite his few grey hairs. Being a confirmed chain smoker, his fingers were heavily stained from the Army Club cigarettes he enjoyed. He was glad he was not wearing riding boots because they were not suitable for walking around, and his flat-soled shoes did not pinch his toes. Carrying his suitcase, the stranger retraced his route back to the Railway Station.

A ticket to Henley Beach

Doug Townsend was thinking about his finishing time of 2.30 p.m. when the stranger approached him at the ticket box and inquired about catching a train to the beach. Townsend knew that Henley Beach was a very popular destination during summer, and he knew of the recent discussions about extending the line further south through to Glenelg. For 7d he then sold his first ticket to Henley Beach.

As there were no first-class tickets to Henley Beach, it was a second-class ticket that he sold. But it was an unusual sale because it would have been a better proposition to buy a return ticket for a shilling, if you intended returning to the city on the same day. A saving of 2d was something to consider. But maybe the man was living or staying at Henley Beach. It was not Townsend's business but he did know that the next train to Henley Beach departed at 10.50 a.m. He only sold two more tickets to Henley Beach that day.

A suitcase deposited at the Cloak Room

The stranger saw the sign to the Cloak Room at the rear of the Railway Station and walked there. Ralph Craig was too busy to take much notice as the stranger placed his neat brown suitcase on the counter. After taking the few pence Craig placed the suitcase in the racks and tore off and handed the stranger the bottom section of the ticket. He knew it was just after 11 a.m. because that was the time the clock stamp imprinted on the section of the ticket he retained.

CHAPTER 3

A BUS TRIP TO GLENELG

It was predicted that Tuesday 30 November would be a warm and cloudy day with a temperature of about 72°F. The stranger was not dressed for comfort, but to the publicly accepted fashion standards of those times – shirt and tie, jumper, sports trousers and jacket and a pair of well-polished matching brown lace-up shoes.

The stranger was happy to have deposited his suitcase in the Cloak Room, and was relieved of the burden of carrying it as he turned his attention to the purpose of his visit to Adelaide.

He had the telephone number of Tessie Johnson, who he knew was now living in Adelaide, in the back of The Rubaiyat that was with him. He knew she was living in the seaside suburb of Glenelg, but unfortunately his telephone call to the number went unanswered. Although a little disappointed, he decided she may be away from her home for a short time and so thought that he could spend some time waiting at the seaside.

Transport to Glenelg

A few inquiries established that the train to Henley Beach did not link up with Glenelg, making it pointless to try and get to Glenelg via that route, unless he wanted a lengthy walk along the beachfront. But Glenelg was easily accessed by tram or bus, both services being under the control of the Municipal Tramways Trust. The stranger was informed that a tram could be caught in Adelaide. He was also pointed in the direction of the bus stop in front of the Grosvenor Hotel directly opposite the Railway Station. That would be the ideal choice he decided and walked across North Terrace. After a short wait he boarded the double-decker bus to St Leonards (now Glenelg North).

Purchase of a bus ticket

At 11.15 a.m. Conductor Arthur Anzac Holderness issued the stranger with ticket number 88708 and collected 7d, the full fare to the final destination of the bus. The punching of the ticket confirmed that it was purchased between the Grosvenor Hotel and the intersection of South and West Terraces, near the West Terrace Mortuary and Cemetery. Holderness could not recall the stranger, but he did know he was one of nine passengers who boarded the bus on that section of the route. Upon reaching South Terrace the full fare changed to 6d, and the bus veered right and travelled along Anzac Highway direct to the beach. Upon reaching its destination, where Anzac Highway formed the dividing boundary between Glenelg and St Leonards, the bus retraced the same route on its return journey to the Adelaide Railway Station.

A walk to Tessie's home

The stranger was one of 40 passengers who travelled on the bus during the journey to the beach. It was then only a matter of a short walk to Moseley Square at the beach end of Jetty Road, the main street of Glenelg, and the entry point to the jetty which is a focal point in the very popular seaside location. It was an easy matter to obtain directions to Tessie's house. With some apprehension he walked towards his long anticipated meeting.

A disappointing result

There was no answer to his continuous knocking on the front door, but it was most unexpected when neighbours advised the stranger that Tessie and her child were not home.

A Pasty

Sometime during the late afternoon or early evening the stranger ate a pasty after purchasing it somewhere in the area. A pasty is common in South Australia: the pastry structure containing minced or diced vegetables was imported by Cornish miners in the colonial period.

CHAPTER 4

A BODY ON THE BEACH

John Bain Lyons was a jeweller with a business in King William Street, the main thoroughfare in Adelaide. He lived at 52 Whyte Street, Somerton Park, a street that ran west from the busy Brighton Road to Somerton Beach, a short distance from his home.

Lyons and his wife would usually walk to the beach each evening, particularly if it was warm, and take a leisurely stroll along the beachfront. That Tuesday evening was no exception and on the last day of Spring in the warm evening they walked along the sandy foreshore towards Glenelg, a short distance to the north.

A stranger on the sand

The house was built in 1884 for Anne Margaret Bickford who had arrived in South Australia in 1839 with her husband, William. He was the first druggist in Adelaide and she established AM Bickford & Sons many years after his death. Later developments saw road building in the area and Bickford Street formed the southern boundary. The house was the Somerton Home for Crippled Children from 1939 to 1976.

Near The Broadway the Lyons turned and commenced their walk home along the same route. When they reached a position near the prominent Somerton Crippled Children's Home which overlooked the beachfront, they saw a man lying on his back on the sand. Mrs Lyons said, 'Look at the way the man is slumped'. They were 14–18 m from the man. They took particular note of certain things about him and the open position he was in. He was lying with his head and shoulders supported by the seawall at the edge of the high water mark. The man was adjacent to and within a metre of the steps that led down to the beach from the Esplanade. They saw that his left hand was by his side, and his feet were crossed and pointing towards the sea. John Lyons said to his wife jocularly, 'I will report this to the Police'. He had no sooner made this remark when he saw the man fully extend his right arm upwards, and then let it fall by his right side. The movements indicated to John Lyons that the man was drunk and attempting to smoke a cigarette. After checking his watch and noting that the time was about 7.00 p.m., he and his wife continued to their home.

Other witnesses
Olive Constance Neill, a telephonist and typist, also noted the warm evening as she waited

for her boyfriend to collect her from outside her place of work in Adelaide. It was early in the evening when Gordon Kenneth Strapps arrived on his motor cycle to collect Olive. They decided to travel to the beach in the hope of finding a cool sea breeze to refresh them.

They arrived at Somerton Beach at about 7.30 p.m. After parking the motorcycle on the Esplanade, they walked to a bench seat just south of the Crippled Children's Home.

They saw a man lying on his back on the sand near the sea wall. He was about 9 m below their position and about 2 m north of the steps from the Esplanade.

Olive could only see him from the waist down because her view was obstructed by the seawall, but he appeared to be a tall, well-built man. She noticed that he was wearing brown trousers and that his legs were crossed. She thought he was wearing brown shoes, and that his left hand seemed to be in a peculiar position.

She observed a male person standing at the top of the steps and looking over at the man on the beach for about 5 minutes. This man was about 50 years of age, of stocky build, not tall and was wearing a navy suit and a grey hat. There were other people either walking on the beach or sitting on seats along the Esplanade.

Olive was concerned about the man lying on his back and she remarked to Gordon, 'Perhaps he's dead'.

Gordon only took a casual glance but he agreed that the man's left hand was out-stretched. He did not see him move, but he thought he noticed a difference in his position. He did not see that his legs were crossed, but recalled that his legs were extended, al-though as he walked up the steps he saw that the left leg had been drawn up, moving it up the sand a bit. He thought he was wearing brown striped trousers that were part of a suit but he could not see his coat.

Gordon was of the opinion that the man was asleep. He noticed there were a lot of mosquitoes, and remarked to Olive, 'As there are mosquitoes here he must be dead to the world to not notice them'.

The street lights were on when Gordon and Olive left the scene at about 8 p.m.

The first day of Summer

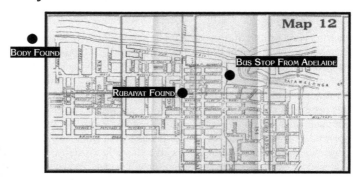

John Lyons was an early riser and he would go for a morning swim regularly, as did other people who lived close to the sea. On the first day of summer John finished his swim by about 6.35 a.m. He then walked along the beach towards Glenelg, where he met with a friend with whom he often swam.

While they were talking John saw some men on horses near the place where he had seen the man lying on the sand the previous evening. He became inquisitive and walked over to the group where he saw the body of a man in the same position that he had seen some 12 hours earlier. Though the man still had his feet crossed, because he had not seen his face, he could not identify him as the same person. He casually examined the body without touching it, and was satisfied that the person was dead. He told the people there that he had seen the man the previous evening. He now thought that the strange arm movement he had seen was not of the man smoking, but the action of a dying man.

Contact with the Police
Lyons returned to his home and telephoned the Brighton Police Station before returning to the body. At the Brighton Police Station, in the next suburb south, PC John Moss received John Lyons's telephone call at about 6.45 a.m. Moss arranged to meet Lyons on the beach in front of the Crippled Children's Home. He knew the area well as it was a location where many people congregated because the stairs provided easy access to the beach.

The Police arrive
Constable Moss examined the cold, damp and stiff body. There were no marks of violence. The deceased male was fully clothed, lying on his back with feet towards the west, with the head resting against the seawall, slightly inclined to the right. His right arm was doubled over, palm upwards, and fingers bent towards the palm. His left arm was lying outstretched on the sand alongside the body. There was a portion of a cigarette on the right collar of his coat, and held in position by his cheek.

In the Coronial Inquest later, Moss stated, 'I made an accurate record of what I found, and was quite sure it had been partly smoked. More had been smoked than what remained. The cigarette was not smoked as far as it could have been smoked, an ordinary person would have smoked it further'.

He examined the cheek, and found no sign of blistering or scorching. He was unable to form an opinion as to whether the cigarette had been kept behind his ear or it had fallen out of his mouth. He considered that it may have been in his mouth, he was smoking it, with his head sideways in the position which he found the head.

Nothing was found near the body to give him any suspicions, and there was no disturbance of the sand. No hat was found in the vicinity.

Clothing
The deceased stranger was wearing brown fawn trousers, a white shirt with collar and tie (red white and blue), a brown knitted pullover and a grey brown matching double breasted coat. He was also wearing clean brown lace up shoes and heavy knitted socks.

A return trip to Adelaide
Moss conveyed the body in a police ambulance to the Royal Adelaide Hospital on North Terrace. He would have to compile a report for the Coroner, and it would be necessary to obtain a certificate from a legally qualified medical practitioner that 'Life was Extinct'.

Life extinct
At about 9.40 a.m. Dr John Barkley Bennett examined the body of the deceased in the police ambulance at the hospital. He certified that 'Life was Extinct'. He thought that death could have occurred up to no more than 8 hours before his examination. Thus, he put the time of death at 2 a.m. at the earliest. He based that opinion on the rigor mortis but he did not make a note of the extent of it at the time. He formed the opinion as to the cause of death from just a cursory look at him, from the cyanosis. There was nothing else about the

body which he noticed.

Apparently Bennett made a further reference in relation to his examination because Professor Sir Cedric Stanton Hicks in his evidence at the Coronial Inquest said, 'A very factual description was given by Dr. Bennett, who said the man appeared to be just like a person who had had a coronial seizure'.

To the Mortuary

Constable Moss conveyed the body to the City Mortuary, or 'The Morgue' as it was more commonly referred to, in the southwest corner of the city, in the vast West Terrace Cemetery in Adelaide's parklands.

Moss was assisted in carrying the body into the Morgue where it was stripped of all clothing, and the naked body was placed on a steel sliding stretcher. A cardboard label was endorsed with the corresponding details from the Registration Book, and tied to the big toe of the body. As a further precaution against false identification, it was a requirement that the registered number be written on an upper arm with an indelible pencil. The pencil lead had to be moistened before it would write and adhere properly: there is no evidence that Moss made the common mistake of licking it to provide the moisture. The body on the steel stretcher was then slid into one of the many racks within a large refrigeration unit.

Clothing searched

Moss then searched the clothing of the deceased and located certain items. His evidence at the Coronial Inquest referred to the following items in particular, 'I particularly noted a railway ticket to Henley Beach, a bus ticket (88708), a metal comb, chewing gum and some cigarettes in a packet. I did not compare the cigarettes with the one that was partly smoked'.

It was later established that the following items were with the stranger: a handkerchief, a pair of underpants (jockey type), a singlet, a train ticket, a bus ticket, a part packet of chewing gum (Juicy Fruit'), two combs, a box of Bryant and Mays matches (quarter full) and an Army Club Cigarette Packet, containing seven cigarettes of another brand (Kensitas).

No identification

At this stage the deceased was not identified, there were no signs of injuries and no apparent suspicious circumstances surrounding the cause of his death. As with all deaths of this nature there was not much the police could do to further the investigation, apart from checking 'Missing Person Records', releasing details to the media and informing relevant police stations whose officers might be able to assist in identifying the body.

A possible identification

Sergeant Lavender of Adelaide's Metropolitan Station submitted the following report to the City Coroner in the evening of Wednesday 1 December in response to information received about the 'Body of unknown man found at Somerton Beach':

> I beg to report that at about 8-45 p.m. this date Sergeant Fenwick of Glenelg phoned stating that the unknown body found at Somerton Beach on December 1st. 1948 might be identified with a person named Edward Cecil Johnson 55 yrs of 32 Arthur Street, Payneham who was known to have a fracture of the left elbow, and little finger missing off the right hand.
>
> Det. Sergeant Leane & O/C. Payneham notified.

Detective Sergeant RL (Lionel) Leane was at that stage one of a very small number of senior members holding that rank within the CIB. He was directly responsible for overseeing general matters requiring direction and the supervision of junior investigators.

Inquiries soon established, however, that Johnson was not the deceased.

The print media pre-empted the result and a small article appeared the following day:

Body Found On Beach

A body believed to be that of E. C. Johnson, about 45, of Arthur Street, Payneham, was found on the Somerton Beach opposite the Crippled Children's Home, yesterday morning. The discovery was made by Mr. J. Lyons, of Whyte road, Somerton. Detective H. Strangway and Constable J. Moss are enquiring.

The autopsy and the specimens

Having just finished assisting in the autopsy, Constable W Sutherland of the Metropolitan Station submitted a report to Metropolitan Superintendant F Homes on 2 December 1948 in relation to 'Specimens taken from the body of an unidentified man found on the Somerton Beach on December 1st. 1948':

> I beg to report that at 7-30a.m. on Thursday December 2nd. 1948 an autopsy was made at the City Mortuary on the body of an unidentified man who was found dead on the beach at Somerton on December 1st. 1948.
>
> The autopsy was performed by Doctor J.M. Dwyer, Legally Qualified Medical Practitioner, of No 105 Port Road, Hindmarsh, who was of the opinion that the cause of death was due to some irritant poison in the stomach.
>
> The undermentioned specimens were retained for analysis by the Government Analyst for any known poison. BLOOD, URINE, PORTION OF LIVER AND MUSCLE, STOMACH AND CONTENTS.

On the same day Sutherland attended the State Government's Department of Chemistry in Kintore Avenue, Adelaide. He was issued with a receipt signed by RJ Cowan, the Deputy Government Analyst:

Received from P.C.C. Sutherland:-
One glass jar containing stomach and contents;
One glass jar containing liver and muscle;
One glass jar containing urine;
One glass jar containing blood;
Said to have been taken from the body of an unidentified man found at Somerton.
It is believed that the specimens were lost when the Morgue closed and its activities were transferred to the Forensic Science Centre in Adelaide.

It would be some time before the full analysis of the specimens would be made available: the results were given in some detail in evidence presented at the Coronial Inquest months later.

Fingerprints

On Friday 3 December Police Photographer and Fingerprint Expert Patrick James Durham, who was stationed in Adelaide, attended the City Mortuary with Mounted Constable Knight. Knight opened a large refrigerator door and partially pulled out the steel stretcher and said, 'That is the body of the man found dead on the beach at Somerton on the 1st of December, 1948'.

Durham and Knight then removed the stretcher and body, and placed it on a stainless steel autopsy table. Durham performed the difficult task of obtaining the fingerprints of the deceased. This required applying ink to the very stiff fingers and then transferring the imprints by a rolling method to the official form for future classification and comparison.

Photographing the deceased

Durham and Knight then performed the more difficult procedure of manoeuvring the body and re-dressing it in the shirt and tie that the man had been wearing. Durham obtained full and side facial photographs of the body.

The stranger was then returned to the refrigerator. Durham and Knight washed their hands with the special foul-smelling soap supplied at the Morgue, and departed the building both knowing that the smell would linger on their hands and clothes for a long time, and would remind them and others of their visit. Eating meals was never pleasant when raising hands to the mouth and receiving a lingering heavy smell of the soap.

THE UNKNOWN MAN

CHAPTER 5

SEARCHING FOR AN IDENTITY

To appreciate the environment and conditions at the time of this investigation, several things must be taken into consideration. The Second World War had not long finished, and items were still being rationed. Ironically, pairs of socks were one such item. Many other items, including petrol, were in very short supply.

The South Australian Police Force was no exception to experiencing the impact of the war on its staff and its operations. Many police personnel had served in the war, and a number had made the supreme sacrifice. The total number of police then was quite small: the detective section comprised about 20 members only. The very strict dress code required a suit or matching trousers and coat and a tie to be worn on duty at all times. Wearing a suitable hat in public was also strictly adhered to. There were no specialist squads concentrating on specific crimes as such in the Detective Section: the general pool of work was distributed and delegated on a needs basis. Transport included bicycles and motorcycles (some with a side car outfit to allow two officers to attend particular duties). A very limited number of motor cars were available. Bus passes were issued for travelling on public transport, which was used on a regular basis. But it was common to perform inquiries on foot, if the distance was not too great.

In contrast, the progress to sophisticated equipment, other facilities and the increase in the number of police is somewhat taken for granted now. In 1948 almost all members knew each other personally, and most detectives were fully aware of all the allocated duties and investigations. Records were maintained in pencil, pen and ink or, if you could afford to own one, your own personal fountain pen. Limited communication was available through the telephone, but most information was controlled, transmitted and received through a central police radio station (VL5AP). Specific intrastate and interstate radio stations were allocated official 'call signs', and nominated scheduled call times were adhered to strictly. All transmissions were officially recorded: all full stops in the text were substituted by the word 'STOP'. 'Trunk' (distance) telephone calls had to be approved by a high authority and were recorded and connected through the switchboard within the Communications Centre.

Depending on the category of an incident, an individual detective or a number of them would be delegated to attend to the matter. Individuals would maintain and retain their own personal files and be responsible to produce those records when and if required. An inquiry of an official nature that required intrastate or interstate attention or some form of investigation had to be structured in the correct format. It had to contain full details and was then forwarded and recorded along the official chain of command. Official reports had to be typed, and it was sometimes a very difficult proposition to not only locate an old Remington typewriter, but to also find one that was in suitable repair. It was sometimes necessary to borrow a suitable typewriter from the office of a member of the hierarchy, because it might be the only one available in reasonable condition. New foolscap or quarto paper was in short supply: it was common to receive reports that had been typed on the back of recycled police running sheet journals, written in pencil, from years before.

There were no photocopying machines and so the availability of carbon paper to produce copies of reports was a godsend. Three copies was the accepted limit unless you were prepared to hit the typewriter keys with a hammer to produce a fourth copy that was very blurred. Official reports to bodies outside the department had to be presented in an original condition with two carbon copies. Documents would not pass through official channels if any simple error was made or any attempt was made to erase mistakes.

Presenting Antecedent Reports to the Supreme Court was the bane of all detectives' lives. Inevitably, after many attempts, a detective would get to the last paragraph, the fingers would tremble, a mistake would be made or the typewriter would sometimes fall on the floor accidently. When a new detective was observed typing one of these reports, it was also common for others to distract him from the office. Another member would then roll the typing material forward to the bottom, type something, and then roll the paper back to the original position. The unsuspecting new detective would then return to the office, continue his typing, and when he rolled the paper forward the required two spaces for the final paragraph a message such as 'Mary had a little lamb … etc.' would mysteriously appear. This distraction only ever worked once per detective!

In 1948 there were no computer facilities to implement a case management system. When an analysis is made of the methodologies used then, it is clear that an extensive and efficient investigation was made into *the Unknown Man*. Many individuals provided varying levels of input into the investigation over many years. Some of those will never be identified and the majority are now dead. It is unfortunate that over time a lot of the original personal notes and recall of individual investigators has either been destroyed or died with them.

There is a large amount of information available from witnesses in statement format, and a considerable amount of information was elicited and recorded during the Coronial Inquest in 1949. This loss of information is no reflection on any individual, and can only be blamed on the passage of time. Culling policies did not exist and there was no obligation on an individual to retain personal notes. Unanswered questions raised in hindsight may never be answered. This will no doubt leave many to speculate.

A coronial investigation
All deaths come under the jurisdiction of the Coroner and it is the responsibility of the police to investigate a death and to present a report to the Coroner. Most of these reports were a simple matter if the deceased was identified and a doctor could certify the cause of death. The Coroner would then issue a Burial Order and await any further information he required. It was not always a requirement that an autopsy be performed: the majority of deaths do not require an inquest to be held. If the death was not suspicious and the Coroner was satisfied with the circumstances surrounding the matter it would be filed.

The death of *the Unknown Man* was to require further attention from the police and the Coroner, not simply because of the mysterious circumstances of his demise but also by the fact that the deceased was unidentified and the suspicion that his death had been caused by some form of poisoning.

Checking missing person reports in South Australia had proved fruitless. Where would the police go from here? Normally the identity of a deceased person is established by fingerprints, dental records, description, clothing, documents, personal identification, media releases and so on, and sometimes a combination of these. Analysing the specimens obtained during an autopsy would require some time to produce results. Even then they may not confirm the poison theory. Nevertheless, it would be reasonable for the police to have assumed that the deceased would be identified quickly, and if poisoning was confirmed then he more than likely committed suicide.

The many articles that appeared in the newspapers and other periodicals throughout Australia during the early years of this investigation do provide some insight into some of the unanswered questions. Some articles contain factual information, whilst others appear to contain information that possibly did originate from official sources and have an element of truth about them. In the absence of confirmation it is difficult to establish what is true.

The initial investigation
In the initial stages of the case Detective Strangway at the Glenelg Police Station was delegated the duty of investigating the suspicious death. He was assisted by Detective Hector (Hec) Gollan and Constable Sutherland. The media was supplied with a photograph and a detailed description of the deceased, and these details were distributed throughout Australia. In addition, official radio messages containing the same information were transmitted to all police headquarters in Australia.

On 3 January 1949 the official documentation containing photographs and a set of the deceased's fingerprints were forwarded to all police departments in Australia. Fingerprints were specifically classified and categorised by fingerprint experts using world standardised methods. This method was adopted to streamline manual filing, retrieval and matching. It was only a matter of a few days before all the reports returned with a negative result in respect to the fingerprints and relevant missing person files.

Missing persons – viewings – general investigations
To maintain a flowing sequential overview of the investigation is very difficult. For that reason various events will be interposed with other events that may not appear relevant to the topic in question. Some of the major events will be highlighted as a single event and will provide all the known information in sequence at that point for completeness.

References to some names and specific details are omitted for confidentiality purposes. That information will be included where names of individuals and details were reported in the media. There were investigations that received considerable media exposure, but the final outcome was never revealed. People who have followed the investigation over the years have continuously requested information in respect to specific subjects. Some information will be included to satisfy their curiosity.

The following items are only a random selection of events that took place during the police investigation. They show the extent of the duties performed in the attempt to identify the stranger. In one short period dozens of sources supplied information that required attention, and in one period it was reported that the body had been viewed by 35 people with eight positively identifying him as four different men. As the mystery deepened, ongoing intense interest was generated throughout the nation as the media reported on the course of the investigation.

The stranger was never identified positively. Many of the men who were reported missing were discounted for various reasons. The majority were eventually located or excluded because they did not match the general description of the deceased. The information in relation to these 'missing' men was forwarded to the MO (Modus Operandi) Section which at that time also housed the Missing Person Files. It is not known how many men were eventually located.

As a result of continuous publicity the police were inundated with information being supplied to the investigators.

The reports arrive
Police in Melbourne advised that a mother from St Kilda believed that the deceased may be her 34 year old son who had been missing for some time. The fact that he had a seriously damaged finger quickly eliminated him.

Jack Thomas McLean

One of the first people who contacted the police was Brian Joseph Dittmar, an ex-soldier, then living at Alberton. He provided the following information:

About four years ago he knew a man named Jack Thomas McLean who was working on coastal boats at Port Adelaide, mainly sugar boats. He was an ex 'pug' [boxer] and he said he had been in trouble with the police at Newcastle and Melbourne, mainly for being drunk. Dittmar knew him for about four months at Port Adelaide. Mclean told him he only took casual work. He had a scar from a bale hook wound on one arm from the elbow up the upper portion of the arm. The wound was not stitched, but allowed to heal without stitches. McLean was a pipe smoker. Dittmar had never known him to smoke cigarettes. McLean also told him that he had worked in foundries, he used to mention Launceston Tasmania as one place where he lived. He also told Dittmar that he resided at Prospect SA, but did not say with whom he lived. He believed McLean was single, he always carried money on him usually more than five pounds.

Apparently Dittmar had already spoken with police and viewed the body of the deceased. He included the following information in his statement:

On Saturday December 5th 1948 I was present at the City Mortuary West Terrace, there I saw the body of a man whom I identify as that of the man McLean. I looked at a scar under the left arm of the deceased it looks like an old scar. There is no doubt in my mind that McLean is the man at the Mortuary, although I now realize it must be nearly four years since I last saw him and not nineteen months as I first said when interviewed. *(Saturday was 4 December. The correct day and date is not known.)*

Police sent a report to the Sydney CIB for any information relating to McLean. On 8 December 1948 a reply was received:

McLean may be identical to John McLean alias Walter Edward Price alias William Price NSW PB [Photo Book] 90/282 and 114/51 and 126/36 and CR 30/181. He has convictions for minor liquor offences this State. He was born 05/06/1892, he was 5'6" tall, medium build. Light brown hair, brown eyes and a scar on his chin. Classification, f.p.c. [Finger print classification] 1 over 1, aa, 14/9.

On 14 December the Sydney CIB advised that McLean appeared on occasions in records of the Mercantile Marine Office in Sydney. They requested the probable age of the deceased and a description, and the name of any ship on which he had been employed.

On the same day the Adelaide CIB advised the Sydney CIB that *the Unknown Man* was about 45 years old, 5'11" [180 cm], of strong build, clean shaven, with fair hair going grey at the temples, grey eyes, and natural teeth but two missing in the front of the upper jaw.

They also advised Sydney that *the Unknown Man* was not identical to McLean. But they requested an urgent reply with any information regarding the possible whereabouts of McLean (alias Walter Edward Price) from the Deputy Director of Merchant Marine in Sydney.

On 16 December the Sydney CIB advised that inquiries were being made at the Mercantile Marine Office, the Electoral Office and many private addresses in Sydney. Inquiries into McLean's identity and whereabouts would continue.

On 22 December Detective Gollan finalised a comprehensive report that outlined information relating to *the Unknown Man*, supplied by Dittmar, about McLean and a full description of *the Unknown Man*, including a dental chart. He requested that a copy of the report be forwarded to each State so that a check could be made with the Repatriation Department in each State concerning any man named Jack Thomas McLean having a military record because that record would show the number of teeth missing and their position in the mouth. In this way some information about McLean might be obtained. He also mentioned that Dittmar had twice viewed the body at the Morgue. Inquiries in relation to McLean produced no records in South Australia. Dittmar's identification was not very satisfactory and it was considered that other verification would be needed before it could be accepted.

On 29 December Constable ND McClelland of the Victorian Police Force replied to the request. Inquiries into Army records at Albert Park did not reveal a Jack Thomas McLean. Royal Australian Navy records at Albert Park were also checked. The Navy did not keep records of merchant seamen, but particulars could be obtained from the Mercantile Marine Office in Melbourne.

On 4 January 1949 Sergeant FH Cross of the New South Wales Police Force reported on his inquiries at the Repatriation Department in Sydney: no person in the records matched McLean. Only members of the Services who were receiving some benefit were recorded with the Department. But records of all members of the Services were recorded with the Record Section at the Victoria Barracks in Paddington. He also suggested that inquiries be made in boxing circles at the Rushcutters Bay Stadium and the Leichhardt Stadium because McLean was said to have boxed in the ring.

On 5 January Senior Constable K Knight of the Victorian Police advised that his inquiries at the Repatriation Department in South Melbourne had not produced a positive result. The Jack McLean with a military record was a much younger man, and there was no record of Jack Thomas McLean.

On the same day the Tasmanian Police reported that they had checked the records of the Army, Mercantile Marine Office, Department of Repatriation, and the Registrar of Births, Deaths and Marriages in Tasmania with negative results.

On 10 January Victoria Police reported that inquiries at the Mercantile Marine Office in Melbourne showed that the only person named John McLean registered at that office had last reported there in 1941. He was then aged 48 years, and his private address was Glebe in Sydney.

On 13 January Detective Constable FR Gorrick of the Darlinghurst Police Station in Sydney reported that his inquiries at the Victoria Barracks did not locate any record of Jack Thomas McLean. Inquiries were also made at the Rushcutters Bay and Leichhardt Stadiums, and also with a number of boxing trainers, without success.

On 22 February 1949 Constable J Arthurson submitted his report:

> On this date a man formally of Victoria and now residing at Port Adelaide, viewed the body, and thinks that it bears a resemblance to a man called Mick McLean. He further states, that Mclean was at one time employed with the Painter's and Docker's in Melbourne and was a member of that Union. He lived at Brunswick, Victoria, and is believed to have lived there with his sister. At one time, Mclean, was in a brawl which took place in a hotel in Flinders Street, Melbourne, and was taken to the Melbourne Hospital, and was later seen in the same hotel on crutches. This man McLean is also believed to have been at one time employed on a boat, and got into trouble with the Police in Queensland for drawing a gun on some person.
>
> He states that McLean was known to the secretary of the Painters and Dockers Union, Melbourne, who might be able to throw some further light onto this matter.
>
> I respectfully suggest that the copy of this report be forwarded to the Victorian Police for favour of enquiry.

On 3 March Senior Constable H Smith of the Victorian Police submitted his report:

I have to report having made inquiries at the offices of the Painters and Dockers, Lorimer Street, South Melbourne, and interviewed the Secretary, Mr. Doyle. He does not know Mick McLean, and cannot recall a person by that name being a member of the union.

Records were perused by the Secretary, and they show that in 1945 there were two McLean's both were elderly men. Roberick was working for Harbour Trust, and Murdock, The Hobson Bay Docking Engineering Co., he is unable to furnish the address of these two men, they are both unfinancial in the Union.

Smith submitted a further report on 8 March:

I have to report having made enquiries in this matter at the Offices of the Melbourne Harbour Trust, 29 Market Street, Melbourne, and I was informed that Roberick McLean left the employ of the Trust in October 1945. His home address was recorded as South Melbourne and nothing has been seen or heard from him since.

On making enquiries at the Office of the Hobsons Bay Docking Engineering Co., 31 King Street, Melbourne, I was informed that Murdock McLean left the employ of the Company in November 1945, his private address being recorded as Newport, and nothing has been seen or heard of him since.

On 18 March the Tasmanian Police returned a comprehensive file relating to McLean after showing photographs of *the Unknown Man* throughout the State. All possible agencies and mining employment offices were checked. No evidence was located that related to McLean. The licensee of a hotel was sure that the deceased was a man he knew as 'Curly', who was a native of Adelaide. He believed 'Curly' was a deserter from the Army in the First World War. He also believed 'Curly' served a jail sentence in South Australia for a serious offence. However, fingerprints excluded him as the deceased.

On 31 May 1949 the Queensland Police advised there was no record in that State of a merchant seaman named Jack Thomas McLean, nor was there any record of a soldier with that name at the Repatriation Office.

Detective Sergeant Leane gave evidence to the Coronial Inquest on this subject:

The response, we have had people coming forward to identify the deceased. I believe one man did identify the deceased as a man named McLean, but it was not positive. It has not been shown to be wrong. Personal particulars did not tally with this man. In all cases where people have written the particulars supplied do not tally, because of teeth, age or other personal particulars. This man said that McLean was a pipe smoker. There was no evidence either on him or in his suitcase to indicate that this man was a pipe smoker. McLean had never been known to smoke cigarettes, and this man was an inveterate smoker, because of the stain on his fingers. This man's hands were hard, but were not rough from performing manual work, and McLean was a labourer. I was not present when the man said the deceased was named McLean. Everything has been done to identify the man, but without result.

Robert 'Nugget' Walsh

On 3 December 1948 Detective Harvey received information from an unknown person that the photograph of *the Unknown Man* in a newspaper resembled that of a Swede nicknamed 'Nugget' who was employed as a packer for Bishops at the East End Market in Adelaide. 'Nugget' was known to a person who was employed at the Bowden Pottery. This person lived in Rundle Street, Kent Town, next to Barrett's Maltsters, and he drank at the Royal Hotel, Hackney.

On the same day Mrs Elizabeth Thompson, a widow, attended the Morgan Police Station and said she believed that the deceased was Robert Walsh, who was also known as 'Bob' or 'Nugget'. She had last seen Walsh in December 1947 when he said he was going to New South Wales. On last Mothers Day she had received a card sent by him as Registered Air Mail, postmarked 8 May 1948 at Crows Nest, New South Wales. She produced a photograph of herself and Walsh to Mounted Constable MS Napier who forwarded it with a report to Detective Gollan.

At about 5.45 p.m. on 6 January 1949 FC Horsnell, Assistant Coroner's Constable, conveyed Thompson of Morgan and Stanley Salotti of Port Adelaide to the City Detectives Office. They had just attended the Morgue and identified the deceased as Robert Walsh. Constable Harry Storch interviewed them and took detailed statements.

Thompson stated that the Sunday Mail delivered to her home on 2 January 1949 had photographs on the front page of *the Unknown Man*. She immediately identified him as Robert Walsh and went to the Morgan Police Station and reported the matter. She took with her a photograph of Walsh that had been taken about 3 years previously. She also took with her the Mothers Day card she had received from Walsh with a £5 note enclosed. She had first met Walsh 8–9 years earlier when he came to her home seeking lodgings. From that time until about a fortnight before Christmas 1947 he had stayed at her home, except when he was cutting wood out from Morgan. He was employed by Mr Ford, Mr French and Jack Shell. Walsh told her he was originally from Wales and his only living relative was a sister who was still there. He did not like his sister because at one time there was an issue over money. On several occasions he went to Adelaide and stayed with people named Turner, who had a boarding house in Gouger Street. On one occasion Walsh brought two men back with him, and they worked with him wood cutting at Morgan. These men were relatives of Stanley Salotti's. Walsh was about 63 years old, a very quiet man who rarely drank liquor and was well liked by everyone. He left her home to go to Brisbane where he wanted her to meet him for Christmas. She did not go. On this day she came to Adelaide to locate Salotti because she knew Walsh had stayed with him at one time. She showed him the photograph of them together, and the photographs in the Sunday Mail. He inspected the photographs and immediately said that Robert Walsh was in them. She and Salotti then attended at the Morgue where they identified the deceased as Robert Walsh.

Stanley Salotti, a driver, stated that he first met Walsh about 3 years ago when he asked him for lodgings. He made enquiries at three boarding houses in the Port Adelaide area to find Walsh accommodation without success, so he allowed him to stay at his house for about a week. Walsh then returned to Morgan where he said he was wood cutting. He described Walsh as an excellent man who had very quiet ways. He was always talking about betting on horses and he formed the opinion that he was a great gambling man. He never mentioned any relatives in Australia, but stated that he had a sister in Wales, who he was not fond of because of a clash over money. Salotti stated his stepson and son-in-law, Alex Salotti and Frank Cherrington, worked with Walsh at Morgan and stayed with Mrs Thompson. He had last seen Walsh at the Victoria Park Racecourse about 18 months ago. He spoke with him for a very short time. Today, 6 January, he was shown the newspaper photographs by Thompson who was certain that the man was Robert Walsh. After examining them closely with her he was certain they were Bob Walsh. With Thompson he had been to the Morgue and identified the deceased person as Robert Walsh.

At about 7.30 p.m. on Friday 7 January 1949 Jack Hannam, a storeman employed by Elder Smith, Goldsbrough Mort & Co. Ltd at Port Adelaide and who lived at the Tivoli Boarding House, 64 Grote Street, Adelaide called at the City Detectives Office. Constable Harry Storch was again on duty and he commenced to interview Hannam. Hannam had first met a man at the Morphettville Racecourse, near the Totalisator betting ring on the area known as the 'Flat'. This was just after the May 1947 Oakbank race meeting. They discussed racing in general, exchanged tips and he introduced himself as Bob Morgan and the nickname 'Nugget', because of his build. He was very quiet, but appeared to bet fairly heavily on race horses. Prior to leaving 'Nugget' stated that he would look him up when he was in Adelaide again. Early in February 1948, by chance, he again met 'Nugget' at the Adelaide Railway Station. 'Nugget' was looking for accommodation so he took him to the Tivoli Boarding House, where he obtained Room 3, adjacent to his room. The Tivoli was often referred to as Turner's Boarding House because Mrs Turner had been the proprietor until about 3½ years ago. Since then it had changed hands on three occasions. At the time Morgan stayed there Len Hefferman was the proprietor. 'Nugget' stayed there for 8–9 weeks, and was employed by the Engineering & Water Supply Department on the Magill line (E&WS water line), as a labourer. 'Nugget' was about 5'8" (173 cm) tall and aged between 42 and 48 years. He was called 'Nugget' because of his build. Hannam never saw him drink liquor and he was a light smoker of tailor-made cigarettes. He and 'Nugget' would talk on a daily basis and he mentioned at one stage he was expecting some mail from along the Morgan line (water line). He also mentioned that he had a Drivers Licence in the name of Robert Walsh, and that he sometimes used the name 'Nugget' McCarthy. He had not explained why he used different names, and he never discussed what country he came from or if he had any relatives in Australia. On one occasion when they were out 'Nugget' had a fit and Hannam had 'brought him round' and assisted him back to the boarding house. Morgan had a very faint tattoo mark on the right forearm, just below the elbow joint. It was a small map of Australia. It appeared as if it had been done locally. Hannam said that he had not seen or heard from him since that time. He attended the Morgue with Storch where he identified the body as Bob Morgan. However, while at the Morgue Storch inspected the right forearm of the deceased, and could not see any signs of a tattoo. The hair on that part of the body was not as thick as on other parts.

On Saturday 8 January Mounted Constable Boyce at Minlaton advised that he had been contacted by a man who believed that the Unknown Man was 'Nugget' Walsh. He had not seen Walsh for about 2½ years, when 'Nugget' told him that if anything happened to him then all of his property should go Mrs Thompson of Morgan. This information was passed on to the City Detectives Office.

On 10 January Detective Gollan forwarded a report containing a photograph for the information of Boyce. On 14 January Boyce contacted the informant and showed him the photograph. He now did not think it was the man Walsh, although he added that it could be him. However, the height of *the Unknown Man* as given in the newspapers ruled out Walsh. The informant stated that Walsh would not have been more than 5'7½" (171 cm) tall at the most. He said that if he was in Adelaide in the next weeks he would be happy to view the body. On 17 January the report was returned to Detective Sergeant Leane for information.

On 10 January Boyce was contacted by another male informant who stated that the photograph in the News was a better one of Walsh than the previous photographs. If the deceased person was either 5'10" or 5'11" (178–180 cm) it was not Walsh. He also cast doubt on the surname Walsh, saying that he was a Welshman and the surname was Welsh and not Walsh. He further stated that after Thompson's husband died, Walsh bought the house for her. He also said that Walsh was a good worker and a very steady and thrifty person. He would no doubt have saved a few hundred pounds. He thought it might be in the interest of certain people if the body was identified as being Walsh. The report was forwarded to Adelaide through Inspector Partridge, the Officer-in-Charge at Wallaroo.

At about 9.00 p.m. on 10 January Constable R Venning, acting under instructions from Detective Sergeant Gully, attended the Morgue with Constable McCallum and James Mack of Norwood. Mack thought that *the Unknown Man* might be a person named Robert Walsh who left some months ago to buy and sell sheep in Queensland. He had expected Walsh to contact him at Christmas time. While he was unable to identify the body positively as that of Walsh, at about 10.00 p.m. that evening Mack telephoned to say that the body fitted the description of Walsh, except for the auburn hair. Walsh's hair was darker. But upon returning home and discussing the matter with his womenfolk, they stated that Walsh had slightly auburn hair. Therefore he now thought it was Robert Walsh.

On 1 February the Police at Port Augusta advised that *the Unknown Man* may have been employed by the Commonwealth Railways on the Alice Springs line. They requested a detailed description of the deceased and photographs to show to present and ex-paymasters who may have travelled the line, and also to persons who may have worked with him.

On 18 February Detective Sergeant Leane supplied two photographs of *the Unknown Man*, his description, dental details and clothing worn at the time of death. Further details could be found on page 25 of the SA Police Gazette of 1949.

On 21 February Inspector Ross forwarded the inquiry through Sergeant Mertin to Constable Copeland to contact Ivor Caird and other staff of the Commonwealth Railways Pay Office at Port Augusta. He did so on that day but no employee could identify the photograph. Caird stated he had associated the photographs in the newspapers with a man known as 'Nugget' who was employed as a fettler on the transcontinental East–West Line. 'Nugget', however, was no more than 5'5" (165 cm) in height and had a very pronounced flattened nose which was clearly not identical with the profile photograph. The photographs were also shown to staff in the Ways and Works Department who employed the fettlers. No-one could identify the man in the photograph as being in any way connected with their Department in recent years. The report was returned to Detective Sergeant Leane for information.

General information and viewings
During the evening of 3 December two men went to the Morgue and said that the body was very similar to a person they knew as Mills. Police ascertained that Mills had a brother living at Kilburn and when he was contacted he said his brother was living with him.

A short time later another person viewed the body but he quickly advised that it was not his relative from Perth.

Later that evening a telephone call was received from a Glenelg resident who thought the man resembled a fisherman from Coffin Bay. He said he would visit on the next Saturday to view the body. It is not known if this happened.

An informant contacted the Richmond Police Station and stated that the photograph resembled a prohibited Bulgarian migrant, who at one time worked in a garden at Lockleys. He refused to view the body.

A Glengowrie person thought the body may have been someone he taught at Goodwood. A viewing of the body was arranged and it was not the person nominated.

Much later on the same night the Prospect Police Station received information that the deceased had resided in a boarding house at 248 Grote Street, Adelaide. Police made inquiries at the boarding house and with neighbouring residents but no-one knew any person answering the description. Further information that came forward excluded the missing person at 248 Grote Street.

On 4 December a resident of Kapara Hospital, Glenelg, advised that he had met a man on the previous Tuesday in the Family Hotel at Glenelg. He said what his name was, and he came from England. He spoke with a foreign accent and had a Military Pension Card. He believed this man had a mental deficiency. A short time later police conveyed the man to the Morgue but he was unsure with his identification. When an officer contacted the Repatriation Commission the next morning, Solomonson was located.

On 5 December another resident went to the Glenelg Police Station and said he thought the deceased person was his brother. He declined going to the Morgue to view the body. Further details were gleaned that established the brother did not in any way match the description of the deceased.

On 6 December a Port Adelaide resident supplied information identical to a previous report relating to a fisherman from Coffin Bay. Inquiries by Constable Forby at Port Lincoln established that the nominated person was still alive.

At 3 p.m. on 7 December a mother was conveyed to the Morgue because she thought the body might be that of her son who she had not seen for about 6 weeks. She could not identify him but her knowledge of his dental description quickly proved he was not the deceased.

After studying the photographs in the paper a St Peters man believed the person had served with him in the Army in the Northern Territory. Arrangements were made to view the body the next day. The man was located living at Geelong in Victoria.

At 7.30 p.m. the police received information from the licensee of the Hyde Park Hotel that a fortnight earlier an unknown man left luggage at the hotel for safe keeping. A person had phoned him subsequently saying his name was Hoddard and asking if he could leave the luggage longer. The police collected the luggage and lodged it in the MO Section. There were two large suitcases containing personal effects, mostly clothing. A photograph and documents indicated the man was ex-Army, having been attached to the Royal Fusiliers in England. He had been a prisoner of war for 3 years. His address was care of the Engineering & Water Supply Department.

At this stage reports from interstate police forces were being received, all acknowledging they were in receipt of fingerprints, photographs and general information relating to the deceased. Unfortunately there was no information or evidence forthcoming that could assist in establishing the identity of *the Unknown Man*.

Label on trousers worn by the deceased

On 7 December the police ascertained from inquiries in the clothing trade that the brown trousers worn by the deceased were not available to the public in South Australia. A tag on a pocket of the trousers was marked 'Stamina Brand – Made by Wilson – From Crusader Cloth' which was a good quality wool blend of fabric made in Australia. On another pocket written in pencil were the markings '560 – T5 – REG – 23' which appeared to be the maker's mark. They were advised that the trousers were probably bought in Melbourne or Ballarat. A request for assistance was immediately made to the Victorian Police who replied on 8 January 1949:

Trousers are made by Wilson Manufacturer 275 Brunswick Street, Fitzroy. The pencil markings mean they were made by number 2 team and could have been made at Kerang, Swan Hill or Fitzroy. There are three thousand pairs made each week and distributed to N.S.W. the whole of Victoria and to Walsh Bros. Perth, W.A. Mr Wilson states that the tracing of the trousers is impossible as no check is kept re distribution.

Further possibilities

At about 9.15 p.m. on 9 December Sergeant Fenwick of the Glenelg Police Station received a report from the Port Germein Police Station that a man had left Port Germein about 3 weeks before and had not returned. He had been staying at the Coffee Palace in Hindley Street, Adelaide. Fenwick contacted the Adelaide Detectives Office, but the description of tattoos showed it was not the deceased.

On the same day Mounted Constable HL Walker of Kalangadoo forwarded a report through his Officer-in-Charge, Inspector Ridgley at Mount Gambier. He advised Detective Sergeant Gill at the Adelaide Detectives Office of a broadcast on the night of 7 December which suggested that a missing person Leonard Berry, who they described, could be the body found at Somerton Beach. Walker had made inquiries and the descriptions of Berry and the deceased did not match. Berry was still missing. Walker located Frank Mildenhall at Kalangadoo who had accompanied Berry from England, and had recently associated with him at Loxton. Berry was from Leeds, Yorkshire and had been treated severely while a prisoner of war for several years. Berry had a large sum of money and had opened a bank account in Loxton, and then went to Adelaide.

Embalming the Deceased

The body lying in the Morgue was beginning to decay and if nothing was done soon it would not be possible to allow people to view it. It was time to call on the expertise of Laurie Elliott of FT Elliott & Son, funeral directors of 89–95 Port Road, Hindmarsh. Elliott had recently returned from England where he had obtained advanced knowledge in the art of embalming. The police asked him to assist and he obligingly agreed. On 10 January he applied embalming fluid to the body and became the first person in South Australia to use the new technique with Formalin.

Some months after Elliott had embalmed *the Unknown Man* a newspaper published a lengthy article, including this mention of the topic:

The Liquid Fuel Company Control Board has granted the undertaker enough petrol for 50 visits to the Morgue for the embalming. For the first three months Mr Elliott averaged four visits a week.

Another newspaper referred to it also:

> During embalming Constable Sutherland found three small scars near one wrist, a scar near the left elbow, and another on the upper left forearm.

Scars on deceased
On 10 December 1948 the scars on the body were described:
- three small scars inside left wrist;
- one scar inside left elbow, curved about 1" (2.5 cm) long; and
- one scar or boil mark ½" (1.25 cm) in length, upper left forearm.

Further general information and viewing
At 7.45 p.m. on 12 December a telephone call was received from an anonymous ex-inmate of the Alice Springs Jail. He said he had served two terms of 4 months during the war for refusing to work. During that time he met a Bulgarian internee, known only as 'Tona'. He said the photograph in the newspaper looked like him.

On the same day a lady from Salisbury stated that the photograph of the deceased looked like her husband. She had married him 7 years ago in Sydney but had not seen him for 22 months. She was from Melbourne. He served in the Army, and left her on a previous occasion. He went under another name and cut all the markings from his clothes. He was a chain smoker. She agreed to view the body.

On 16 December the licensee of the Botanic Hotel in Adelaide contacted the police and nominated a typewriter mechanic who was employed by the government as the deceased. He had left a hotel in Alice Springs in August and said he was going to Darwin. He did not pay his board. Since his departure two letters had arrived for him, the last was dated 4 November 1948. The police spoke with a brother of this person who said his two brothers were both in Alice Springs at one stage. One was now wool classing in Mt Gambier and the other was not at home. He would advise them to contact the police.

On 20 December the Victorian Police requested news of any further developments because they intended to publish the photographs and details in their Police Gazette.

The police at this stage had checked all boarding houses in Adelaide and no information had come forward to assist in identifying the body. The many follow-up investigations being conducted were to the detriment of other police work. But they generated detailed reports which were despatched to police interstate for information, distribution and attention. All details had been distributed nationally through the media and this had generated considerable input from many people. Nevertheless, the investigation was reaching a stalemate and it was thought necessary to 'cast the net' to an international audience.

International distribution of fingerprints
Copies of the official reports generated and of the deceased's fingerprints were posted to all English-speaking countries on 21 December 1948. During January 1949 notification about the deceased's fingerprints were received from the selected countries. They all proved negative. A reply of note posted by the Federal Bureau of Investigation, United States Department of Justice, Washington DC on 5 January was received by the South Australian Commissioner of Police, WF Johns, on 17 January:

Commissioner of Police
Box #676, G.P.O.
Adelaide, South Australia

Please refer to file IE

My dear Commissioner:

I wish to acknowledge the receipt of your letter dated December 21, 1948, submitting the fingerprints of an 'Unknown' deceased person.
Please be advised that a search of these prints through the Identification Division of the FBI has failed to disclose any record.
Assuring you of my desire to be of all possible assistance to you in matters of mutual interest, I am

Sincerely yours,
(signed J.E. Hoover)

John Edgar Hoover
Director

In later years Hoover signed his name J Edgar Hoover. The Federal Bureau of Investigation produced a very informative monthly Bulletin to Law Enforcement Agencies throughout the world. It was a common practice among groups of detectives on their fortnightly payday to contribute 6d into a 'sweepstake'. The competition entailed guessing the number of times a photograph of Hoover would appear in the next issue of the FBI's Bulletin. The 'sweep' was normally won by someone nominating a number between 10 and 25.

No positive results
On 22 December the specimens taken from the deceased and delivered to the Government Analyst for attention had not revealed any known poison. Testing was continuing.

Dental records
On the same day Detective Gollan compiled a lengthy report containing the description of the deceased. His compilation included a record of the deceased's teeth;

TOP OF MOUTH	
Left Side	Right Side
8 7 6 - - - 2 -	- 2 - - 5 6 7 8
8 7 6 5 4 - - -	- - - - 5 6 7 8
*The numbered teeth are the missing teeth	

A copy of this information was forwarded officially to all interstate police forces.

CHAPTER 6

INVESTIGATIONS ENTER A NEW YEAR

Information from the public

On 2 January 1949 a person from Edwardstown contacted the police and stated that he had noticed an article in the Sunday Mail that mentioned that the missing man may have been from a boat which was tied up at Port Adelaide for 2 months in 1945. He stated that in 1945 he was engaged in painting a Dutch boat named the Thedens of the KPMLine, which was there for about 2 months for repairs. Also, he had worked on the Van Heutz which was at the port for the same time in 1945.

At 10.15 a.m. on the same day a woman from Torrensville contacted the Adelaide Detectives Office and stated that the deceased resembled a man who worked at British Tube Mills with her 5½ years ago. She nominated this man as Kelly and said he was well known to another man (who she nominated) working there at the same time. The last time she heard of the man who might assist was when he was running a sideshow at Glenelg.

At about 6.15 p.m. on 5 January a man from North Adelaide came to the Adelaide Detectives Office and nominated the same person as the woman from Torrensville. He knew the man who worked at British Tube Mills about 6 years ago. The man was conveyed to the Morgue where he viewed the body. He stated that it was definitely not the person.

Clark from Woomera

At 3.30 p.m. on 2 January a man arrived at the Adelaide Detectives Office to assist the investigation. Upon reading the Mail he thought the body might be that of a man, Ray Clark, he had worked with at Woomera. Clark was 38 years of age, born in Queensland and had been working in Melbourne recently. He was a prominent boxer some years before and so was well known to Jack Delaney, the former welterweight champion of Australia. He was about 5'10" (178 cm) tall, of medium build, and with slightly reddish complexion and hair. He had some teeth missing and his face and ears showed signs of boxing. Clark was engaged by the Commonwealth Department of Parks and Interior in Canberra to work with surveyors at Woomera.

He had left Woomera on about 20 November 1948 saying he was going to Adelaide until after Christmas. The informant stated he came to Adelaide from Woomera on 27 November 1948 to run a sideshow at the Attunga Carnival at Toorak. He also said that if Clark was still in Adelaide he would have been to see him at the carnival, because he had shown an interest in sideshows.

The informant went to the Morgue with Constable FC Horsnell to view the deceased. He stated that the body very much resembled Clark. But he said he was not definite, and he would locate Jack Delaney to see if he could assist.

The following item appeared in a newspaper:

MYSTERY OF BODY ON THE BEACH

Adelaide:- The mystery of the identity of a man whose body was found on the beach at Somerton, near Adelaide, on December 1, is becoming a major problem for police investigating the circumstances of his death ... Police are now concentrating on a claim that the dead man's name was Ray Clark and that he came from Queensland to work on the rocket range.

At 9.15 p.m. on 3 January an Adelaide man came to the Adelaide Detectives Office as a result of what he had read in the News. He believed the deceased was Ray Clark whom he had worked with and shared a room with at the Woomera Rocket Range. He knew Clark very well. He was conveyed to the Morgue to view the body, but it was not Clark. He did not know the current whereabouts of Clark but there was some connection with a fish café in Hindley Street.

On 5 January the police received a letter from a surveyor in Coburg, Victoria. The man nominated the same Ray Clark because of the description published of the deceased. Clark had worked for him at the Woomera Rocket Range. He said the man was a pugilist and he seemed to be very 'punch drunk'. He said he had been to the war and had received head injuries in North Africa. He once told him that he had been a barman at Young & Jackson's Hotel in Melbourne for years, and that he had a wife and child living in Sydney. The Head Surveyor at the Rocket Range said that he had been sent away for medical attention on account of the head injury. When Clark was in Woomera he had a Royal Australian Air Force motor licence in another name and a Sydney address. The man was well known to Sergeant Dunlop of No. 2 ACS of the RAAF at the Rocket Range. He believed that Dunlop had moved to Mildura.

On 2 January another Adelaide man was taken to the Morgue by Horsnell to view the deceased. The man stated that the body looked similar to a man named Sarrogon who he had worked with in 1916 on a farm at Overland Corner. The informant said he saw this man about 10 years ago in Adelaide. He was not sure of the spelling of the name. Horsnell was not impressed with the identification.

At 7.30 p.m. on the same day a man associated with a fuel company contacted the police and stated that the photograph in the Mail looked like a man he nominated as working at one stage at a service station on the corner of Military Road and Henley Beach Road. This man had also been a plumber and an iron worker. Police at Henley Beach made inquiries that revealed the man was still working at the service station.

At about 5.25 p.m. on 3 January a painter, and now a casual gardener and residing in Adelaide, was conveyed to the Adelaide Detectives Office by Constable Curtis. He thought that the body was that of a man, name unknown, who was employed as a fireman on an Indian boat that had berthed at Port Adelaide in November 1948. He would not disclose his reasons for thinking this, but said he would like to view the body.

On the journey to the Morgue he asked Constable Storch if the body was found on the beach in a sitting or lying position. He also asked whether the body had been examined by a doctor as to whether any poison had been injected into it. He was told that an autopsy had been performed and as far as was known at this stage it had not disclosed any poisonous substance being present.

After examining the body, he said it was the fireman. They returned to the Adelaide Detectives Office where a statement was taken from him. The painter stated that he had seen the man 2 days prior to his death (29 November 1948) walking in Ferris Street, Somerton. He was dressed in a khaki shirt and shorts, wearing boots but not wearing a hat. He had very sunburnt skin. He saw the man jump the fence of a house and drink from a tap in the front yard. He had seemed very distressed and was waving his hands. He had jumped back over the fence into Ferris Street and walked around a corner out of view. The painter was then working in Ferris Street at about 10 a.m., but would not disclose who he was working for.

Storch asked him why he would not disclose his suspicions regarding the man, and he stated that he had not completed his inquiries. He said that he knew an Indian family of English extraction in the area, and he thought that the man was trying to get friendly with their daughter. As a result they injected some poison into him.

The man stated that he knew a nominated detective personally. Storch was not impressed with the witness.

A missing friend from New South Wales

At about 8 p.m. on 4 January 1949 Detective Sergeant Leane received a telephone call from a staff member of the Australian Broadcasting Commission who stated that he had received information from Canberra that *the Unknown Man* might be a man who had been living in Goulburn, New South Wales. He had been missing since November 1948. The deceased's details were transmitted to the police at Goulburn that day and they immediately commenced their inquiries. Detective Sergeant BJ Catt interviewed the brother of the missing man who had reported him missing on 3 January. He had seen the photograph and details in the Sunday Telegraph on 2 January, and he believed it was his brother.

His missing brother had left Sydney on 25 November 1948, travelling to Adelaide with the intention of seeking employment as a cook in the shipping industry. He described him as aged 45 years, 5'10" (178 cm) tall, medium build, fair complexion and hair thin on top and at the temples. He had a round solid face, a determined solid chin, hazel or grey eyes and an appendix scar on his abdomen. He was formerly a cook in the Royal Australian Navy. The missing brother had a first-class rail ticket from Sydney to Albury (on the Victorian border with New South Wales), and he intended to pay his own fare for the remainder of the rail journey to Adelaide. His brother did not know the clothing he wore and could not describe his teeth.

He stated his brother had a wife in Sydney who could supply more details. He thought she might have his discharge papers from the Navy and that they might contain details of any scars. He had contacted his sister-in-law on 29 December, and she had not heard from her husband.

Catt recommended that his report be forwarded to the CIB in Sydney, with the view of the wife at the nominated address to be interviewed as to whether she has any tidings of her husband. If a detailed description of him is obtained and any other information that may assist the Adelaide Police, it is to be forwarded direct to them.

On 6 January Sergeant L Moore of the Sydney MO Section reported that 'he could find no person on their Missing Friends Files that answered the description of the person found on the beach at Somerton'.

On 9 January Detective Constables FR Gorrick and SC Workman reported that they had contacted the wife of the missing husband. She last saw her husband on 25 November and has not heard any news from him since. He was going to Adelaide by train. He was a cook in the R.A.N. and she has never seen his naval discharge papers. He held the rank of C.P.O. Cook and supplied his service number. She said that the description given by the brother was accurate apart from him having bushy eye-brows, a noticeable dimple on his chin and he had a full set of false teeth in his upper and lower jaws. When she last saw him he was wearing a fawn sports coat with a greyish herringbone pattern, (which she had purchased for him at David Jones) navy blue trousers, black naval shoes, green shirt, red tie, a blue naval gabardine top-coat and a green hat with a feather in the side. She is of the opinion that the unidentified man is her husband.

On 12 January the report from the Darlinghurst Police Station was forwarded through official channels to South Australia's Commissioner of Police 'with a view to an effort being made to establish whether or not the person referred to herein is identical with the unknown man whose body was found on Somerton Beach, Adelaide on 2nd ultimo'.

On 17 January the report was forwarded to Detective Sergeant Leane, who did not consider the description of the missing person as matching that of the deceased.

At about 7 p.m. on 7 January Constable Storch spoke with a man from Kilkenny at the Adelaide Detectives Office. About 2 years ago the man was in Mrs Molloy's boarding house at 192 Semaphore Road, Semaphore. Another man came to the house and he shared a room with the man. He could not remember his name but thought that Molloy would. The man stayed at the boarding house for about 10 weeks. He handed a letter with further details to Storch. He said the man's face was similar to that shown in the newspapers, but he refused to view the body.

On the instructions of Detective Sergeant McGrath, Constable Canney interviewed a man from Largs Bay on 7 January. The man had gone to the Morgue with Constable Horsnell and had identified the deceased. He said the man was well known to him and had done casual work along the Murray River between Mildura and Renmark early in 1939. He had seen him frequently and he often referred to ice and snow at home during the winter but did not say what country he came from. He described him as 5'10" (178 cm) tall, well built and with sandy hair that was inclined to be wavy. He could not remember him having a scar on the ear. The informant had enlisted in 1940 and had not seen the man since then. He believed the man would be about 44 or 45 years of age. He felt certain that the body was of the person he nominated but he was unable to give definite proof other than the similarity of the features and general appearance of the body.

At 11 a.m. on 7 January Detective Sergeant A Evans had a conversation with a tool inspector at General Motors (Holden's) Ltd. He and several of his workmates were of the opinion that the deceased was a former employee with the Christian name Handel and an English surname. Born in Sweden on 10 November 1899, he was a member of the Merchant Navy in the First World War. A butcher by trade, he was employed in the Tool Section from 27 August 1946 to 17 February 1948. It was believed he lost his wife about 6 months earlier. His last known address was 271 Gouger Street, Adelaide.

A missing son in Queensland
At 3.15 p.m. on 8 January the Brisbane CIB radioed a lengthy message to the Adelaide CIB. They provided details from a father in Dalby, Queensland who had not heard from his 22-year-old son since a letter contact on 25 November 1948. The son had said he would be home soon. He gave his address in Williamstown, South Australia. A lengthy description was given of many scars and prominent birth marks. However, before 10 p.m. on the same day a reply was transmitted to the Queensland CIB:

RE YOUR MESSAGE 6 UNABLE TO CHECK WHEREABOUTS AS NO-ONE HOME AT WILLIAMSTOWN ADDRESS TONIGHT STOP UNIDENTIFIED MAN BETWEEN 40 AND 50 YEARS OLD STOP DO NOT THINK HE WOULD BE IDENTICAL STOP

Forming a dedicated investigation team
Detective Sergeant Leane was one of the most senior and experienced detectives in the Adelaide CIB. He had a very good working knowledge of Adelaide and its suburbs. He, along with other officers, played a major role in supervising and directing aspects of the investigation but they were yet to produce any evidence to identify the deceased or to explain the circumstances surrounding his death. It was obviously a suspicious death and despite all inquiries to date, nothing concrete was forthcoming to help the investigation solve the mystery. Indeed, the investigation was becoming a little fragmented due to the many other commitments of personnel. It had every indication of becoming a 'hard slog' and a centrally located and dedicated team of investigators to devote time solely to this

matter was required.

On 8 January Leane was placed in charge of an Investigation Team which included Detective Gollan, and Constables Sutherland and Horsnell. They were centrally located in the Adelaide Detectives Office.

A fresh start

On 8 January 1949 the Commissioner of Police received a letter from a woman in Tasmania, who had read an article in the local newspaper about *the Unknown Man*. In the sad and touching letter she stated her husband had been away from home for 8 months though she saw him about 5 months ago in another town. He was not in the best of health, but had told her that he would be home soon. She blamed the war for his frayed nerves. They were unable to get a house to live in, but they were very devoted and had a lovely little girl. She described her husband as being 26 years old, going a little grey, tall, fair and with grey blue eyes. He had a nasty war wound on the left thigh and a skin graft on the right leg. She enclosed a photograph of her husband and said he must be under an assumed name.

On 26 January Leane replied to her letter and returned her photograph.

Search for a truck in Sydney

On 10 January Detective Gollan submitted a report for inquiries to be made in New South Wales in respect to information supplied by a person from Norwood who had viewed the deceased. He stated that the deceased looked like the driver of a truck he had spoken to at Kent Town on 27 October 1948. The truck was a red buckboard type, with the rear portion covered with canvas. It had no tailboard and had soft carpets stacked on the tray. On the driver's door was the address 104 Pitt Street, Sydney. He stated that there was a strong likeness between the driver and the deceased though the former appeared to be shorter.

On 1 February Sergeant MT O'Neill reported that there was no number 104 Pitt Street. Sergeant King of the North Sydney Police Station advised that the highest number in that street was 84. He also enquired at the Department of Road Transport in Sydney with a view to tracing the lorry. However, he was advised that it would be impossible because there were more than 130 000 lorries registered in New South Wales.

O'Neill had also noticed an article in the Daily Telegraph about 'Keane'. He took it upon himself to check all records of 'Missing Friends' reported in New South Wales during the previous 12 months, and there were no reports containing this name. He attached a copy of the article to the information he forwarded to South Australia.

On 10 January a member of a family living in the farming community at Minlaton, believed that the photograph of the deceased was similar to a man who was employed by them during the harvest period. He left there on Sunday 21 November 1948 and said he intended to return on 24 November. They did not believe that he really intended to return because he took his work clothes with him. It was known that he wrote to a lady at Whyalla. They believed he originally came from Winton in Queensland. The local policeman recalled him obtaining a drivers licence at the beginning of November. From his conversation with him he believed he was a Victorian. He did not match the description of the deceased.

Detective Brown joins the investigation

On 11 January Detective LD (Len) Brown joined the Investigation Team. At this stage the police began directing their attention to the possibility that *the Unknown Man* may have abandoned or deposited personal possessions prior to his death. They knew that this would be a mammoth search, taking into account the several hundred hotels and boarding houses throughout Adelaide and the suburbs. Many had already been checked. It was decided to request public help through the media, which might help streamline the process.

Luggage as clue to beach body

Police today appealed to all boarding housekeepers and hotel licensees to advise them if they have any unclaimed luggage left before December 1.

The appeal is made in connection with inquiries into the unidentif ed body found on Somerton Beach on December 1.

Detectives say the victim must have left his belongings in the metropolitan area the day before his body was found but they have been unable to trace them.

He did not bear the appearance of a man without means of support who might have slept on the river banks. He had shaved on the day of his death.

With a knowledge of past cases where intending suicides have travelled to Adelaide to end their lives, detectives have checked at the railways luggage off ce for unclaimed baggage, so far without result.

On 12 January under instruction from Detective Sergeant Gully, the police went to the Adelaide Railway Station and collected Doctor Black, the South Australian Railways doctor. Black thought he knew the identity of the deceased but he was unable to identify the body he was taken to view at the Morgue.

On the same day Constable R. McCallum attended a shop at 44a Wakefield Street, Adelaide where he was informed that one morning near the end of November a man had left his kitbag in the shop intending to pick it up at lunchtime. He never returned. The female attendant could not describe the man. The kit bag contained clothing and an old razor strop. On one item of clothing was the name 'Moran', apparently as a result of it having been dry cleaned. Detective Sergeant Evans was to make inquiries to locate the person.

At about 6 p.m. on 11 January the manager of Newday Furniture in Hindley Street, Adelaide reported to the police an incident that he and his wife had witnessed on the Glenelg foreshore a couple of days prior to the reports of the body being found. The man was sitting on a seat with his head hanging in the crook of his arm for about 1½ hours. On one occasion his hat had fallen off and two young men walking past put it back on his head and walked on. The manager felt he might be able to identify the person.

At long last – a possible breakthrough

Detective Sergeant Leane had been inquiring with the staff at the Cloak Room at the Adelaide Railway Station to ascertain if there was any unclaimed property that might correlate with *the Unknown Man*. On 14 January he learnt that there was an unclaimed suitcase that had been booked in on 30 November 1948 with ticket G52703. He was advised that the automatic time register indicated that the suitcase was booked in between 11 a.m. and noon.

A visit to the Cloak Room

Later that same day Leane sorted through unclaimed property in the Cloak Room. On ticket G52703 on the unclaimed suitcase on a shelf was written 'The charge for each article (Motor Bicycles excepted) is for day of lodging and one clear day thereafter 4d. For each subsequent day 4d'. He took possession of some items from the suitcase for checking. The suitcase was left there on the chance that someone might claim it. After making some observations and comparisons he was satisfied that the suitcase and its contents were linked to *the Unknown Man*. It was a normal brown suitcase, in good condition with no stickers or travel identification attached. It also appeared that a label had been removed from one side. He took formal possession of the suitcase on 19 January.

Contents of the suitcase

Leane made a close examination of the contents and recorded the items contained therein. He particularly noted the coat worn by the deceased, three items of clothing in the suitcase that the names 'Kean', 'T. Keane' and 'Keane' were written on and items that he associated with stencilling.

THE UNKNOWN MAN

Def nite Clue In Somerton Mystery

Detectives obtained their first real clue in the Somerton body mystery yesterday, when they examined clothing found in a suitcase recovered from the cloak room at the Adelaide Railway Station.

Det-Sgt R.L. Leane, who with Detective L. Brown and Plainclothes Constable D. Bartlett, is engaged on the case, said yesterday that he was satisf ed beyond doubt that the clothing in the suitcase belonged to the man found dead at Somerton on December 1.

He had concluded this after closely examining a card of brown cotton found in the suitcase. Of an unusual type, it was identical with the cotton used to repair the lining of a pocket in the dead man's trousers, to sew buttons on a pair of trousers found in the suitcase.

A puzzling feature about the clothing found in the suitcase was that with the exception of the names "T. Keane" and "Kean" on a singlet, all name tabs had been removed from the garments.

Lamp Test

Mutilated name tabs on other pieces of clothing in the suitcase were placed under an infra-red lamp yesterday in an unsuccessful effort to read them.

Police believe that whoever removed the name tabs from the clothing either overlooked the names on the two pieces of clothing, or purposely left them on, knowing that the dead man's name was not "Keane" or "Kean".

Another piece of evidence connecting the suitcase with the dead man was the discovery in the case of a small brown button identical with buttons on the dead man's trousers.

Articles found in the suitcase were a red checked dressing gown, pair of red slippers, pyjamas, shaving gear, an electrician's screwdriver, a stenciling brush, and a table knife which had been cut down into a short and sharp instrument.

Comparison of items by Leane

During the Coronial Inquest Detective Sergeant Leane gave evidence of a comparison he made between items found on the deceased's body and in the suitcase:

The name tabs were missing from the coat, they have been torn out of the pocket of the coat which he was wearing, but they are identical in size. Those he was wearing are of Crusader Cloth, they could have been made in any State of Australia. The clothes in the case were well kept and tidy …. Most of the pencils are Royal Sovereign, 3 of them are H type, which would be drafting pencils. The knife, stencil brush, and scissors, were found in the case. The brush is used for stencilling the brands cut out. Mr. Cowan made a test on the brush, and found that it had been used. He could not find out what the substance was, but a black substance came out of it. The case is practically new. Wherever it came from has been taken off the end of it; the luggage label has been removed, I mean. A number of the articles in the case are minus the tags.

We noticed that the coat has been stitched with brown cord. That coat was being worn by the deceased. In the suitcase was found a needle and thread of similar texture. The trousers pocket in the case had been mended with a similar thread. It appears to be rather a masculine mending. The trousers worn by the deceased were mended with a similar thread; he had sewn buttons on his trousers with a similar thread. The thread is a common thread. The shirt in the suitcase and the shirt the deceased was wearing were similar shirts; also a pair of Jockey underpants found in the case were a similar brand to those worn by the deceased. There was one brand new handkerchief in the case, which is similar to the handkerchief found on the body. The trousers and the coats were a similar size. The trousers were an identical size – they were measured. The coat in the case was smaller. The fitting of the coat he was wearing might have been a little bit large, and the one in the case might have been a little small. They could have been the coat of one man. The dressing gown is of reasonable quality, and there is a pair of slippers to match. They have been worn fairly well.

A visit to the School of Arts and Crafts
Leane went to the South Australian School of Arts and Crafts with certain items that had been in the suitcase. He described his visit to the inquest:

> I interviewed Mr. Gray, the headmaster of the School of Arts and Crafts, North Terrace Adelaide and after studying catalogues he came across a knife the replica of this one in shape. It is an ordinary table knife cut down. Inside the folders produced is tinned zinc, an alloy used for stencilling. Mr Gray then produced a piece of similar zinc, not quite as heavy, and stated that in his opinion the knife was used to start the letter off, he then finished the letter by cutting around with the scissors.

Possible links to America
The coat that *the Unknown Man* had been wearing was examined for Leane by Hugh Pozza in Adelaide. Leane's evidence at the inquest explained the results of that examination:

> I interviewed Hugh Possa, tailor, of Gawler Place, and he is of the opinion that it is an American type coat, because there is a gusset in the front of the coat shown in American Catalogues. He pulled the coat to pieces and viewed the stitching, and there is a feather type stitch in it which he states could be made only in America, where the only machines which could do that were. The coat was partly made, then fitted. It was mass produced but made to measure. The body work is performed, and then the person is fitted before it is completed. He thought it was made in the United States; it could have been made by someone who was in Australia but who learnt the trade in America because of the machine. Such clothes are not imported. He had either been in America, or had bought the clothes off somebody who had been there.

Professor Cleland examines the clothing
At some stage Leane gave the property to Professor John Cleland of the University of Adelaide. The Professor's evidence at the inquest included the following:

> I made an examination of the clothing which was on the body of the deceased, and also the contents of the suitcase found at the Adelaide Railway Station, and many of my observations have already been expressed in evidence. In the suitcase was an orange coloured linen thread. I found a similar thread in the clothing on the body and in the clothing in the suitcase. In the suitcase was some orange coloured thread. This was examined microscopically and corresponded in colour and size of fibres to similar thread used to sew up a trouser pocket in the suitcase, buttons on the trousers taken off the deceased, and to repair where the coat collar of the deceased had given way. The colour was a warm sepia colour, which is an unusual colour.

I put on the deceased's double-breasted coat, and it buttoned on me with some difficulty, and a sports coat in the suitcase similarly could be buttoned with a squeeze. The sleeves of each of these garments came down the hand about the same extent though perhaps the sports coat sleeves were not quite as long.

The trousers in the suitcase and those worn by the deceased seemed to be of equal length. The shoes taken off the deceased made an excellent fit to Mr. Cowan, but the slippers in the suitcase he thought were a trifle smaller.

The coat in the suitcase may have been a trifle smaller than the one the deceased was wearing. The sleeves were shorter. Both were too small for me. For a smaller chested or smaller abdominal man, the coat on the body might have been a trifle too large, and the one in the suitcase a little too small, in other words, they would have both fitted the one man.

I found the stump of a blade of barley grass in the inside of the lower part of the trouser leg in the suitcase, and another stuck in the sock worn by the deceased, but I do not pay much attention to that, as barley grass is widely distributed at this time of the year, in all states. It is a grass which throws up its seeds as one walks through it.

The shoes on the body were remarkably clean. They looked as though they had just been polished. There was a little sand around the toe marks, but they were not quite what one would have expected had the deceased been walking about Glenelg from noon until he was seen lying on the beach. I would expect them to have shown loss of gloss in such circumstances.

I did not feel too convinced about the tags on the clothes – it appeared that they had been removed, but I did not find any thread to indicate they had been recently removed.

CHAPTER 7

NATIONAL ASSISTANCE SOUGHT

A s a result of locating the unclaimed suitcase the Investigation Team was satisfied it belonged to *the Unknown Man*. Unfortunately there was no documentation or information that would assist in establishing his identity, apart from laundry marks on a pair of trousers, and the names 'T. Keane', 'Keane' and 'Kean' on a few items of clothing.

The names and markings were photographed for circulation purposes. Police records were checked for the names but the result was negative. A list of laundry and dry cleaning businesses were compiled, and they and the photographs were distributed throughout the State. Various media outlets were provided with relevant details in order to gain public assistance, as the following article which appeared in a local newspaper shows:

COTTON MAY BE CLUE TO MYSTERY

A thread of cotton may yet prove the means of solving one of the strangest mysteries to confront police – the identity of the Somerton beach body.

While searching unclaimed luggage at Adelaide Railway Station yesterday, detectives found a suitcase containing a pair of trousers, a pocket of which had been stitched with unusually coarse thread.

They have now established the thread is identical with that on the buttons of the trousers worn by the victim. The trousers found in the unclaimed luggage bear three sets of dry cleaning numbers (see picture.)

A check will be made with dry cleaning firms throughout the Commonwealth.

The luggage was handed in to the railway parcels office

on November 30 – the day before the body was found at Somerton.

The victim has been five times "identified" as five different men, and police now feel hopes of establishing his name from viewing the body are unlikely to succeed.

Police Photographer Aebi today photographed the dry cleaning marks and Det.-Sgt. R. L. Leane is arranging to circulate them throughout Australia.

A request for national assistance

On 18 January Lionel Leane compiled a very comprehensive report for the interstate police and media. He included photographs, the background to the situation, recent developments relating to the suitcase, a list of the property located and the details printed on the clothing. He mentioned the names Kean and T. Keane.

Interstate replies

Queensland Police returned a report on 7 February, advising that they had conducted an inquiry in conjunction with one of their own investigations concerning the body of an unidentified man found dead at Mount Cootha, near Brisbane, on 30 January 1949. A detailed list of all the businesses they had checked was supplied. At the places they visited it was stated emphatically that the laundry marks displayed by the police were not theirs. The details and photograph appeared in the Brisbane Truth on 30 January and the Queensland Police Gazette of 12 February (p. 56).

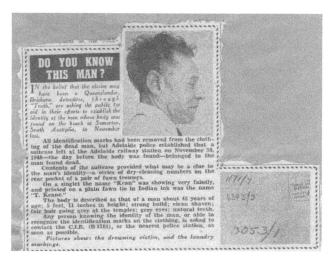

Victoria Police returned a report on 8 February. They stated that the photographs of *the Unknown Man* and of cleaners' marks on clothing suspected of belonging to him were reproduced in Melbourne's newspapers and the Victoria Police Gazette.

They reported that several people had said that they could positively identify the deceased. In most cases the description they furnished differed so vastly from him that it would be superfluous to include them in the inquiry. The following people furnished some information.

A woman said her brother had left Yarraville in November and had not been seen since. He sometimes went to Adelaide. He had a scar under his right shoulder from an operation to remove two ribs. She thought he looked like the photograph.

A woman from Geelong stated that the photograph was very much like her husband, whom she had last heard of at the Stockwell Hotel, Stockwell, South Australia.

A man from a department in Law Courts Place, Melbourne stated that the photograph looked like a former Apollo Bay man, whom he nominated, who was involved in a Court matter in Adelaide in late 1948.

A man from Reservoir stated the photograph was very much like a man, whom he nominated as living at an address in Adelaide. He also gave his place of employment.

Example of interstate inquiry – a full circle

An interstate request for assistance through official channels involves several people. The file passes through the chain of command where it receives specific reference numbers for recording and indexing purposes. The following is an example of the process:

18 January Detective Sergeant Leane submits a comprehensive report for inquiries by New South Wales Police.

18 January Superintendent W Sheridan forwards the report to the Commissioner of Police, Ref: CIB 132/13.

18 January The report is received by the Commissioner of Police, Ref: M/10/673.

21 January (Time stamped between 9 and 10 a.m.) Received by Police Dept. NSW. Ref: N. 7702/3347.

21 January The Commissioner of Police forwards the file to the Superintendent of Detectives in the CIB: 'Forwarded for information, necessary attention and report, please as

desired by the Commissioner of Police, Adelaide, hereon. Photographs (3) attached'.
Received on the same day by the CIB in Sydney Ref:12448/242 see also 55/63.
4 February Sergeant M Marzol reports to the Superintendant of the CIB:

I have to report that all available particulars to hand, in connection with above subject matter, have been circulated per medium of the New South Wales Gazette issued on the 2nd instant (copy attached), and a direction given for inquiries to be conducted throughout this State, and any results to be promptly communicated to the Criminal Investigation Branch, Sydney.

The papers are returned in order that consideration can be given to the request of the South Australian Police to have some publicity given the matter per medium of the Sydney press. Three photographs attached.

The information was forwarded to various locations, including the North Eastern District, Newcastle where on 7 February a file was given the reference no. S.1461/388. On the same day Superintendent Clifford forwarded the file to the Inspector of Police at Newcastle:

The attention of the Inspector is directed to page 51 of the Police Gazette issued on the 2nd instant, relative to the subject matter. In accordance with the directions contained therein, immediate inquiries should be made at all dry-cleaning establishments and any other appropriate inquiry made, so far as your Sub-District is concerned, and a report furnished when this has been done. Of course, should any information of value be obtained, such should be communicated direct to the Criminal Investigation Branch.

Inspector Noble either typed out a Sub-District Memo himself or engaged the services of a good typist to produce carbon copies which were forwarded to the Inspectors in Charge of the Cessnock, West Kempsey and West Maitland Police Stations.
18 February Cessnock replied with a negative result.
21 February West Kempsey replied with a negative result.
22 February Inspector SJ Stewart of West Maitland returned his file to Newcastle: 'I have to report that this matter has been brought under the notice of all Stations in this Sub-District and reports are now to hand and are attached'.
Inspector Noble received the reports from the Sub-Districts and submitted the following to the Superintendent:

Forwarded. The above matter was circulated by Sub-District Memo. Reports have now been received from each Station to the effect that the necessary inquiries have been made as directed and the notice of all Police has been brought to the Police Gazette dealing with this matter.

No useful information has come to light other than the report of Sergeant 3/c Handcock of Hamilton Police, wherein he stated that laundrymen are of the opinion that the laundry marks on the clothing are of English origin, this by reason of dealing with items at the laundry, bearing laundry marks known to have been made in England.

23 February The Superintendent at Newcastle forwarded the file to the CIB Branch:

THE UNKNOWN MAN

'Forwarded for information. The necessary inquiries have been made throughout the North-Eastern District, but no useful information has been obtained. However, attention is directed to the final paragraph of Inspector 3rd Class Noble's accompanying minute'.

On 24 February Constable E Day of the Sydney CIB submitted his report to the CIB's Superintendent of Detectives:

I have to report having noted the contents of this file. To date the following action has been taken in an effort to ascertain the identity of a dead man, whose body has been at the City Mortuary, Adelaide, South Australia, since 1st December, 1948.

As set out above in the report of Sergeant 3rd Class Marzol detailed information in connection with this matter appears in the New South Wales Police Gazette for the information and attention of all police. (Specimen attached). The press was supplied with the particulars of the inquiry and subsequently the Daily Telegraph and the Daily Mirror newspapers published articles in their editions of the 16th February, 1949. (Cuttings attached).

I have made inquiries at the Marco Productions Pty. Ltd., 583 Pacific Highway, St. Leonards, manufacturers of the trousers the deceased was wearing and ascertained that their records go back to 1945 and the number appearing on the trousers is not included in the numbers recorded since that year indicating that the trousers* were manufactured prior to 1945. (*The deceased was not wearing these trousers. They were located in his suitcase.) I also made inquiries at Charles Parsons and Co. Ltd., 71 York Street, City, and Robert Reid and Co. Ltd., 34 York Street, City, both of which firms handle "Marco" products in their business as wholesalers but was unable to obtain any suitable information that might indicate to which retailer the particular trousers were sold.

On the 21st instant I interviewed Mr. Barclay of the Chamber of Manufacturers of N.S.W., 12 O'Connell Street and he indicated that he was prepared to insert a photograph in the Dry Cleaner's Journal, a monthly publication widely distributed in the dry cleaning trade of what appears to be dry cleaner's marks on the deceased's trousers and the necessary printer's block was obtained from the Daily Telegraph newspaper for this purpose.

Inquiries have been made at the Commonwealth Electoral office and numerous "T. Keane and T. Kean" appear on their records. A large number of the addresses obtained have been visited and no suitable information has been obtained to date.

On 17th instant information was received at this office that the dead man might be the husband of [a nominated person] of Waverly. She was subsequently interviewed and shown photographs of the unidentified dead man, and she states that she is of the opinion that it is identical with her husband, who left her three years ago to take up rural work in the Dubbo-Bourke district. A report has been furnished requesting inquiries be made with his mother at Dubbo and a close male friend of his living in Bourke. The results of these inquiries are not yet to hand. (File No. CIB 49/915)

Inquiries are being continued in this matter and perhaps this file might be returned to me in due course for further report. (Two comprehensive newspaper cuttings dated 16/2/49 attached).

On 27 February Senior Constable HJ Small of the Woy Woy Police Station submitted this report in reference to the note in the New South Wales Police Gazette:

I have to report that I interviewed a male person of Woy Woy this date in regard to a statement made that he believed he could assist in establishing the identity of the body of a man found on the beach at Somerton, SA on the 1st. December, 1948.

He stated that he knew a man named Thomas Kean or Keane many years ago whilst serving with the Defence Forces in Western Australia and whom he considers strongly resembles the description published of the unidentified body.

Description of Thomas Kean or Keane is as follows:- Height about 6'1", well built, fair to auburn hair, freckled complexion, prominent cheek bones. He was last seen by this person at Fremantle, WA, in 1920 and was then 24 or 25 years of age, he was serving with the 10th. Coy. Royal Australian Coast Artillery at Port Arthur's Head, South Fremantle and held the rank of Gunner.

He was shown the photograph of the unidentified body appearing in the NSW Police Gazette and considers that there is a marked resemblance to the man he refers to, taking into consideration that the photograph was taken after death. I examined a group photograph which included Gunner Thomas Kean or Keane and I cannot agree that there is a resemblance in the features but the general description of the two men are very similar.

The informant is a retired army non-commissioned officer and is, so far as can be ascertained, a reputable person. He informed me that he has not corresponded with Thomas Kean or Keane and has had no intimation of his whereabouts since he saw him last in 1920.

The above report was received by Sergeant ED Benson of Woy Woy and was forwarded to the Inspector of Police in, Newcastle on 28 February 'for forwarding to the Criminal Investigation Branch, Sydney, for information'.

On 15 March Detective Constable WH Moye and Constable EP Day of the CIB in Sydney, jointly submitted a report to the CIB's Superintendent of Detectives:

We have to report that since our last report on 24th February, 1949, in connection with this matter the remainder of the persons bearing the name "T. Keane or Kean" have been interviewed or other satisfactory evidence of their existence has been obtained.

The Dry Cleaner's Journal containing the photograph of the dry cleaner's marks on the deceased's trousers has been in circulation for several days but no information has yet come to hand concerning their origin.

The man mentioned in our previous report as possibly being identical with the dead man has been interviewed at Dubbo.

Attached hereto is file no. S1461/324 containing a report by Senior Constable Small of Woy Woy, N.S.W., in which he sets out a description of a man named Thomas Kean or Kean, last heard of in West Australia in 1920. Also in this file is a report by Inspector Noble of Newcastle in which there is a suggestion that the dry cleaner's marks may have an English origin.

Every effort has been made by us with a view to having this man identified, but without result. Perhaps this file might be returned to the South Australian Police for their information. Their attention is particularly invited to the reports of Inspector 3rd Class Noble and Senior Constable Small which may be of some assistance to them in this inquiry. This matter will receive constant attention by us and should any information be forthcoming it will be immediately forwarded on to the South Australian Police for their information.

The file containing all the above details was forwarded to the South Australian Commissioner of Police for the information of the Investigation Team.

Missing friends
Reports nominating men who had worked throughout South Australia from the West Coast to the South East were received from members of the public who suggested numerous reasons for the person they nominated to be the deceased, but the suggestions were all rejected.

A letter was received from a woman in Western Australia who believed the deceased was her missing son-in-law. Her details of injuries excluded him, and her letter was filed at the Missing Persons Section for reference and she was advised accordingly.

CHAPTER 8

ATTEMPTS TO LOCATE KEAN

The following information is supplied as a result of responses to the Police reports and media publicity generated as a result of the names Keane and Kean found in the suitcase of the deceased.

New South Wales and Victoria

In January Leo Francis Kain from Five Dock in Sydney viewed the body of the deceased and said it resembled his brother Thomas Hugh Kain. His brother was a 'wanderer' and could be in any State, and he has not seen him for 20 years. His description now is about 50 years of age, 5'10" tall, thick wavy hair and a fair complexion. Leo believed his brother was working on wharves in Melbourne, Victoria. Detective Col Streeter compiled a report on 10 January and the information was forwarded to Victoria Police for inquiries to be made.

On 19 January the Victoria Dock Police Station reported that they had made inquiries at the Victoria Dock Labour Compound. They perused the records of wharf labourers employed on the waterfront in Victoria. No person of that name or description had been employed on the waterfront since 1941 when the records were compiled.

On 24 January Constable V Spiers reported that no Thomas Hugh Kain was on the electoral rolls. There were two people with the name Thomas Kain – born 1900 of Coleraine and born 1900 of Cardross.

On 29 January Constable G Jewell of the Coleraine Police Station reported that he had spoken to Thomas Kain. He had no knowledge of a Thomas Hugh Kain. He nominated the relatives he had living in Adelaide and the South East of South Australia. Thomas Kaine had since moved to Red Cliffs.

On 17 January a request was forwarded to Sydney Police to re-interview Leo Francis Kain to ascertain if he could supply any further information. On 3 February Constable JT Wylie of Five Dock Police Station advised that Leo Kain had been expected home from South Australia days ago, but he was now expected to return home on about Sunday 6 February.

Constable JT Wylie of Balmain Police Station later reported that he had re-interviewed Leo Kain. He had spoken to his sister who said the brother had a permanent scar on the nape of his neck as a result of a carbuncle being removed.

On 10 February Constable Thomas interviewed a Thomas Kaine at Red Cliffs. He said he was not related to, and did not know either Leo Francis Kain or Thomas Hugh Kain.

On 12 February the brother who originally viewed the deceased wrote to Detective Sergeant Leane from Sydney. He mentioned viewing the body and that since then he had remembered that his brother had a large scar on the back of his neck where a carbuncle had been removed. The scar should still show.

Queensland

On 10 January the report submitted by Detective Streeter relating to Thomas Hugh Kain missing from Five Dock, Sydney, along with a copy of the report compiled by Detective Sergeant Leane in respect to the property located at the Adelaide Railway Station, and the names 'T. Keane' and 'Kean' were forwarded to the Queensland Police.

On 29 January Constable RK Greenwood of the Brisbane CIB received information

THE UNKNOWN MAN

from a man living at Yarrol via Monto. He stated he could give some information about the unidentified man. He was detained for a period at the Round Mountain Detention Camp in Brisbane in 1945 for being 'AWOL' (Absent Without Leave) and he remembered a Corporal Thomas Keane being on the staff at the camp. Keane was working under the supervision of Major Murphy. Keane was a single man who had been a cane cutter in North Queensland. He described him as being 40 years, 5'11", stout and hair turning grey. He remembered that on the night Keane was discharged during April 1945 he was assaulted in Brisbane. He did not know if the assault was reported to the police. The informant stated he had seen the article in Smiths Weekly and the Courier Mail.

On 31 May Queensland Police advised that the above mentioned person was identical with Thomas Lawrence Kean who died in Brisbane Hospital on 24 March 1949.

On 30 January a builder of Belmont in Brisbane contacted Constable GH Fursman. He said he had read about *the Unknown Man* in that day's Truth. He advised that about 2 years ago he was employed by the Housing Commission on a building project at Stafford, and he believed that a carpenter employed there was the man in the photograph. His name was either Tom Kean or Keane, but he could not supply any further details. However, on 31 May Queensland Police advised that this person had been located.

On 30 January Constable Fursman received a report from a man from Bowen Hills in Brisbane in relation to that day's papers request for information about the man who 'drowned' at Somerton last November. The man stated that about 25 years ago he knew a man named Tony Keane, who was a sawmiller in Yarraman. He was single and about 35 years old. He left there and was heard of shortly afterwards in Toowoomba. He thought he resembled the description and photograph in the newspapers. On 31 May Queensland Police advised that this person was not the deceased.

On 31 January a letter was received from a man who referred to an article in the Courier Mail regarding a T Keane found dead on the beach at Somerton. He stated that in 1942 when he was attached to the 29th Infantry 'B' Company in the Goondiwindi area, there was a Quartermaster T Keane who was about 5'11" and about 50 years of age. As far as he knew he was a single man.

On 31 May Queensland Police advised that not only was this soldier Thomas Lawrence Kean who had died in the Brisbane General Hospital on 24 March 1949, but also that they had checked all records in respect to the names supplied and could not locate any information that would assist in identifying the deceased.

Western Australia – Kean to Kane
On 24 March a report was received by South Australia Police from the New South Wales Police. The report related to inquiries in that state in particular information that nominated a T. Kean or Keane in West Australia. The report was forwarded to Detective Sergeant Leane.

On 25 March Detective Sergeant Leane put the following notation on the file:

Perhaps this file could be forwarded to the Police, Western Australia with a view of having inquiries made concerning the present whereabouts of Thomas Kean or Keane as mentioned in Senior Constable Small's report, or any Keane who may be missing from that State during the past 6 months., and reported as a Missing Friend as I am of the opinion that the body found at Somerton is that of a man named Keane.

On 6 April the report was forwarded to the Western Australian Commissioner of Police and on 12 April it was forwarded to Detective Sergeant Richardson of Perth CIB for attention.

31 May Detective Sergeant Richardson submitted the following forwarding minute:

I respectfully report having made inquiries for the person named Thomas Kean or Keane as mentioned in the attached report by Senior Constable Small about the City but without success.

It is mentioned that a person by that name, and of similar description to the body found at Somerton Beach, South Australia was in 1920 a gunner in the Royal Australian Artillery at Fremantle.

Perhaps further inquiries could be made at Fremantle.

On the same date the report was forwarded to Inspector Lewis for attention.
On 31 May Inspector Lewis of the Fremantle CIB received the report (Reference B109/49 and IO779/48). He minuted his report to Detective Daniels on the same date with:

'For inquiries at the Royal Australian Artillery Depot in Burt Street regarding Thomas KEAN or KEANE, particulars of whom is supplied in Senior Constable Small's report dated the 27th. February '49'.

On 16 June Daniels of the Fremantle CIB completed his inquiries and reported to Lewis:

I have to report having made inquiries at the Royal Artillery Barracks, Fremantle, in regard to the within mentioned "T.Keane or Kean", as described by the nominated person of Woy Woy, N.S.W.

I interviewed Captain Hannaby, Sergeant Gower, Marcus Williamson and others who have been attached to the Artillery Depot since the time mentioned by the nominated person. They are all unanimous in the opinion that the man referred to by this person was one Thomas Kane, who fits the description given by him and served at Arthur's Head etc at that time.

They do not agree that Kane resembled the photo of the unidentified body on the beach at Somerton, S.A. Neither do they remember anyone named Tom Keane, who was supposed to have served at about that time.

During the war, most of the old records at the Artillery Depot are believed to have been destroyed and nothing could be found to show that anyone named Thomas Keane served at about that time.

An old record however was discovered showing that Thomas Kane was discharged in 1922 and the above mentioned members recall that he then went kangaroo shooting in the north of this State and it is thought he eventually went to Queensland.

I have also interviewed all persons named Keane or Kean in the Fremantle District, but none of them can assist at all in this inquiry.

If it is considered likely that the unidentified body could be that of Thomas Kane, who has served at Arthurs Head, it has been suggested that further particulars re him could be obtained from a man named Harry Skipworth, who is now a farmer at Gutha, via Morawa. Skipworth is stated to have been friendly with Kane and it is thought that they perhaps kept in touch with one another after they were discharged.

On 17 June Inspector Findlay forwarded the file to Inspector Clifford of Geraldton Police Station 'to arrange for Harry Skipworth of Gutha to be interviewed, in connection with this matter, which should be expedited'.

On 21 May Constable Kelliher received the file; marked: 'For early attention please'.

On 27 May Constable Kelliher of Morawa Police Station returned the file to Inspector Clifford with the following report:

I have to report having interviewed Mr. Harry Skipworth, of Canna, where he is employed as a Pumper for the West Australian Government Railways, regarding the unidentified body of a man found on the beach at Somerton, South Australia, thought to be that of Thomas Kane, late of Arthur's Head, Fremantle.

Skipworth informed me that he has not seen Thomas Kane since he was discharged from the Artillery in 1922.

Skipworth was shown the photos of the Deceased, which are attached to this file, and he states that they do not in any way resemble Kane, besides Skipworth states that the photos are of a person between forty to fifty years of age, and if Kane is still living he would now be about seventy years of age.

The report arrived back with Detective Sergeant Leane on 11 July 1949 through the official chain of command. It contained the following note:

Inquiries show that the man referred to by the nominated person was one, Thomas Kane, who was discharged from the Artillery Depot in 1922 and went kangaroo shooting, and it is thought, eventually went to Queensland.

Further inquiries show that the body found at Somerton is definitely not that of Thomas Kane.

There is no record of anyone named KEAN or KEANE missing in this State.

Keanic

The following newspaper article makes reference to the name Keanic. There may have been journalistic licence associated with the article.

New Clue May Identify Somerton Man

The man who was found dead on the Somerton beach on December 1 and who has not been identif ed despite world-wide police investigations, may have been a Bulgarian named Keanic, according to information received by the police recently. In view of the fresh evidence Det. Sgt. R. L. Leane has recircularised the man's description throughout the world under that name. Police believe that they now have a def nite lead towards establishing his identity.

Recently an Egyptian, who speaks seven languages and is employed by a Hindley Street butcher, identif ed the name "Keanic" written on the tie worn by the dead man, and said that he believed him to be a Slav, probably a Bulgarian. After a minute examination of the name tag in the suitcase, he told police that the last two letters had been partly obliterated by wear, and that the name could have been mistaken for Keane. Police had previously hoped to identify that man as "Keane", the name also found on clothing in the suitcase which they are certain was left by the dead man at the railway station shortly before the discovery of the body.

This opinion was reached after the finding of a type of rare grass seed near the body which was identical with one found in the suitcase. The case of clothing contained a seafarer's stencilling outf t which, according to shipping authorities, would be used only by a member of a ship's crew for marking cargo and supplies. A small piece of paper printed in Turkish which was found in the dead man's pocket has lead police to assume that he was able to speak that language.

On 29 April Detective Senior Sergeant Leane submitted the following report:

> I beg to report that on the morning of the 1st December, 1948, an un-identified body of a man was found on the beach at Somerton, South Australia. Although continuous enquiries have been made, since that, by pathologists, the cause of death has not been ascertained.
>
> A suitcase has been recovered from the Adelaide Railway Station Cloak Room and has been definitely established as the property of the deceased. In the suitcase was found a neck-tie, which bore a name, in marking ink, which at first was thought to be "T. KEANE". Further inquiries have been made and a Mr. Moss Keipitz, an Egyptian, employed in Adelaide has been interviewed and shown the neck-tie.
>
> Mr. Keipitz is of the opinion that the name on the neck-tie is "KEANIC" pronounced "QUANIC" and that name is of European origin, either a Czechoslovakian, Yugoslavian or from the Baltic country. He viewed the body, which helped him to form his opinion. He further stated that the initial, which was thought to be a "T" is a "J" written in Arabic.
>
> May I respectfully request that this report be forwarded to the Police at Canberra for inquiries to be made at the Department of Immigration, Customs and Dead Letter

Office at the General Post Office. It is thought that this person may be a displaced person or a deserter from an overseas vessel.

On the same day the report was forwarded to the Chief Officer of the Commonwealth Police in Canberra.

On 14 May Constable AJ Urquhart submitted the following report:

I have to report that I have made a thorough search of the records held at the Department of Immigration, Canberra, but no trace can be found of the name "Keanic" or a close variation. My search included all classes of Immigrants and ship's deserters. I also searched the records of the Customs Department and the Canberra Branch of the Commonwealth Employment Agency Canberra General Post does not retain unclaimed letters. They are forwarded to Sydney Dead Letter Office after a lapse of 10 days.

Perhaps this file could now be returned to the Commissioner of Police, Adelaide, for information please.

On 29 April Detective Sergeant Leane forwarded an identical report to the Victoria Police with the following request:

May I respectfully request that this report be forwarded to the Police in Melbourne for enquiries to be made at the Department of Immigration, Customs and Dead Letter Office of the General Post Office. It is thought that this person may be a Displaced person or a deserter from an overseas vessel.

On 26 May Senior Detective Adam from Russell Street, Melbourne, submitted the following report:

I have to report that as requested by the South Australian Police, I have made enquiries at the Dead Letter Office, G.P.O., also a Branch which deals with foreign displaced persons and ships deserters, but there is no trace of any person named "Keanic" or "Quanic".

The Immigration Department in Melbourne only deals with persons admitted to Victoria, not other States. There is no further information to hand in this State which would assist in the identification of the person found at Somerton.

51

NEW SOUTH WALES

POLICE  GAZETTE

AND WEEKLY RECORD OF CRIME.

No. 5.] WEDNESDAY, 2 FEBRUARY. [1949.

ATTENTION OF ALL OFFICERS.

SPECIAL INQUIRY.

Sydney.—Above are photographs of the unidentified body of a man found on the beach at Somerton, South Australia, on the 1st December, 1948. The centre block illustrates cleaner's mark on the pocket of a pair of Elasta-Strap trousers, subsequently traced, and evidently the property of deceased. The dead man is about 45, 5 ft. 11 in., strong build, fair to auburn hair turning grey at temples, grey eyes, natural teeth, two of which are missing from front of upper jaw; dressed in grey-brown double-breasted coat, brown trousers, brown knitted pullover, white shirt and collar and brown shoes and socks.

A 24-inch brown fibre suit-case, containing clothing, unclaimed at the luggage-room at Adelaide Railway Station since the 30th November, 1948, bears evidence of being the property of deceased. Identification tabs had been removed from the clothing found in the case, but close examination of a singlet revealed the name "KEAN" in marking ink, on a plain fawn neck-tie the name "T. KEANE" was similarly marked, the only other article bearing marks was the trousers with cleaner's marks "1171/1," "4393/3" and "3053/1" (illustrations above) in indelible pencil on the hip pocket. Other property in the case comprised a red and grey small check pattern dressing gown; a pair of red felt slippers, size 7; a card of sewing thread; a table knife, the blade of which had been reduced in length and ground to a dagger-like point which would suggest it had been used for skinning purposes; a pair of scissors, the blades reduced to 2 inches and sharply pointed; and a stencilling brush. The last three mentioned articles might reasonably suggest the likelihood that deceased was a station hand or had been engaged in a similar rural pursuit.

The foregoing facts provide scope for inquiry throughout this State, and Police generally are directed to co-operate in this direction. In country districts the Officer-in-charge of a station will see that all dry cleaning establishments are contacted and other appropriate inquiries made within his patrol. In the Metropolitan District each Divisional Officer will arrange for similar action to be taken.

Officers are directed to give this matter particular attention and communicate immediately with the Criminal Investigation Branch should any information be obtained which may lead to the identification of the deceased person.

CHAPTER 9

THE UNKNOWN MAN IS BURIED

At some stage, shortly after Detective Sergeant Leane collected the suitcase from the Railway Station he handed for examination all of the clothing associated with the deceased, including the items he was wearing, to Emeritus Professor John Burton Cleland, a legally qualified doctor in the Department of Pathology at the University of Adelaide.

In his evidence to the Coronial Inquest Professor Cleland stated that:

In examining the clothes, (trousers worn by deceased) in a fob pocket which was rather difficult to find, just on the right of the fly, I found a piece of paper. After I found it and put the paper back, it took me a good deal of time to find it the second time as it was a pocket which could be easily missed.

(The fob pocket on the inside of the waist band of trousers was very common in that period. The piece of paper with the words 'Tamam Shud' on it was tightly rolled up into a cylinder shape and it was hard to find the second time.)

Leane in a statement mentioned that '*On the 19th. April, 1949 Professor Cleland informed me that he had found a small piece of paper in the Fob Pocket of the deceased's trousers produced, bearing the words Tamam Shud*'.

Detective Brown's evidence to the inquest observed, in part, '*I saw the slip of paper "Tamam Shud" I received it from Detective Leane with instructions to make enquiries about it. It was found in the fob pocket of the trousers on the body by Professor Cleland*'.

The mysterious 'Tamam Shud'
The finding of this small, torn piece of paper with the words 'Tamam Shud' was a general topic of discussion, but no-one could identify what it related to. Frank Kennedy, the Police Roundsman for the Advertiser, was a well-read man. After hearing about this mysterious slip of paper, he made contact with Detective Brown. In one conversation Kennedy said to Brown, 'If you are looking from where the words 'Tamam Shud' came from, find a copy of The Rubaiyat of Omar Khayyam. Some copies end in Tamam and some in Tamam Shud'.

Detective Brown toured the many bookshops of Adelaide in an attempt to find a copy of the Rubaiyat that contained the words 'Tamam Shud' that were identical to the words found in the trousers of the deceased. It did not take him long to realise how popular this particular book was. There were copies at many locations, produced by numerous publishers, but never the one particular version he was looking for.

At one time Detective Brown stated:

On Wednesday 8th. June, 1949 I went to Beck's bookshop in Pulteney St., Adelaide and made a search of a number of copies of a poem named RUBAIYAT and written by Omar Khayyam. This poem has been translated to English by a man named Fitzgerald and is a very popular poem and can be found in practically every library and a large number of homes.

In one particular copy by Collins Press, England I examined the printing on the slip

*of paper with the print at the end of the poem, namely 'Tamam Shud' and found that the
lettering in each came from the same font of print.*

*I have made inquiries and examined a copy of the Persian English Dictionary written
by a man named Wallaston (sic). The words "Tamam Shud" appear in this dictionary
and means 'To end' or 'To finish'."*

Brown's evidence at the inquest elaborated on his statement:

I went to Beck's Book shop in Pulteney St., Adelaide where I looked through a
number of copies of the poem, until I found one copy at the end of which appeared
the words "Tamam Shud" in the same font of type as the words on the slip of paper
I possessed. I held that copy up to the light, and passed this slip of paper over the
words "Tamam Shud" in that copy, and they are identical in size and length. That
copy was published by Collins Press of England, and is distributed to Australian
distributors although printed in England.

I was not able to find a copy which did not have printing on the back (meaning that
the words 'Tamam Shud' had not been removed) as from the slip of paper produced. I made enquiries at the public library, the lending library, and the circulating
library, and also the University Library, in an endeavour to find a copy that might
have the words "Tamam Shud" torn from it. I caused enquiries to be made interstate, and also at Brighton, Somerton, and Glenelg, but no copy can be found with
the words 'Tamam Shud" torn from it.

The paper on which the words are written is known as coated wood free art paper,
substance of 28 X 36, 56 lbs to the 500 sheets. That is the paper which is before
me. I did not compare this paper with that in the Collins Book. If this is a Collins
impression, the one which I saw would be a different impression. The type of paper
I have is the type used in book manufacture. It appeared to be much the same sort
of paper as appeared in the Collins Book. Different impressions of the same book
might be printed on different paper. These words appear at the end of the first edition, at the end of the second edition the word "Tamam" appears.

I have made enquiries as to the meaning of the words. I made enquiries from
Mr. Whiting, of the public library, and in a Persian-English dictionary compiled by a
man named Wallaston (sic) the words "Tamam Shudan" appear and these words
mean, "To end or To finish". In another copy of the Rubaiyat written by another
translator the ending of the poem merely states "Finis". I take it "Tamam Shud"
means the same. "Shud" appears to be the verb, and "Tamam" the noun "to end".
The poem itself simply means that we know what this world has in store for us, but
we do not know what the other world has in store, and while we are on this earth
we should enjoy life to the fullest, and when it is time for us to pass on, pass on
without regrets.

Photographing 'Tamam Shud'

The police made arrangements to have the torn slip of paper containing the words
'Tamam Shud' photographed and duplicated into a number of copies. The photographs of
the words were then cut into small neat rectangular shapes to make them available as examples for future intestate inquiries. They were also made available to the media throughout Australia. In some cases they were believed to be actual copies of the original piece of

torn paper, resulting in references being made in some articles that the deceased neatly cut or trimmed it himself, prior to his death.

The following two portions from Melbourne and Adelaide newspapers refer to the piece of paper containing the words 'Tamam Shud' having been cut.

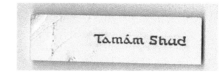

Because the top of the scrap of paper had been cut clean, it did not fit into the torn part of the page. But the bottom of it corresponded with the printer's trimming at the foot of the page, and police are satisfied that the piece was torn from the book.

As the scrap of paper found on the dead man had been trimmed, police were unable to identify the book merely by fitting it into the torn page. Proof will now rest with tests on the paper and the print.

The following article appeared in a local newspaper:

Cryptic Note on Body

The translation by Public Library off cials yesterday of a cryptic note discovered in the clothing of the unidentif ed man found dead at Somerton on December 1 has caused detectives to intensify their enquiries in an effort to solve what is considered the strangest case of its type in the history of the SA police force.

The note which was printed on a scrap of paper, read "Tamam Shud."

The words "Tamam Shud" are to be found at the end of the last verse of the English translation of the Rubaiyat of Omar Khayyam.

Tamam Shud is believed to be a contraction of the Tamam Shudan, which according to Wollaston's

English – Persian dictionary, means "to end" or "to finish."

Detectives believe that the dead man cut the words out of a book.

In an effort to trace the book photographs of the scrap of paper will be sent to interstate police.

Report for national inquiries – search for The Rubaiyat
On 10 June Brown submitted a lengthy report to be forwarded to all States:

I beg to report that on the 1st. December, 1948, the body of a man was found on the beach at Somerton S.A. All efforts to date have failed to establish the identity of this man.

On making a search of the clothing on the deceased, a small slip of paper bearing the words "TAMAM SHUD" was found. Until recently the meaning of these words could not be found, but it has now been established that these words mean

"To Finish" or "To End" and is found in the conclusion of the Poem RUBAIYAT written by Omar KHYYAM a Persian Philosopher. This work has been revised by Fitzgerald and it has been found that the lettering as per attached photographic copy comes from a font of print used by the Collins Press, England, for whom W. Cooppen of 527 Little Collins St., Melbourne, Victoria and Australian Publishing Co. Pty Ltd., Bradbury House 55 York St., Sydney, N.S.W. are the Australian distributors.

As the slip of paper bearing these words was in good condition, and was in the fob pocket, it suggests that the slip was torn from one of these copies in circulation shortly before death. I respectfully ask that this information be forwarded to the Police in [State nominated] requesting that a check be made of the Lending and circulating section of the Public Library to see if these words have been torn from any publication in their possession. A photographic copy of the print is attached. This copy is slightly larger than the original."

Interstate response

All States replied with a negative result. On 20 June Constable AH Southern of the CIBanch in Sydney reported:

I have to report having interviewed Mr. Pentelow, Deputy Principal Librarian, Mitchell Library, McQuarie Street, Sydney, this date, in connection with the within mentioned matter, and he informed me that hundreds of copies of the Fitzgerald edition of the "Rubaiyat" had been obtained in the past, both for use in the Sydney Library, and also for disposal per the Country Order Branch of same, and as the volumes are not minutely examined for damage or deletion after use by readers, it would be an impossibility to identify any particular reader who might be responsible for the deletion of the portion of the volume containing the phrase referred to in this file.

I also interviewed Mr. W. Goodchild, Secretary, Australasian Publishing Company, 55. York Street, Sydney, and was informed by him that the copies of the poem referred to edited by his company would number in the thousands and would be distributed throughout the Commonwealth.

It would appear that no information can be obtained in this State which would assist the Adelaide Police in this matter in any way. Perhaps this file might now be returned to the South Australian Police for information.

Detective AB Duncan of the Queensland Police reported:

I have to report with reference to the attached file from the South Australian Police, that I have made inquiries at the Public Library, William Street, Brisbane, along the lines suggested in the attached report.

The circulating section of the Queensland Public Library has only recently commenced operation, and there was no circulating Section in the year 1948. There is only one copy of the book 'RUBAIYAT OF OMAR KAYYAM' at the Queensland Public Library, and this is a very old edition. It has been examined closely and it appears that the words 'TAMAM SHUD' were not included in that edition. In any case there is nothing to suggest that those words or anything else were removed from the book at the Queensland Public Library.

This additional information which is now in the possession of the South Australian Police has been given some prominence in the local papers here, but no further information has been received which would assist. The proprietors of several leading Brisbane lending libraries have also been contacted in connection with this matter, but no useful information has been obtained.

Perhaps this file could now be returned to the South Australian Police for their information.

The Western Australian Police also reported that all libraries had been checked, and no copy of the Rubaiyat with a missing page was located.

Time was running out
The body of the deceased was slowly deteriorating and it was reaching a point when it would soon not only become impossible to continue to preserve the body, but also to take people to the Morgue to view it. Discussions were also taking place in various circles in relation to making arrangements for the burial of the deceased.

The last viewing – Tommy Reade
Information was received that the deceased may be Tommy Reade who had been employed on the steamer 'Cycle' until about 3 years previously. Police made inquiries aboard the 'Cycle'. As a result two crew members were probably the last people to inspect the embalmed body of the deceased. He was not identified as Tommy Reade.

A cast of the deceased
There was no information forthcoming suggesting any possibility that *the Unknown Man* would be identified in the near future. The police had to consider alternatives to photographs as a means of identification once the body was buried. It was decided to approach the South Australian Museum to discuss the feasibility of producing a cast of the upper body.

As a funeral date had been set, the work had to be done quickly and without any publicity. Paul Lawson, taxidermist, had discussions with the Director of the Museum and it was decided that he would be engaged to produce the cast.

On 2 June Lawson was taken to the Morgue by detectives where he viewed the body and a general discussion took place in relation to producing a bust cast. He then planned the work.

The next day he travelled to Koster's Pottery Works to obtain clay to make a mould cast.

On Monday 6 June he made his final preparations in readiness to commence the task the next morning at the Morgue. On 7 June, with the assistance of Detective Brown and other police, he removed the body from the refrigeration facility and commenced to make a mould of the head and upper body. It was a very difficult process because the body began thawing and the moisture had to be continually wiped with towels. Making a mould of the ears was not attempted at this stage but arrangements were made to continue the work the following day.

During the Wednesday at the Morgue a telephone call was received from Constable

Dinham regarding the funeral arrangements. Meanwhile, Detective Brown and another police officer discussed the case as Lawson completed a suitable mould of each ear. The ear moulds were cast and Lawson commenced piecing together the remaining mould.

The next day he was completely engaged in piecing together the mould, filling it with plaster and breaking away some of the clay moulding.

On June 10 the remaining mould was removed and the project was inspected by Brown who expressed his approval of the product. Professor Cleland had requested that a sample of the brain be obtained by Lawson and so he commenced to remove some of the stitches that had been placed in the head during the autopsy. In a further conversation Lawson was advised that because of the impending funeral and time constraints not to continue with obtaining specimens, but to complete making the mould. He was advised not to replace the stitches he had removed.

At this stage the cast had not been completed: it required further drying and some finishing off processes. The Monday after the weekend was a public holiday. So Lawson did not return to work on the cast until Tuesday 14 June.

The bust was completed on 15 June when it was inspected by Professor Cleland, Detective Sergeant Leane, and Detectives Brown and Noblet. It was apparent to everyone present that Cleland was very displeased that his request for a sample had not been met.

Lawson handed the cast to Constable Horsnell on 16 June, and it was conveyed to Police Headquarters for photographing. On the same day Lawson was served with a Summons to appear before the Coroner's Court, at the IOOF Building, 11–13 Flinders St, Adelaide, on the morrow at 10.30 a.m. to be examined by the Coroner.

Lawson's evidence to the Coronial Inquest follows:

I carry out my work at the Museum, North Terrace. On 7th June 1949 I went to the City Mortuary with Detective Brown, and he pointed out a body to me. I proceeded to make a cast of the features of the body.

I first made a mould, and reproduced in that mould the cast. The cast in Court is the cast which I made. It should be a perfect reproduction of the deceased. There would be a slightly difference in appearance of the deceased when alive than at the time when I made the mould. The naturally fleshy parts of the face would have shrunk and sagged slightly.

The formalin which was used to embalm him would shrink it in a general direction. It was the effect of the embalming substance more than death which caused the shrinking.

I examined the body. His feet were rather striking features, suggesting, this is my own assumption, and he had been in the habit of wearing high-heeled and pointed shoes; I base that on the fact that the calf muscle was high and well developed, such as found in women.

The feet were comparatively broad at the joints of the toe and the foot, but the big toe and the little toe were joined together towards a common apex, in other words wedge shaped. That peculiarity I found more pronounced that is usual.

His shoes had been of a good fitting quality as there were no undue calluses. I noticed nothing unusual about the toe nails or finger nails. I should say they had been reasonably well cared for. I would not like to say if he had been in the habit of cutting or filing the nails. They were not broken as though he was nervous. I could not say if they were broken by manual work or not.

I have not seen the tendency of his calf muscle so pronounced in others as in this case. I had occasion recently to take a cast of a girl's legs, and she had been in the habit of wearing low-heeled shoes. I have also studied girl's legs fairly critically. From that observation I would say that low heels will not develop the calf muscle to such an extent as high heels will.

The nape of the cast presents an unusual appearance. I would attribute that to the post mortem examination and lying on the block. Apart from that, that is the replica of the body that I saw. I have made a study of making casts for museum purposes, so I have had reasons for making investigations and comparisons of calf muscle.

Lawson also supplied a statement which, in part, read:

> On looking at the deceased's legs I am of the opinion that he was used to wearing high heel riding boots. I form that opinion because the muscles of his legs were formed high up behind the knees, similar to the muscles of a woman who wears high heeled shoes.

The funeral
The Elephant and Castle Hotel is situated on the northeast corner of the junction of West Terrace and Gilbert Street, Adelaide. The popular hotelier there was Leo Kenny, originally from the West Coast of South Australia, and a member of the large and well-known Kenny family. Apart from many local residents, workers and businessmen coming to the hotel, it was also the local 'watering hole' for workers and visitors to the West Terrace Cemetery opposite the hotel. These patrons included cemetery staff, funeral directors, police, pathologists and suppliers of headstones.

Not as a pauper
For 6 months the most topical subject of conversation at the hotel was the mystery of *the Unknown Man*. At times this subject might even have pushed the usual discussions on horse racing, cricket, football and politics into the background. So it was very fitting that discussions took place there that finally decided *the Unknown Man* would not be buried as a pauper.

The funeral was conducted on Tuesday 14 June 1949. As the service concluded, Captain EJ Webb of the Salvation Army said, 'Yes, this man has someone to love him. He is known only to God.'

The report on the funeral is best summed up by a local newspaper:

Few see burial of Somerton body

The body of the unknown man found on the beach at Somerton more than six months ago was buried at West Terrace Cemetery at 9.30 a.m. today.

Arrangements for the funeral were kept secret to prevent the attendance of curious sightseers.

This afternoon grave-diggers will place a small wooden cross on the grave bearing the words "Unknown Man". *The inscription was 'Unknown Somerton Body' (refer to photograph).*

Police had to call on a newspaper reporter and a publican to assist as pallbearers.

To prevent the victim being buried as a pauper, the cost of the funeral is being met by the SA Grandstand Bookmakers Association.

Time old method

The body, which has been embalmed in a manner similar to that employed by the Egyptians 2,000 years ago, is expected to stay preserved for many years, should it be necessary to exhume it.

The grave is in specially selected dry ground in the cemetery.

The burial service was conducted by Capt. E.J. Webb, of the Salvation Army.

The coroner's warrant to bury was made out for "the body of an unknown man found on the beach at Somerton on December 1, 1948. Age, address, and occupation unknown."

A copy of the burial warrant cannot be located.

No wreaths

The funeral, comprising a hearse and one car, left the parlours of F.T. Elliott & Sons, Port Road, Hindmarsh, at 9.15. There were no wreaths.

Before the casket was sealed the coroner's constable (PCC Sutherland) who has been associated in inquiries since the mystery began, viewed the body.

Mr. L. A. Elliott, who is a member of the British Institute of Embalmers and the British Embalming Society, embalmed the body 10 days after it was found. He believed it is the longest period a body has been kept embalmed in Adelaide.

The embalming was done by injecting special fluid into the veins.

The case has aroused great interest among embalmers in England, and a full report is being sent away by Mr. Elliott.

Mr. Leo Kenny, licensee of the Elephant and Castle Hotel, opposite the City Morgue, acted as a pallbearer. He has followed the case with great interest.

The City Coroner (Mr. T. E. Cleland) will attempt to unravel some aspects of the mystery associated with the man's death when he opens an inquest at 10.30 a.m. on Friday. Among the 20 witnesses will be University professors, pathologists, and analysts.

As an interim measure a wooden stake with a small plaque containing the following stenciled words was placed on the grave:

UNKNOWN SOMERTON MAN

A few days later a headstone was erected on the grave. The work was the gift of Mr. A. Collins, a Keswick monumental mason, who was given permission by the Police Department to put a concrete kerb round the grave, and to cover it with a

THE UNKNOWN MAN

concrete floor sprinkled with marble chippings.

**HERE LIES
THE UNKNOWN MAN
WHO WAS FOUND AT
SOMERTON BEACH
1st Dec 1948.**

***

A CROSS bearing the words "Unknown Somerton body" has been erected over the grave of the unknown man who was found on the beach at Somerton six months ago. His body was buried at West Terrace Cemetery yesterday.

CHAPTER 10

THE CORONIAL INQUEST

Coroner Thomas Cleland had been following the unfolding events and mysteries surrounding the death closely. The deceased had not been identified, the cause of his death had not been established and there were very unusual circumstances.

In very broad terms, a coroner has a wide range of powers and the rules of evidence differ from normal criminal proceedings in some instances. A coroner can summons any witness or accept their evidence in the form of a statement. There are provisions for cross-examination of witnesses on the coroner's behalf. Hearsay evidence is admissible and witnesses can decline to answer questions on the grounds that they may incriminate themselves.

Under the law, it was inevitable that a Coronial Inquest would be held into *the Unknown Man* and Coroner Cleland instructed the Coroner's Constable in Adelaide thus:

Body found lying at Somerton
I have fixed Friday the 17th June for this inquest.
I have directed that the following witnesses be summonsed.
JB Lyons
Dr JB Bennett
PC Moss
GK Strapps
Miss OC Neill
Dr Dwyer
RJ Cowan
Prof JB Cleland
Prof Sir Stanton Hicks
Conductor Holderness
Det Sgt Leane

Witnesses to prove the following.
Teeth of deceased, or perhaps Dr Dwyer can give the necessary evidence.
Photographs of deceased and fingerprints.
Witnesses from M.T.T. to prove the time or of issue of the bus ticket.
Witnesses from S.A.R. to prove. (a) date and time of issue of rail ticket found on the body. (b) The clerk who issued the ticket. (c) Times of arrival of interstate and country trains on the day in question. (d) Times of departure up to 11.15am of trains for Henley Beach. (e) Receipt of suitcase and the fact that it has not been claimed.
A witness, if one can be found, as to the words "Tamam Shud".

Please take action that the names and addresses of these witnesses may be obtained, and forwarded down to Mr. White A.G's office as soon as possible, and advise me of what they can prove to me.

The inquest, which commenced on 17 June 1949, is reported and commented upon at length.

INQUEST INTO THE DEATH OF A BODY LOCATED AT SOMERTON ON 1.12.48.

REMARKS OF THE CITY CORONER ON OPENING THE INQUEST

The report I have received indicates –

(1) that the identity of the deceased is quite unknown;
(2) that his death was not natural;
(3) that it was probably caused by poison;
(4) that it almost certainly was not accidental.

The alternatives to be considered, therefore, are whether the deceased died by his own act, or by the act of someone else.

Because we do not know who he was we are ignorant of the motives which may have actuated him or someone else. This ignorance is a disadvantage in investigation, and it emphasizes the necessity of ascertaining what is known and of recognizing what is only inference.

The natural and simple explanation of the circumstances which will be detailed in the evidence may be that the deceased died by his own act, but as we are dealing with circumstances which are not ordinary, it may be that the natural explanation is not the true explanation.

Until the circumstances exclude the possibility that the deceased died through the act of someone other than himself, the possibility of murder must remain under consideration.

Consequently it is most necessary that in giving evidence witnesses should be careful to distinguish between what they know of their own knowledge, and what they infer from what they know.

I am required to find, if I can, who the deceased was, and how, when and where he died. I will, I fear, be unable to answer these questions unless further evidence should be obtained. For this reason I have directed that a cast be made of the deceased's features, and that the cast be photographed. These photographs may give a better idea of the deceased's appearance than those which have been published previously, and they will be available for publication.

The deceased remains unknown despite the energies of the police, and the wide publicity the death has received. It would seem that the deceased has not been missed because there appeared to be sufficient reason for his disappearance from his usual surroundings – such as the expressed intention of going elsewhere to live.

If the photographs, or the suggestion I have first made, should lead any member of the public to believe he can supply information which may be of assistance, will he please communicate with the police.

Comment: Take into account that the year was 1949, and then consider what facilities were available to record the depositions of evidence given. The depositions were recorded on a typewriter and transcribed into a combination of a question being asked and the given answer translated into a general gist of the subject. At the completion of evidence each individual witness would read their depositions and correct any misleading errors. There is no comparison to the court facilities of today, that produce transcripts which record every question, answer and all other relevant comments verbatim.

The general evidence relevant to the known movements of the deceased produced no controversial issues that troubled Coroner Cleland. Unfortunately, although every possible avenue was pursued there was no evidence to identify the deceased. The cause of his death was a complex issue and could not be resolved completely, despite the input from several experts. Evidence in respect to the cause of death is produced by the following witnesses:

Life extinct

John Barkley Bennett LQMP

I have a few notes which I made at the time, at 9.40am on 1 December, 1948. I examined the body in the ambulance outside the Adelaide Hospital, in a police ambulance. Life was extinct when I examined the body. I thought death could have occurred up to 8 hours before my examination, not more than 8 hours. I would put the time of death at 2 o'clock at the earliest. I based the opinion on the rigor mortis but I did not make a note of the extent of it at the time. I formed the opinion as to the cause of death from just a cursory look at him, from the cyanosis. There is nothing else about the body which I noticed.

Post-mortem examination

John Matthew Dwyer LQMP

At 7.30am on 2 December 1948 in the presence of Constable Sutherland I made a post mortem examination at the City Mortuary on the body pointed out to me as being found on the foreshore at Somerton on 1st December.

The post mortem rigidity was intense, and there was a deep lividity behind particularly above the ears and neck. The pupils were smaller and unusual, uneven in outline and about the same size. Certain drugs may be associated with a contraction of the pupils. Even barbiturates may do it, but it is by no means a distinguishing point, except in broad groups. There was a small patch of dried saliva at the right of the mouth. The impression was that it ran out of his mouth some time before death when he was probably unable to swallow it, probably when his head was hanging to the side. It would run vertically. It had run down diagonally down the right cheek.

Sunburn markings were present up to the level of the crotch, and they were probably from the previous season. The fingers were cyanotic, there was sand in the hair, but none in the nostrils or mouth.

The scalp, skull and brain were normal, except that small vessels not commonly observed in the brain were easily discernible with congestion. There was congestion of the pharynx, and the gullet was covered with a whitening of the superficial layers of the mucosa with a patch of ulceration in the middle of it. The stomach was deeply congested, and there was superficial redness, most marked in the upper half. Small haemorrhages were present beneath the mucosa. There was congestion in the 2nd half of the duodenum continuing through the third part. There was blood mixed with the food in the stomach.

Both kidneys were congested, and the liver contained a great excess of blood in its vessels. The heart was of normal size, and normal in every way. The impression it gave me was that it was the heart of a man in good physical training. The reason why I say that is that the muscle was quite tough and firm. Both lungs were dark with congestion. The heart, if anything, was contracted.

The question had been raised of the taking of an overdose of a drug which would cause the heart to contract. I could not say that that did not happen, but I feel there is not enough evidence for me to say that that was the cause. I would not like to be dogmatic on the question, but I feel that the explanation is that the man was in good physical condition, and his heart was in keeping with that. I could not rule out the other possibility. Both lungs were dark with congestion, but otherwise normal.

The spleen was strikingly large and firm about three times normal size. The points to which I gave consideration in my summary were the acute gastritil haemorrhage, extensive congestion to the liver and spleen, and the congestion to the brain.

There was food in the stomach. I would say that the food had been in the stomach for up to three or four hours before death. It is difficult to give an opinion on that, because if the person is in a state of anxiety, that digestion may be suspended.

I have made microscopic examination of the disease, and there was pigment in it, although I cannot say of what disease. It does not resemble malarial pigment, and I can only keep an open mind on the matter.

The blood in the stomach suggested to me some irritant poison, but on the other hand there was nothing detectible in the food to my naked eye to make a finding, so I sent specimens of the stomach and contents, blood and urine for analysis.

There was one point in the microscopic examination which was fairly definite, in that there was destruction of the centres of the liver lobules revealed under the microscope, and apart from signs of congestion there was nothing else in the other organs.

There was a peculiar cellular reaction under the oesphageal mucosa, but I have not found an answer to that. I am quite convinced that the death could not have been natural, as there is such a conflict of findings with the normal heart. Some factor must have influenced the heart to bring about that state of affairs, or alternatively the centre which controls breathing.

I feel quite certain that death was not natural. I think the immediate cause of death was heart failure, but I am unable to say what factor caused heart failure. Something stopped the blood from being pushed along, because of the cyanosis. When I sent in my report the poison I suggested was a barbiturate or a soluble hypnotic, and I think that is still consistent with the finding.

Assuming Dr. Cowan found no barbiturate or any common poison, I was astounded that he found nothing, as I thought he would. I know he is a chemist of considerable experience, and if he did not find any I accept his finding. There are changes which could occur, particularly with certain quick acting barbiturates.

There are other poisons which do come into the picture which would be decomposed very early after death. In support of my statement concerning the disappearance of certain barbiturates, I can put in an extract from a book dealing with the matter.

Dwyer then presented the extracts on poisons to the inquest:

To City Coroner 31 May 1949.

On this day I am forwarding extracts from 'Poisons, Their Isolation and Identification' by Frank Bamford, late Director of the Medico-legal Laboratory Cairo. Second edition revised by C.P. Stewart, Reader in Clinical Chemistry University of Edinburgh. The foreword is written by Professor Sydney Smith. Published by Churchill 1947.

Page 194. The simple ureides and the thio-barbiturates (pentothal e.g.) adaline and bromural appear to be entirely destroyed. Roche Lynch reports five cases, three of them fatal, in which he failed to find these drugs in the urine or viscera, although in every case bromine was detected. [Note: there is no bromine in pentothal but there are usually traces in the body.]

Page 195. A patient sometimes dies of sulphoral poisoning long after the administration of the drug has ceased, and even after its complete elimination from the body (Sydney Smith, Godamer).

Page 222. It is, however, the common experience of toxicologists that they have failed to detect certain alkaloids when there has been strong evidence of their administration; this occurs in the case of addicts whose ability to tolerate large doses is possibly due to the acquired power of the organs to destroy the drugs.

While these quotations do not enable any conclusion to be reached concerning the cause of death in the Somerton case the information does offer a possible solution to the dilemma.

Dwyer's evidence continued:

The substance of the extract is that in certain cases although it seems certain barbiturates have been ingested, there is no sign on analysis.

I think that is a possible explanation, that barbiturate was taken or administered; it caused death, and became decomposed. That must be considered, but I do think it is under ordinary circumstances a likely explanation. It is a possible explanation, but an unusual one. If the man was alive at 7 o'clock and dead by midnight, if it were a carefully judged dose of barbiturate – there are records of barbiturates, in one case 72 grams of sodium amytal, which is quiet a heavy dose and one would expect it to leave signs, and the patient recovered.

Nembutal has been stated to cause death in cases of 7.5 and 6.7 grams, another one is a name which I will not mention and it has caused six cases of death in doses of 30 to 38 grains. There are poisons which act very quickly, but most poisons require some time to cause death.

Barbiturate in usual cases of suicide may not cause death for 36 to 48 hours, and usually those barbiturates are taken in large doses. There is a big variation in the amount which people can stand. Even the quick acting one would require a massive dose to produce death by midnight if the man were alive at 7 o'clock, one would think. If the dose were massive, one would expect to find it on analysis. On the whole, I think it is probably correct that barbiturate is not the cause of death, except that as I said earlier it is a possible explanation.

It is my opinion that in view of the chemist's finding it is unlikely that barbiturates are responsible for death. On the other hand, being driven as far as one can possibly go, I find that the cause might be the cause which I originally suspected.

A large number of the back teeth were missing. I think that from the food that it was probably a pie or pasty which he had eaten as his last meal. I did not get the impression from looking at his mouth that he was in the habit of using a dental plate. Dental plates were not present when I examined the body.

I would not stress the size of the pupils in the case of the dead man; it is my habit to point out the findings as I find them.

The blood in the stomach, I would have noticed if it was produced by the post mortem. It was present prior to the post mortem, and because there were numerous hemorrhages I formed the opinion it was mixed with food during life. I think the question is still open, but in view of the congestion I think failure of the heart is more likely than failure of the respiratory centre.

I looked to see if the man had been vaccinated, but I do not think there was an obvious sign of vaccination. There was a slight scar on the left upper arm. In my experience, the man might have been a member of the forces and had been vaccinated, and it did not leave much sign.

I saw no evidence of a hypodermic needle having been used. I considered the possibility of one having been used, especially if it were used in an unusual place. There were two marks between the knuckles and the back of the right hand, they appeared to be recent abrasions just before death, they were in the hollow of the knuckles, but they did not appear to be significant.

I do not think there was any injection of curare or tubariu, which cause death from asphyxia.

I do not think it is possible there had been an overdose of insulin, as there was no evidence of a disturbance. I think the question of insulin can be discounted on the findings of the liver. If a man had access to diphtheria toxin, that certainly could be a possible explanation, but it would be very unusual. He would have to have access to a place where diphtheria toxin was being manufactured. A very small amount of that would cause the haemorrhages.

Botulism can be ruled out because of the time, the death in those cases do not occur shortly after an administration. Deliberately taken by the mouth, the poison of botulism could be fatal. On the other hand there would be an incubation period of 12 hours. I hardly think it worthwhile going into the question, but it did enter my mind the possibility of poisoning by nicotine, but Mr. Cowan has said none was found.

There are possibilities of the aconite or aconitine being used, and there are chemical difficulties about their isolation. I do not think I can say anything else.

Knowing how reliable Mr. Cowan is in his analysis, I have to think along the lines that poison was the cause of death, which cannot be found on analysis. The poison must have been taken a few hours before death, and I have to find out a cause for the change. Apart from the special case of barbiturates, there is no case of poison known to the average person which could not be discernible on analysis. I can think of prussic acid, but its action is so rapid that death is practically instantaneous, so that there would not have been time for the finding in the organs to have developed, particularly the microscopic finding.

Deputy Government Analyst – Robert James Cowan

On 2 December 1948 I received from P.C.C. Sutherland a glass jar containing stomach and contents, one containing liver and muscle, a bottle containing urine, and a bottle containing blood. Mr. Sutherland told me they were taken from the body of an unidentified man found at Somerton the previous day.

At his request I carried out analysis of those specimens, but was unable to find signs of any common poison in any of them. I tested for common poisons. Cyanides, alkaloids, barbiturates, carbolic acid, are the most common poisons. If any of the poisons for which I tested were the cause of the death, they would not be absent from the body after death if they were taken by mouth.

There are cases of which I heard in which barbiturates are the cause of death and yet are absent on analysis. I think it is unlikely if they were taken by mouth that they would not be detected in the stomach contents.

I cannot say if a man were alive at 7 o'clock in the evening and dead about midnight, it would need a massive dose to cause death. I found no common poison present, and I do not think any common poison caused death. I cannot suggest anything, other than I think it is most unlikely that a common poison caused his death.

Off hand I am not aware of poisons which can cause death but decompose in the body so that they are not discernible on analysis. I would say that it would be highly probable that any poison causing death would be discoverable on analysis. I am still speaking of poisons taken orally, as distinguished from poisons injected. The difference would be that on injection some of those poisons would be destroyed in the tissue, by the liver, and even by the kidney, whereas in the stomach, you would expect to find that which was in excess to that required to kill the person.

I feel quite satisfied that if death were caused by any common poison, my examination would have revealed its nature. If he did die from poison, I think it would be a very rare poison. I mean something rarely used for suicidal or homicidal purposes. I cannot make any suggestion as to what that might be.

I think that death is more likely to have been due to natural causes than poisoning. I failed to detect any poison in the stomach or organs, and this causes me to make that statement.

Insulin is not rare, but used as a poison for homicidal or suicidal purposes it would be rare. I was taking insulin as being a poison. I just do not know how a poison could be defined. When I spoke of rarity of poisons, I was speaking of rarity of their being used as poisons, not the rarity of their existence.

Evidence of Professor John Burton Cleland LQMP, Emeritus Professor of Pathology at the University of Adelaide

Professor Cleland commenced giving evidence at 10.30 a.m. on 21 June. A large portion of his evidence has been included elsewhere in topics under discussion. The following evidence is relevant to the subject of the man's death:

I agree with Dr. Dwyer's estimate that the man was somewhere between 40 and 45; I would say he was between 40 and 50.

I saw the body after it was embalmed …. I have considered the circumstances disclosed in the evidence, and I came to the opinion, taking all the circumstances into account, that death was almost certainly not natural, and in all probability that some poison had been taken, with suicidal intent. I came to this conclusion before I found the piece of paper bearing the words "Tamum (sic) shud". Bearing in mind that those words mean something like "the end" that supports my opinion considerably: I think the words were put there deliberately and indicated that intention that he was fed up with things.

I have read the account of the post-mortem, and there is nothing to indicate death from natural causes. He was a comparatively young man. The vessels of the heart and the brain are described as free from theroma, so that if his death was to be attributed to natural causes, one would have to think of some vagal inhibition, which would mean a sudden and unexpected death for which no preparation could be made, or possibly something like a diabetic coma, which would begin to overcome a person anywhere before they had time to retire to a place in which to lie down.

Death from vagal inhibition is quite sudden, and is the result of a shock. If he died from such a cause and that, the shock must have occurred in the spot where he was lying when he died. Of course, people from time to time die of a natural death, and we cannot find any organic lesion to account for it.

I agree that the words 'Tamam Shud' would exclude a natural death, one would not expect that they would be on the body if the death were natural, also because of the circumstances of the position of the body. I think if he did commit suicide whatever he took commenced to have a soporific effect on him before he had made his way as far along the beach as he had intended, that he had only time to descend the steps, found he was becoming drowsy and lay down with his head and shoulders resting against the seawall, in a position which is within a yard of the steps, on a summer evening, which would be frequented by several people at least.

I do not remember if there was any post-mortem evidence of lividity of the neck and shoulders. Supposing the respiration was failing, his face might get dusky, and the blood might gravitate down to the ears after death. The lividity around the ears and neck was perhaps surprising in view of his position, but it was explainable. It would depend on how much his head was supported, it may have been slightly supported, perhaps no more than one's head supported on a pillow.

My opinion is that not only was death not natural, but was probably caused by some poison. I would accept Mr. Cowan's evidence that he found no poison present, as he is a competent analyst. It is possible for certain poisons to be excreted from the body before death so that they are not noticeable on analysis.

Barbiturates and Alkaloids may not be detected on analysis. On the other hand, such negative findings must be rare, and if they had been taken, it would be a very remarkable coincidence that common poisons of that nature should have given that difficulty in detection, and at the same time the person concerned seemed to have taken undue trouble to hide his identity. It makes one rather think that he may have gone to equal trouble to use something which caused a quiet death, something unusual, which was unlikely to be found.

It would presuppose some knowledge, either a medical man or someone associated with a laboratory, or possibly as Sir Stanton Hicks suggested, an illness in the family for which some drug had been prescribed which would achieve the result intended. If a common poison were used and not found, even in the presence of ordinary circumstances, the dose must have been enough, and just enough, to cause death.

As far as I can estimate he probably died at or before midnight, and that is a comparatively quick death from poisoning, barbiturate and so on, and one would infer that to produce death so quickly a large dose had been taken, and that would be readily detected.

Every poison we have suggested seems to be discounted. We found no evidence of vomiting. A possible stain on his trousers did not look like vomit, and we did not detect any evidence of potato, and he had been eating potato. The internal organs were somewhat congested, but not deeply congested as might be expected from failure of respiration.

If he had given himself a hypodermic injection of tuberine, which is curare, he should have died a death from asphyxia. It does not seem there is sufficient evidence from the post-mortem to suggest that.

Most of the common poisons would give vomiting or evidence of convulsions, something which would have drawn attention to the deceased. Cyanide would be very quick, and no bottle was found, nor was there any smell of cyanide.

Barbiturates are the things which could have caused death, if only they could have been found. If a barbiturate, it would probably be a sodium compound, which are absorbed faster and broken down more rapidly, but even in such a case it would appear that 50% would remain and be detectible.

A drug which had been prescribed medically, as I have mentioned, would be difficult for the ordinary person to obtain. Of course, the man may have been a chemist or pharmacist. There was no sign of vomiting, and any trace of those substances would be difficult to detect. They would require a hypodermic injection, or I suppose they might be taken by mouth.

It is difficult to find any poison which fits the circumstances. There always seems to be some little point which prevents us from accepting any particular poison as being the cause of death. It is impossible to be certain, but in my mind there is very little doubt but that the death was unnatural.

The man was not circumcised, which would point to his not being a Mohammedan or a Jew and I could not be certain that there was no vaccination mark. Of course, all persons serving in the forces would be vaccinated, but in some cases the vaccination marks are hard to see.

A mark made by a hypodermic injection could be overlooked, notwithstanding all care. Of course, he would have to do away with the syringe and bottle. Apparently he had discarded most of the contents of his pockets, including his money. The absence of money suggests he had deliberately emptied his pockets. One can hardly think of the last penny having been expended in his last meal or whatever his last purchase was, unless of course he had been robbed after death.

In the event of a man taking an overdose of insulin by injection if one had thought of the possibility, the heart blood might have shown an unusual low percentage of sugar. I think Dr. Poynton told me a case which he had seen where a man had taken a large dose of insulin, and he was supposed to have died in an hour and a half or two hours of taking it. I am trying to remember what he told me. It may have been a peaceful death, or it may have been hypo-glycemic. Some patients who go into that type of coma do have convulsions.

I think it is probably quite possible to inject into the finger and leave no puncture mark.

I examined a microscopic section of the liver, but it did not seem to me to offer any explanation as to the cause of death. Insulin has to be taken by injection. A lot of people take insulin nowadays, and if they got hold of the idea that it could be used for suicidal purposes, they might do so.

Evidence of Sir Cedric Stanton Hicks, Professor of Physiology and Pharmacology at the University of Adelaide

Prior to Sir Cedric Stanton Hicks giving evidence, Coroner Cleland read a portion of Dr Dwyer's evidence to him. Sir Stanton then gave evidence:

I have become aware of various facts in connection with the death of this unknown man. (Reads portion of Dr Dwyer's evidence.) I have formed an opinion as to whether death was natural or not. I think it was not a natural death.

I am in agreement with the other medical evidence with regard to that. Being no signs of violence about the body, first of all I accept the findings of Mr. Cowan, who is a very competent and conscientious chemist, and then acting on the possibility of there still being an undiscovered barbiturate, I would expect to find death from respiratory failure and an enlarged left ventricle of the heart, which was not the case. The post mortem findings exclude the possibility of barbiturate being the cause of death, in my opinion.

I accept the evidence that the man probably died at 2 o'clock at the earliest, and that he was seen to move at 7 o'clock the previous evening. I consider that a dose of morphine which would have killed a man in that time would have been easily detectible and measurable.

In cases where death is said to be due to barbiturates, and in which barbiturates have not been found, in cases mentioned, the poison is sulphonal. It is a possibility, but not in this case because of the condition of the heart, and I might add because of the viscera. There have been cases where death has known to be from barbiturates, but such has not been found on analysis. In the case of sulphonal, it is possible that the dose was the bare minimum sufficient to cause death and to leave no trace on analysis. It is my opinion that to cause death in seven hours the dose would have to be massive.

I could perhaps give my reason for suspecting a possible group, they are, one, that the heart was contracted, and two, that the lungs and in particular the liver and spleen were engorged, and three, that the wall of the stomach was not engorged but there had been blood extravasated into the cavity of the stomach.

These facts, because they are facts, suggest to me the action of a poison which caused the heart ultimately not to relax and fill in the normal way, and that prior to its stopping in the unfilled condition, there must have been some time during which its filling was getting less and less. If the heart were filling less and less as time went by, that would mean that more and more blood would be remaining on the input side of the heart, and that would explain the engorgement of the viscera found at

THE UNKNOWN MAN

the post-mortem.

The fact that there was blood in the gastric contents suggests to me that there had been some violent contractions of that organ, or that there had been some inflammation of the organ. No inflammatory agents were detected by Mr. Cowan, nor did the post-mortem examination suggest that some irritant metallic poison might have been involved, or an acid. Therefore I incline to conclude that a member of a group of drugs causing the heart to stop systole might have been used. The first word in the exhibit is the name of the group, and the other words are members of the group.

On the members of the group, I would say that there are several variants of number 1, and I had in mind more particularly number 2, which would be extremely toxic in a relatively small dose, I mean even in an oral dose, and would be completely missed by any of the tests applied and would in fact be extremely difficult if not impossible to identify even if it had been suspected in the first instance. I mean it would not be identified in ordinary chemical tests. Such a substance would be quite easily procurable by the ordinary individual, I do not think even special circumstances would be required.

They might even have been procured from a case under treatment, but I think you would have to prove that to a chemist. It would imply intelligence and shrewd observation, but not necessarily a knowledge of the way in which it would cause death because that might have been unpleasant.

The only missing fact which would have made me confident is the absence of signs of vomiting, but there is sufficient variation between individuals to account for it or he may have vomited before he took up his position by the seawall, but I confess that I would have been more confident in drawing a frank conclusion had there been signs of vomit somewhere about him.

I have been proceeding on the assumption that this was self-administered. If it had not been self-administered, and the body brought there, that would remove any doubts as to the time at which death took place, as well as any other difficulties.

If death had occurred seven hours after the man was seen to move, it would imply a massive dose. The drug which I have mentioned in a massive dose could have caused death in that time, and could still have been undiscoverable. The circumstances are consistent with its administration, and some of them even suggestive of it. Nothing is inconsistent with it.

There is one point in Dr. Dwyer's evidence in which he refers to some changes in the liver lobules. He has not extended his observations upon that, and I therefore infer that they are not very significant. I infer that if they had been significant, he would have laid greater emphasis upon them, and then one might have had to consider something which had been operating over a longer period of time. My own conclusion is that they are not significant.

I can think of no other group of which the two poisons are two representatives, there being several others, which could have caused death in the way in which it occurred.

There would have been convulsions with the poisoning in the group mentioned. I understand there was no sign of disturbance in the sand, and I can only assume that so many people walked in the sand that there was no evidence that there had not been convulsions. I am only going by what I was told, that there had been a lot of people around the body, and sand being what it is it would be impossible to draw any conclusion. That is something as well as the vomiting about which I would have liked further evidence. There must have been convulsions, which of course does not mean that there would be violent movements of the body, but there must have been convulsions.

If told that he was in the same position at seven o'clock the night before he was found, and still in the same position when found, I could not draw any inference from that because he could have had convulsions without changing his position.

Convulsions may precede death, they do not necessarily precede death, but I would expect them to. The question of whether or not convulsions precede death would relate to the physical state of the individual. If he were in a dilapidated condition, I would expect convulsions, but in this case I would expect some. Convulsions are mainly of the arm. I suppose you could call the movements which you described to me as a convulsive movement.

The popular idea of a convulsion is that it is violent, but it does not necessarily mean movements of the arm, although they can be strong movements. The convulsion is a movement, not just a stiffening. This movement at seven o'clock could well have been the last convulsive movement.

The state of the liver would exclude insulin. It is not possible the man was a diabetic who died in a diabetic coma, because the state of the liver did not support that. Further, there would have been noticed on his breath the smell of products associated with diabetic coma, after his death. It would be noticed around his body when it was opened. The finding of glycogen in the liver excludes the possibility of insulin causing death.

A very factual description was given by Dr. Bennett, who said the man appeared to be just like a person who had had a coronary seizure, and that is also in keeping with the conclusion that I have come to. The substance could have been taken orally. Had it been taken by injection it would have acted more rapidly.

Evidence relevant to the cause of death
In addition to the opinion of the above, evidence on the cause of death was given by Detective Sergeant Leane:

There is no fact that I know of which points towards suicide and abolishes the possibility of murder. I believe he died an unnatural death, but how I cannot say. A physical specimen as he was would not just go to the beach and die. The words "Tamam Shud" means the end, or the finish. That could have been placed in his pocket by the person who caused his death, so I cannot attach any special significance to that.

Inquest Adjourned – Sine Die
When the inquest was adjourned on 21 June Coroner Cleland remarked:

The body of the deceased was found on the shore at Somerton at about 7a.m. on the 1st December, 1948. Dr. Bennett who examined it at 9.40 a.m. was of the opinion that death occurred round about 2 a.m.

The body was clad in clothes of fairly good quality. All tags which might have led to the discovery of identity had been removed. The deceased was lying on his back with his feet towards the sea, his head and shoulders supported by the sea wall. The head was inclined to its right and between the right cheek and the right lapel of the coat was a partly smoked cigarette, but the coat was not scorched nor the cheek blistered. The only articles in the clothing were some cigarettes and matches, two hair combs, a packet of chewing gum, a single uncancelled railway ticket from Adelaide to Henley Beach, a bus ticket which was proved to have been issued at about 11.15 a.m. on the 30th November on the Adelaide – Somerton bus and which would have carried the holder from Adelaide to Somerton, and lastly a piece of paper on which were printed the words "Taman (sic) Shud". The paper, which was in the fob pocket of the trousers, and which was not found for some time afterwards, was, I am satisfied, torn from a copy of the second edition of Fitzgerald's translation of the Rubaiyat of Omar Khyyam. The printed words are the concluding words of the poem and mean "The end." (The book was a first edition.)

At 7 p.m. on the 30th November, a man was seen lying precisely where the body was found and in a similar position. He was seen to raise his right arm to its full extent. The arm fell limply. At about 7.30 p.m. a man and a girl saw the man in the same place. They did not see him move, but one of them gathered the impression that his position changed somewhat, and that in a way that they could not define he was lying unnaturally.

A little over a month later an unclaimed suitcase was found at the luggage office at the Adelaide Railway Station. There was internal evidence that it had either belonged to the deceased, or was connected with his death. Tags had been removed from clothing, the clothes were of a size with those found on the body, a similar and rather unusual thread had been used to mend clothes in the suitcase and those on the body, and there was other evidence which led to the conclusion.

It was thought that the deceased must have arrived by train at the Adelaide Railway Station, left his case at the luggage room, purchased a ticket for Henley Beach but missed his train, and then travelled to Somerton by bus. Neither the luggage room attendant, nor the officer who issued the Henley Beach ticket, nor the bus conductor can remember seeing him. No one has come forward to say that he was seen at Somerton between the arrival of the bus and 7 p.m.

A postmortem examination was made. Small vessels not commonly observed in the brain were easily discernible with congestion. The stomach was deeply congested: there was superficial redness; small haemorrhages were present beneath the muscosa. The heart was normal – the heart of a man in good physical training. The muscle was quite tough and firm. It was, if anything, contracted. There was extensive congestion of the liver and spleen. A microscopic examination revealed that the centres of the liver globules were destroyed. Dr Dwyer who made the postmortem examination was of the opinion that the immediate cause of death was heart failure, but being able to find anything that would have caused heart failure, he concluded that death was unnatural; and he retained appropriate specimens from the body for analysis. But on analysis no common poison was found.

Three medical witnesses are of the opinion on the postmortem findings that death was not natural. The words "Tamam Shud" support this conclusion, and indeed put its accuracy beyond reasonable doubt. There was no indication of violence, and I am compelled to the finding that death resulted from poison. But what poison?

No doubt minimal doses of certain common poisons could have caused death and have been eliminated from the body before death. But on the expert evidence no such minimal dose could have caused death so quickly, and a more massive dose would certainly have left traces which would have been detected on analysis.

The only poison which Sir Stanton Hicks can think of, and which is consistent with the postmortem findings, is one of the group he mentioned. But here again there are difficulties. There was no vomit, although there was some evidence of convulsion.

I have been discussing the circumstances on the footing that the body found on the morning of the 1st December was that of the man seen in the evening of the 30th November. But there is really no proof that this was the case. None of the three witnesses who speak of the evening of the 30th saw the man's face, or indeed any part of his body that they can identify. If the body of the deceased was not that of the man mentioned and if the body had been taken to the place where it was found, the difficulties disappear. If this speculation, for it is nothing more, should prove to be correct, the original assumption that it was the deceased who left the suitcase at the luggage room, bought the rail and bus tickets, removed the clothing tabs, and put the printed words "Tamam Shud" in a pocket, would require revision.

The evidence is too inconclusive to warrant a finding. There is no evidence as to who the deceased was. Although he died during the night of the 30 November – 1st December, I cannot say where he died. I would be prepared to find that he died from poison, that the poison was probably a glycoside and that it was not accidently administered; but I cannot say whether it was administered by the deceased himself or by some other person.

I therefore adjourn this inquest sine die.

THE UNKNOWN MAN

CHAPTER 11

INVESTIGATIONS INTENSIFY

The inquest generated considerable publicity throughout Australia, but no information was forthcoming to assist the police investigation. There were leads to follow up, people continued to nominate missing friends, interstate police maintained their inquiries, but what the police really needed was the copy of the Rubaiyat with the page containing the words 'Tamam Shud' torn from it.

Bust of deceased to SA Museum

On 4 July 1949 Detective Sergeant Leane reported:

> ... that on 17th. June, 1949 an inquest was opened by Mr. Cleland, City Coroner concerning the death of the unknown man found dead on the beach at Somerton S.A. on the 1st. of December, 1948. This inquest failed to establish the identity of the deceased.
>
> Mr. Lawson a preparater at the Museum, Adelaide was entrusted with the preparing of a cast of the head and shoulders of the deceased and produced this cast at the inquest on the 17th. June, 1949.
>
> The cast is a particularly good replica, and from an identification angle, is a great success.
>
> Police inquiries have failed to establish the identity of the deceased, and it is respectfully requested that the Museum Director be approached with the view of having the cast displayed at the Museum for general inspection. If this were done it would be available for public inspection, and may lead to the identity of the deceased being established.

Pressure from the press

At times the media can assist to speed up decision makers and no doubt the following short article achieved that.

Leane's request was eventually approved and the bust was placed in a room at the South Australian Museum, but it was not put on public display at this stage.

Cast of body for Museum?

The plaster cast of the bust of the Somerton body may soon be on display in the Museum. It is believed the Police Department will ask Museum Authorities to do this in the hope somebody might recognize the man.

The Rubaiyat

The newspapers were doing their utmost to assist the police, and the following are just two of the many articles that were produced.

Remote book clue in mystery death

Although police realize they are acting on a million to one chance, a search for a book with a torn page which may throw some light on the Somerton body mystery is continuing throughout Australia.

A torn page of Fitzgerald's translation of the "Rubaiyat of Omar Kayyam" was found in the pocket of the victim.

Det.-Sgt. Leane and Det. Brown believe the torn book may still be on the shelves of a library. They think that if they can find it, they can trace the man to the city or town he was in before he came to Adelaide. With this information, it may be possible to establish his identity.

Melbourne police have made a search of public libraries and libraries in Victorian provincial towns, but have failed to find the torn volume.

Although a number of city and suburban libraries have been checked here, others in country districts have not yet been investigated.

The cause of death will probably never be known.

A plaster cast of the victim's head and shoulders which was exhibited at the inquest, is now in a store room at Adelaide Museum. No request for it to be displayed has yet been made by the authorities.

Possible Clue in Somerton Body Case

A bus conductor informed police last night that he believed he knew the whereabouts of a book which, if it were correct one, might provide a very important clue in the Somerton body mystery.

Detective-Sergeant R. L. Leane has been trying for several months to trace a copy of the 'Rubaiyat of Omar Khayyam' from which the dead man is believed to

have cut a piece of paper bearing the words "Tamam Shud" (meaning "The End") and placed it in the pocket of his trousers.

Last night Mr L. F. Wytkins, bus conductor, of Partridge Street, Glenelg told police that several months ago he found a book answering the description of the one required by the police. He handed it into the lost property off ce at the Tramways Trust.

Mr. Wytkins said he was not sure when he found the book, but he believed it to

be about the time the man's body was found on the beach at Somerton.

Although it is nearly eight months since the body was found, enquiries throughout the world have so far been unable to establish the man's identity. An inquest recently failed to reveal the cause of death.

Detective-Sergeant Leane believes that if he can find the book from which the clipping was taken, he might be able to trace from where the book came and possibly the person who owned it.

At long last – the missing link

On Friday evening, 22 July Ronald Francis, a businessman from Jetty Road, Glenelg read in The News about the police trying to locate a copy of The Rubaiyat. He already knew about the body being found on Somerton Beach because it was a topic of conversation in the area, as well as receiving publicity in the media.

Francis immediately recalled that his brother-in-law had left a copy of that book in the glove box of his little Hillman Minx which he normally parked in Jetty Road. He could not recall him collecting it, and so it was probably still there. He went to the car and looked in the glove box – yes, the book was still there. To his amazement a section had been torn out of the rear page, in the position described by past newspaper reports.

Francis could not wait to telephone his brother-in-law, with whom an excited conversation then took place:

Do you recall late last year when we all went for a drive in my car, just after that man was found dead on the beach at Somerton? You were sitting in the back with your wife and when we all got out of the car, the book you were reading, you put in the glove box of my car, and you left it there.

His brother-in-law replied:

No it wasn't mine. When I got in the back seat, the book was on the floor; I fanned through some pages and thought it was yours, so when I got out of the car I put it in the glove box for you.

The conversation after that went in all directions and it was obvious that the Police had to be notified. Maybe it was the book they were looking for!

The book is delivered to SA Police

The following morning Francis went to the Adelaide Detective Office and showed the book to Detective Sergeant Leane, who could not believe what he was seeing. After the months of intensive investigation and many frustrating false trails and dead ends, here at last was something that might point the inquiry in a new direction. Indeed, not only did the copy of The Rubaiyat have a portion torn from the last page where the words 'Tamam Shud' should be, but also it was located a short distance from where the body had been found.

Leane listened with interest to the circumstances leading to how the book was located. When Francis requested that his identity not be disclosed, and gave his reasons why, it was not a difficult decision for Leane to make, and he readily agreed to the request. He knew he would be hounded to reveal the identity of the person and curious people would continually speculate on the subject. But did it really matter if the discoverer was a doctor, chemist, dentist, jeweller, business person or a male or female? He adhered to the request because he knew that Francis would be hounded if his identity was known: not revealing the identity was not going to complicate matters.

Other promising lines of inquiry in the past had all reached a dead end. Was this going to be the same? The lead certainly looked promising, but Leane knew that the torn paper found in the trouser fob pocket of *the Unknown Man* would have to match the missing section of the book now in his possession. He also knew two things were required: to find an identical copy of The Rubaiyat to compare the font and positioning of the two words, and to have both pieces of paper examined forensically.

Leane soon noticed what appeared to be a telephone number written in pencil on the rear cover of the book. *(Although there has been mention of other telephone numbers I have seen no evidence of them.)* It would certainly require checking, but how significant was it? A simple inquiry with the Postmaster-General's Department would establish the name and address of the subscriber, and then he could delegate someone to follow that line of inquiry. Through a large magnifying glass he also saw capital letters written in faint pencil on the back of the book. They meant nothing at this stage, but would require assessment.

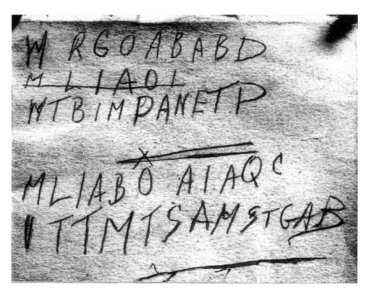

Newspaper articles

Many newspaper articles supplied a summary of the police investigation, and some selected passages are reproduced here.

'TAMAM SHUD' HINT

Whose body was it? No one identif ed it, even though the body was kept embalmed for months and thousands of people examined it, or the photographs that were circulated throughout the world.

Last month the body was buried.

Clues were baff ingly few. Every identifying mark had been cut off the clothing

Search In Vain – And Then So the one faint chance the detectives had was to find a copy of the Rubaiyat of Omar Khayyam with the last page missing.

They began their search by circulating public libraries throughout Australia – on the grounds that the body was that of a poor man who would be unlikely to own such a book.

Nothing came of this line of inquiry, but a newspaper paragraph was published giving the story.

Last night an Adelaide business man recalled that some time in November last year he found a book thrown on the back seat of his car while it was parked in Jetty Road, Glenelg.

Today he handed detectives the book. On the last page the words "Tamam Shud" had been torn out.

Phone Number In Book

On the back of the book are several telephone numbers and a series of capital letters written in pencil. The meaning of this has not yet been deciphered.

POLICE TEST PAPER, BOOK

Microscopic examination of the slip of paper found in the clothing of the Somerton body, and of the book from which the slip is believed to have been torn, is being made by police today.

The nurse
Detective Errol Canney was delegated to check the telephone number found in The Rubaiyat, and to make any further inquiries necessary. He obtained the name and address of the subscriber, who was in the Glenelg area, and he went there and spoke with the female who occupied the premises. She said her name was Tessie and that she had recently married Prestige Johnson. *(She was not married)* After a general discussion the conversation turned to the subject of The Rubaiyat with her telephone number pencilled on it. Canney hoped that the plausible explanation she offered would provide the identity of *the Unknown Man.*

Tessie told Canney that some years before she had given a copy of The Rubaiyat to an Army lieutenant, who she had met on a couple of occasions at the Clifton Gardens Hotel, while nursing at Sydney's North Shore Hospital. The name she supplied was Alfred Boxall and she knew he lived in Para (sic) Street, Maroubra, and that he was attached to the Water Transport Company, Australian Army Service Corp. The exact conversation that transpired between Canney and Tessie is not known, but information supplied by the nurse satisfied him that an investigation could be made to identify Boxall. He expected that inquiries would most likely identify him as *the Unknown Man.* So it was only a matter of confirming the identity of Boxall and linking him to an address for further inquiries to be made.

Breaking news
The morning newspaper of Tuesday 26 July 1949 included an article from which these selected passages are included. References made in respect to information allegedly supplied by the police, the nurse or the Boxall family are in italic.

BODY MYSTERY DEEPENS
Phone number found on cover of book

The Somerton body mystery deepened today with the discovery of an Adelaide woman's telephone number on the cover of a book linked to the case.

A fragment found in the victim's clothing is believed to have come from the book "The Rubaiyat of Omar Khayyam."

Police have discovered also that the woman gave a similar copy of the book to an Army lieutenant in Sydney about three and a half years ago, and that the lieutenant later tried to contact her in Melbourne, when she wrote back saying she was now married.

Police have also discovered that the Somerton body was found within a quarter of a mile of the woman's home.

Today, police in Melbourne and Sydney are checking on the missing people to see if the Army Lieutenant is among them.

Det.-Sgt. R.L. Leane yesterday obtained the opinion of an authority that the piece of paper bearing the words "Tamam Shud" was of the same texture and colour as that of the book handed to police on Saturday.

The book had been thrown into the back seat of a motor car in Jetty road, Glenelg, shortly before the victim's body was found on the beach at Somerton on December 1.

Woman's story

All efforts yesterday to obtain a similar copy of the book from the city book shops failed. If police could obtain a similar copy, they would be able to check on the print used in the words "Tamam Shud."

The woman whose telephone number appears in pencil on the cover of the book told police that when she was nursing at North Shore Hospital in Sydney about three and a half years ago, she gave a similar copy to a lieutenant who served in the Water Transport section of the Army.

Later, she said, the lieutenant wrote to her mother's home in Melbourne. She replied to his letter, telling him she was married.

Subsequently, the woman told police, she and her husband settled in Adelaide. Last year a man called at the house of a neighbour, inquiring for a nurse he once knew.

This afternoon the woman is being shown the plaster cast of the Somerton victim, which is now in a storeroom at Adelaide Museum.

Acting on the possibility that the "Rubaiyat" in their possession did belong to the lieutenant, police set out to decipher a number of block letters pencilled on the back of the book.

Although the lettering was faint, police managed to read it by using ultra-violet light.

In the belief that the lettering might be a code, a copy has been sent to decoding experts at Army Headquarters, Melbourne.

POLICE are looking for anyone who has an exact copy of this book "The Rubaiyat of Omar Khayyam." It was published in New Zealand by Whitcombe and Toombs (sic).

Interstate inquiries
At 10.30 a.m. on 26 July radio messages were sent to the police in New South Wales and Victoria respectively:

TO: C.I.B. SYDNEY

IS THERE A PERSON NAMED ALFRED BOXALL MISSING FROM YOUR STATE STOP WAS AN OFFICER IN THE WATER TRANSPORT COMPANY AUSTRALIAN ARMY CORP STOP ABOUT THREE YEARS AGO LIVED AT PARA (sic) STREET MAROUBRA STOP MAY BE IDENTICAL WITH SOMERTON BODY STOP

TO: CHIEFPOLICE

HAVE YOU AN ALFRED BOXALL MISSING FROM YOUR STATE STOP WAS AT ONE TIME AN OFFICER IN WATER TRANSPORT COMPANY, AUSTRALIAN ARMY SERVICE CORP STOP MAY BE IDENTICAL WITH SOMERTON BODY STOP

A visit to the Museum
In the afternoon of 26 July Leane and other detectives conveyed the nurse to the South Australian Museum where she was shown the plaster cast of the deceased. Her reaction to seeing the bust was described as 'completely taken aback, to the point of giving the appearance that she was about to faint'. She stated that she could not identify the bust as anyone she knew.

Searching for an Army lieutenant

Variations appeared in other newspaper articles produced along similar lines, and selected passages from one are included here. References made in respect to information allegedly supplied by the police, the nurse or the Boxall family are in italic.

Suggestion of a code

Another newspaper article indicated the possibility of a coded message on the book.

Army Off cer Sought to Help Solve Somerton Body Case

Detectives investigating the Somerton body mystery yesterday interviewed a woman who had given an Australian Army lieutenant a copy of the "Rubaiyat of Omar Khayyam," which she believed could be identical with the book found in a motor car at Glenelg last year.

The book handed to the police was found in the back seat of an Adelaide businessman's car in Jetty road, Glenelg, shortly before the body was discovered on December 1. The words "Tamam Shud" had been torn from the last page of the book. Similar wording was printed on a piece of paper found in the clothing of the dead man.

Tests made yesterday revealed that the piece of paper found on the body was of the same texture and colour as the torn page in the back of the book. Yesterday's discovery caused local police to enlist the aid of Sydney and Melbourne CIB's in an effort to trace the man mentioned by the woman. The police have also forwarded to the Army Headquarters, Melbourne, a copy of a series of letters printed in pencil on the back of the book. They believe that it is possible that the letters may be some coded message.

Police located the woman from a telephone number, also written in pencil on back of the book. *The woman who wishes to remain anonymous, told police that when she was nursing at the North Shore Hospital, Sydney, about 3½ years ago, she gave a copy of the "Rubaiyat of Omar Khayyam" to an Australian Army lieutenant who was serving in the water transport section.*

The woman said that she subsequently went to live in Melbourne, where she was afterwards married. After her marriage she received a letter from the man. She replied telling him that she was now married. Sometime last year, she could not remember the month, she was told that a man had come to some flats next door to her home and enquired for a nurse. She did not know, however whether this was *the same man.*

It was after this incident that the body was found on the beach at Somerton, not far from the woman's home.

After seeing a plaster cast of the head and shoulders of the dead man, the woman said she could not say whether the dead man was the lieutenant she had known.
It was pointed out yesterday that the features of the dead man had altered materially before the cast was made.

An amazing coincidence was revealed yesterday when another Adelaide businessman called at police headquarters with a copy of the "Rubaiyat" which he had found in his motor car at Glenelg about the time the body was found. This book was a different edition.
Between 4 p.m. and 11 p.m. yesterday police headquarters received 49 telephone calls from people stating that they possessed copies of the "Rubaiyat."
In many instances the copies were not identical with that of the book linked with the case. Four or five were of the same publication.

SOMERTON BODY MYSTERY

Belief book is right one

Police today obtained further evidence to substantiate the belief that they hold the actual book from which the mystery Somerton victim tore the last words "Tamam Shud" – meaning "The End."

Following an appeal in "The News" yesterday for a similar copy of the "Rubaiyat of Omar Khayyam" to that found in the back of a car at Glenelg last November several people came forward with the book.

A comparison of the type used in the printed words "Tamam Shud" was found to be identical with those on the back of paper found in the victim's clothing.

Yesterday police traced a telephone number pencilled on the cover to an Adelaide woman who had given a similar copy of the book to an Army Lieutenant in Sydney 3½ years ago. This man was last heard of in Melbourne, and eastern States police are still trying to locate the man. *The reference to Melbourne is not correct unless it is to a report that a letter was sent to her mother.*

If the Army lieutenant is missing, he might be the Somerton "Mystery Man." If he is still alive, police will then try to learn what he did with the copy of the book.

Efforts to decipher several rows of block letters, believed to be a code, on the back of the book are continuing.

A Navy "code cracker" is tackling the task this afternoon.

Indication of the public interest in the mystery was shown last night and again today, by 60 phone callers, who have offered copies of the book. Most of them are different editions from the one required.

Det.-Sgt. Leane today renewed an appeal to dry-cleaning experts throughout Australia to make a search of their records for the following entries:-

1171/7 4393/3 3053/1

The numbers were found in clothing in an unclaimed suitcase at the Adelaide Railway Station luggage off ce, and may be linked with the victim.

The search for Boxall

On 27 July Sydney detectives were able to ascertain that the last known address of Alfred Boxall was 19 Parer Street, Maroubra. Boxall was not home when they went there, but they established that he was at work at the Randwick Bus Depot. They then went there and their conversation quickly established that Boxall was alive and that, 'Yes, he did receive a copy of the Rubaiyat from a nurse at the Clifton Gardens Hotel during the war, and he still had the copy at his home'. They conveyed him to his home and a copy of The Rubaiyat was produced.

Disappointing results again

At 1.10 p.m. on 27 July a radio message was received from the Sydney CIB:

To: C.I.B. ADELAIDE

RE YOUR NR 259 STOP ALFRED BOXALL ALIVE AND WELL RESIDING NR 19 PARER STREET MAROUBRA STOP

THE UNKNOWN MAN

If the police needed any further confirmation that the deceased was not Alfred Boxall it arrived in a radio message from the Victorian Police at 5.15 p.m. That afternoon:

To: C.I.B. ADELAIDE

RE YOUR MESSAGE NR 360 OF 26TH INSTANT STOP ALFRED BOXALL NOT REPORTED MISSING AND HAS NO CRIMINAL HISTORY THIS STATE STOP MILITARY RECORDS REVEAL ALFRED BOXALL NX83331 BORN 16TH APRIL 1906 STOP NEXT KIN SUSIE ISOBEL BOXALL NUMBER 19 PARER STREET MAROUBRA NSW STOP ONLY DESCRIPTION 5 FT 7 INS, GREY EYES, DARK COMPLEXION, DARK HAIR, MEDICAL HISTORY OF THIS MAN RECORDED AT DEPARTMENT OF REPATRIATION SYDNEY STOP PHOTO BEING FORWARDED BY AIRMAIL STOP

This subject, naturally, also received attention in the press throughout Australia and the following articles are but two of many. The second is from Adelaide's The News of Thursday 28 July 1949. References made in respect to information allegedly supplied by the police, the nurse or the Boxall family are in italic.

EX-OFFICER FOUND – AND HIS "RUBAIYAT"

SYDNEY, July 27.

The latest clue in the "Tamam Shud" mystery at Somerton beach (SA) broke down in Sydney today.

Sydney detectives, at the request of Adelaide police, interviewed a former army lieutenant whose body it was believed might have been that of the man found on Somerton beach last December.

The clue was given by a former army nurse, now married and living in Adelaide, who told police that about three years ago she had given the man, Lieut. Alfred Boxall, a copy of Omar Khayyam's "Rubaiyat" when he was in hospital. *There was no such hospitalisation*

She thought the book might have been identical with one found in a car at Glenelg.

After enquiries in the city and suburbs today detectives traced Boxall to Randwick bus depot, where he is employed on the maintenance staff.

Boxall told the police he had been employed at the bus depot for ten years except during his army service.

The copy of the "Rubaiyat" given to him by the nurse was later shown to the police.

Boxall said he had given the book to his wife in June, 1945, and it has been in her possession ever since.

References made in respect to information allegedly supplied by the Police, the nurse or the Boxall family are in italic.

Mystery may be unsolved

The Somerton body case is becoming more involved than ever.

A high police off cial said today that if the body were not identif ed soon, the mystery would probably remain unsolved. *Three and a half years ago an Adelaide woman gave a former Army lieutenant a copy of the "Rubaiyat of Omar Khayyam" similar to the one from which the Somerton victim tore the last words "Tamam Shud" meaning "The End."* Sydney detectives yesterday interviewed the lieutenant Alfred Boxall, at his employment at Randwick bus depot.

The copy of the "Rubaiyat" given to him by the Adelaide woman was shown to the police. Boxall said he had given the book to his wife in June, 1945. Boxall's wife yesterday showed a Sydney newspaper reporter her husband's copy of the "Rubaiyat." The book was completely intact and undamaged. There was no writing in any of the pages. *This must have been a different copy because the copy given to Alf Boxall was inscribed on the inside of the book. Mrs. Boxall said her husband gave her the book at Christmas, 1944.

Television interview with Boxall

Alfred Boxall was interviewed by ABC-TV in his home in Sydney in 1978. References made in the transcript below in respect to information allegedly supplied by the police, the nurse or the Boxall family are in italic. The conversation took place after a representation of The Rubaiyat of Omar Khayyam being found in a car at Glenelg.

Narration   A 'phone number in the back of the book led to the woman and she identified the bust of the dead man as Mr Alf Boxall, a man she had met during the war. *(The woman did not make an identification.)* But the police eventually found Mr Boxall alive and well and living in Sydney."

Interviewer   Mr Boxall what was the first you heard of all this mystery about a man on Somerton Beach?

Boxall   Well, very embarrassing business. I ah, I was in the Pay Parade at Randwick Bus Depot, when one large policeman came up and in a loud voice demanded to know, who I was, had I ever been in the Army, had I ever been here, there, and all the rest of it, and without any warning one of the policemen said to me; Did you hear about a body being found on a beach in Adelaide? And ah, I quite candidly, I wasn't sure because I wasn't particularly concerned about a body being found on a beach in Adelaide.

Interviewer   What I am getting at is did they say, did they think, the body was you or that in some way you were responsible for the body. What did you think?

Boxall   Well, the first impression I received was that the gentlemen from Adelaide were highly annoyed when after I answered a few questions, they realized that I, who I was, that I was obviously the person referred to by someone in Adelaide, and ah, the fact that I was there and still alive, completely upset their apple cart and they were very displeased. *(No police from Adelaide were present. Boxall was interviewed by the NSW Police.)*

Narration   During the war Mr Boxall was based near the Clifton Gardens Hotel in Sydney. He and some other service personnel were sometimes allowed into the hotel after the normal six o'clock closing time. It was here that he met the young lady who said her name was Jestin. She was introduced to Alf Boxall by the girlfriend of a fellow officer. Jestin who seemed to be a rather shy girl, said she worked as a nurse at the North Shore Hospital. He told her he was soon to go on active service, and at a second meeting she handed him a copy of the Rubaiyat of Omar Kayyam. Inside the front cover she had written an inscription.

The film then shows Boxall collecting a book from a bookcase and walking back to the table. The focus is on the book and the inscription.

Boxall   Number 70 … (Opens book)
Interviewer   Now this is the verse that …
Boxall   Yes.
Interviewer   … and it's from verse 70 and it says, 'Indeed, indeed, the penitence of before I swore. But was I sober, when I swore? And then, and then, came spring and rose in hand. My threadbare penitence, apieces tore.' Well that is about being sober and being repentant, and …
Boxall   Yes.
Interviewer   … and you are all at the pub. Is it something to do with, did you have a heavy night or something?
Boxall   Oh no, it couldn't possibly have been, because these visits over there, so swift and sudden, I mean, they were never really arranged, they were never really arranged as can you come, can you come and so on, you would sneak down the stony stairs, around the little bay and into the pub and you, I might have a couple of 'snorts' and so forth and away.

CHAPTER 12

CODE BREAKERS AND SPY THEORIES

After the letters were revealed on the rear cover of The Rubaiyat Detective Sergeant Leane sought the assistance of the Navy Office at Port Adelaide. On 29 July 1949 a photograph of the letters and a copy of a similar Rubaiyat were forwarded to the Director of Naval Intelligence in Melbourne.

Naval Intelligence replies
On 25 August the Navy Office at Port Adelaide responded to Leane:

Somerton Beach Mystery

With reference to our earlier conversations in conjunction with the above subject matter, submitted is a copy of the letter received from the Director of Naval Intelligence, Melbourne.

From the manner in which the lines have been represented as being set out in the original, it is evident that the end of each line indicates a break in sense.

There is an insufficient number of letters for definite conclusions to be based on analysis, but the indications together with the acceptance of the above breaks in sense indicate, in so far as can be seen, that the letters do not constitute any kind of simple cipher or code.

The frequency of the occurrence of letters whilst inconclusive, corresponds more favourably with the table of frequencies of initial letters of words in English than with any other table; accordingly a reasonable explanation would be that the lines are the initial letters of words of a verse of poetry or such like.

Copy of Omar Khayyam's Rubaiyat is returned herewith.

Release of the code
When Leane reproduced the list of capital letters from the copy of The Rubaiyat and later released the details to the media, he could never have envisaged the impact they would have on the public of Australia.

These letters and details, depicted by the media as a code, unleashed the greatest array of amateur code breakers this country has ever known. Some people were convinced they had solved it, others claimed to have solved it, but would not reveal their solution unless a reward was made available, and many people are still pondering over it since it first appeared. People have become obsessed, frustrated and produced theories that range from the sublime to the ridiculous.

Since July 1949 comprehensive feature articles have been produced in the media on a regular basis. The articles have continually titillated confirmed followers, and entrapped a new generation into the web of mystery. In the current times upsurge in people compiling family histories there are often queries about whether the deceased may be the missing link that has been eluding the genealogist.

Adelaide, Thurs. – 26 August, 1949.

Navy decoding experts have admitted that they cannot crack a code which might identify a body found on Somerton Beach last December.

A Glenelg man found the code message in a copy of Omar Khayyam's Rubaiyat, which someone threw into the back seat of his car in November.

A month later police found the body of a man on Somerton beach, but their only clue to his identity was a slip of paper in a pocket bearing the Persian words, "Tamam Shud," meaning "the end.". (This should perhaps read 'A day later' as the body was found on 1 December 1948.)

Police believe the printed quotation was torn from a copy of the Rubaiyat.

Navy experts worked vainly on the code for weeks.

Police today released the code letters in the hope that somebody might offer a clue to their meaning.

The letters are:

M R G O A B A B D
M L I A O I
M T B I M P A N E T P
M L I A B O A I A Q C
I T T M T S A M S T G A B

The code breakers
People from all walks of life from all over Australia have attempted to give meaning to the letters. They have sent their findings to the SA Police and newspapers, along with a variety of theories and scenarios to support their reasoning. The contributions have ranged from minor to very comprehensive and detailed. Some have attempted to convert the letters to numbers, others have used the writings within The Rubaiyat as a 'key', and many have either invented their findings or used the known events to suit them.

Unfortunately, the contributions and deductions have been made from information in the newspapers, which contained errors and a lot of speculation. Also, people living interstate were usually hampered in applying inductive and deductive logic to scenarios, due to their restrictive access to limited and selective information. Besides this, much of the reporting continued to reproduce the 'code' in a capital letter format, rather than use the readily available photograph. This was probably due to cost, availability of space and time constraints.

Contributions to the debate
It is almost impossible to reproduce most of the contributions analysing the code: the following are a very small selection of items.

The following newspaper reports and selected passages are a mere selection of the many that appeared throughout the country.

Within days a squad of code and cipher experts were working on the bizarre arrangements of letters but no intelligent sentence or message could be deduced from them.

The ranks of those working on the puzzle swelled when the list of letters was published. Practically all were amateurs but many knew what they were doing. Not that a solution that made sense resulted.

Requests for a reward
The editor of The News in Adelaide received a letter on the 'Somerton Mystery' in which the writer sought a reward:

I have not heard of a reward offered by the Police Department, for a clue to the above. I have spent quite a lot of time in finding the "Key" to the code; but by sheer patience and concentration, I have not only deciphered the code, but have also found the initials of the deceased for the police to query upon. Should a reward be payable to deciphering the code, I hereby claim same. If you are interested in a big scoop, I will give you the whole lay out for a reasonable reward. Further I will come to Adelaide to prove it to you, and the police, if you send a car out and arrange with (place of employment) for my absence.

One man, after viewing the photograph, told police it was obvious to him the man on the Somerton Beach was the famed Russian Soldier Marshal Kliment Voroshilov. He said he had carefully studied the two faces, measured the distance between the eyes, noted other facial characteristics and had come to the conclusion the man found on the beach had to be the marshal. The implication was Voroshilov had been murdered by enemies and dumped on the beach. He was, according to the fantastic theory, on a secret espionage mission in Australia.

Unenthusiastically, police made a quick check and told the theorist that marshal was living in Moscow and was now 75 years of age.

New Bid to Read Mystery Code

A Sunshine dry cleaner, Mr Bill Harvey has had a shot at the code which is baffing police investigating the Somerton (Adelaide) body-on-the-beach mystery. Mr Harvey suggests that the code hides two names – one of them, "SAM STERLING, A.B." Mr Harvey believes the code is similar to codes often used by children.

'Imagination'

"The system is to write messages leaving out the important letters and relying on imagination to do the rest." he said.

"A friend who has something to do with codes says that the double t's indicate it doesn't conform to a set pattern. He believes only imagination can solve it.

Mr Harvey takes a step further the suggested solution by Mr E. Jessup of Eumeralls Road, Caulfeld, who thinks the code points to a "Mr Goddard" possibly a seaman aboard an Indian Ship. This is how Mr Harvey Works it out:-
MRGOADABD "This looks like Mr Goad or Goddard aboard...."

"Skip a line, as we did as children to the third line – MLIABOAIAQC. This might mean 'mail (or Malay) boat in A-class quarters.'

"Back to the second line – MTBIMPANETP. This could mean 'Might be another important enterprise....'"
"Then to the last line – ITT-MTSAMSTGAB. It might read 'In time to meet Sam Sterling, A.B. (Able Seaman)'

"So the message could read – 'Mr Goad (or Goddard) to be aboard mail boat in time to met Sam Sterling. A.B. Might be another important enterprise."

Drank 10 Pots of Tea To Keep Awake

Mr. C. Rusten, of the Alberton Post Off ce, who worked all through one night in an effort to decipher the lettering which appears on the back cover of a copy of the Rubaiyat of Omar Khayyan drank 10 pots of tea to prevent him falling asleep.

Police believe that the lettering could provide a vital clue in the Somerton body mystery. The book was found in the back seat of a motor car at Glenelg shortly before the body was found at Somerton last December.

Mr. Rusten, who has a knowledge of code from being a former lighthouse keeper on Cape Willoughby, said yesterday he worked out the following message by a standard code:- "Go B Wait by PO. Box L1 1 a.m. T TG" (signature).

Police informed Mr. Rusten that Box L1 was at Bowden.

The opinion that the lettering was more cryptic than cipher was expressed in a letter to "The Advertiser" yesterday by Mr. V. A. Reynolds, of Magill Road, Magill.

Mr. Reynolds, who was a signaller in the World War I., suggested the following interpretation:- "Wm. Regrets. Going off alone. B.A.B. deceived me too. But, I've made peace and now expect to pay." "My life is a bitter cross over nothing. Also I am quite conf dent I've this time made 'Tamam Shud' a mystery. St. G.A.B. (Or signature) G.A.B."

The same person also sent a letter to the Adelaide Detectives Office:

I note the piece in the Advertiser yesterday (Wednesday) headed "Drank 10 pots of tea to keep awake." I drank no tea for 3 nights; but last night I busted the "code" wide open. I'll defy anyone to say that I have not got the "Key" and that my deciphering is in-correct. I even know the initials of the deceased. Yesterday I sent a letter to The Editor of the News informing him of my success. I asked him if the Police Department were offering a reward to such a vital clue as I could give them, as I believe the Somerton Mystery is solved. Further I informed "The Editor" that I would sell him the whole works in lieu of a reward. I further stated that if he agreed; he could send a car to (place of employment) and I would get time off from (place of employment) come to the News Office and decipher the code in his presence, and of the Police also. I do not know whether the Editor has contacted the Detective Office, about the "Code": or not. Anyhow as I have stated, I have busted the "Code" wide open, and if I may say so the poor chap in my opinion was murdered, and taken to Somerton after death. I would Mr Johns, [as] Police Commissioner [ask you] to contact the Editor of the News about my letter to him yesterday, and see if he is agreeable re terms. I did hear today by chance that the Police have offered a fair reward. If that is so, I am claiming the reward right now. I am quite willing to come to the News Office or Detective Office, and in the presence of Commissioner Johns and Staff and all interested parties I will lay the 'Code' wide open. If you are agreeable; then please send a Police Car out to (place of employment) Friday morning, and I will come in to you (sic) office and give you the low down. It will be necessary to contact (employer) re my leave of absence. I alone know the code."

"The Mirror invited readers to work out their own solutions to the mystery, to decode a message on which Army experts in Canberra are still working.

There must be a streak of amateur sleuth in most of us.

Hundreds of readers did turn detective. And some of their solutions were good enough for further enquiries by detectives in Sydney, Brisbane and Adelaide.

Does old bank account hold secret?

A Sydney schoolboy provided the Adelaide detectives with the most promising lead. Angelo Morabito, of Naremburn, wrote; "Being a student of inquisitive nature I set about breaking down the message code to assist you if possible."

Angelo tried various combinations and various permutations. Several times he lost himself and had to start again. Each time he came to the same conclusion – the letters represented not other letters – even letters in French, Italian and Egyptian, which he speaks fluently – but numbers. But the final number was complicated by a cross placed over the "O" in the fifth line. (The cross was over the fourth line.)

The number Angelo came up with was "504320 – with a cross – 02.""

Why the cross?

"The cross on the line means either a 'crossing over.' An extension number or the erasing of one of the O's, that is a crossing out," he wrote. Angelo also discovered that allowing for the extension, there was such a number in the Adelaide directory. Apart from being near the top of the Mirror's amateur detective squad, Angelo Morabito is also a very considerate schoolboy.

"I didn't want to inconvenience anyone just because of a childish phone call," he said, "So I didn't dial the number." So we did. The number, allowing for the crossed "O," is the telephone number of the Currie St, Adelaide branch, of the Commonwealth Bank. Did the bank have the same number in 1948? Obviously not, because the system of direct dialling has been introduced since.

But the accountant at the bank told us the number in 1948 was "something like 50432". (The telephone number in 1948 was 6204.)

Adelaide detectives said: "It is an inquiry that takes very little time or trouble." So they are looking now for an old account at the Currie Street branch in some name like 'Keen."

Executed by Melbourne underworld?

One Mirror "investigator" had more than just an idea to go on.

The Tamam Shud, he said, was more than just a page torn from a book.

It was the usual signature of a man who had twice stood trial for murder.

Every big baccarat player in post-war Melbourne he said knew who "Tamam Shud" was.

He was the enforcer!

In the hey day of a man called "Twist" he said and "Freddie The Frog" Harrison – himself executed – "Tamam Shud" was known and in nether world of sly grog and illegal baccarat, feared.

Obviously the dead man had fallen afoul of the underworld and had been executed.

In fact, Melbourne detectives had investigated the same theory years before.

But this apparently promising lead had been a dead end.

Another reader believed the code was no more than a chess annotation.

But three chess experts eventually ruled the theory out."

A letter from a Queensland resident

In response to an article which was published in the Brisbane Telegraph about a fortnight ago, I wish to submit a "Translation" of the "Code" mentioned.

I wish to point out that some variation is possible on some particular words, also that, apparently, in the first line, some persons initials are used.

Also, if it should prove helpful or perhaps, successful, I would like to hereby submit my claim to any reward which may be offering for the cleaning up of this mystery.

Translation

Mr. R. Gone Out And Down At B.D. (Billiards D. Boxing D. Beach Display, Initials)

My Trouble Being in My Pregnancy, Am Not Expected To Please

My Love I Am Bored, Out Alone In A Quiet City,

It Tempts Me To Send A Message Straight To

G.A.B. (i) Gabriel (ii) G. At B. (iii) G. And B. (iiii) Glenelg And B.

An Adelaide attempt

An Adelaide man who classed himself as an expert in codes thought he had practically solved the Somerton Mystery. He worked out the code as: 'At B. Samba' and he thought the body may have been at the home of B Samba (Distinguished Service Medal) before it was dumped at Somerton, if such a person existed.

An offer to assist from Queensland

An attached clipping from a Brisbane paper explained this letter.

I was employed in "Ciphers" during the war, and I have a good knowledge of both codes and ciphers, and have been a keen amateur in cryptography since the war. Where experts fail, it is hardly likely that an amateur will succeed – but on the other hand an amateur cryptographer is more likely to bring a fresh approach to the problem for amateurs are a suspicious race; always trying to trick the other fellow.

I notice the newspaper refers to a "code" and not to a "cipher" message. Even so, I should like to try to solve this message. If necessary I am prepared to spend 12 months upon it.

If you decide to let me have a copy of the message, will you also, please forward any information that may aid in breaking the puzzle. Should the message be a transposition, (which is not likely, or the naval men would have cracked it) even such a thing as the number of the unattended car mentioned, could form a clue.

I undertake not to mention the message to any person, other than to an officer of your own department. Trusting I can be of aid.

A letter from a Victorian resident

I believe I have found a solution of the four rows of letters found on the back of the copy of the Rubaiyat of Omar Khayyam found in the car belonging to a doctor at Glenelg, and from which the last line "Taman (sic) Shud" had been torn out, the line mentioned was found in the pocket of the dead man who was found on Somerton Beach in December 1948.

Taking the letters to be initials of words they could be thus:

Must Really Go Over And Demand A Better Deal.

May Try Bribe Inside Man Perhaps A North East Territory Policeman.

May Leave In a British Overseas Aircraft I am Quite Confident.

I Tried Three Months To See A Mess Steward To Get A Berth.

This or some of the obvious alternatives may be the correct meaning.

Attempt by a New South Wales resident

SOMERTON SANDS MYSTERY

POSSIBLY – MR. A. GODDARD

POSSIBLY – M.B.I.E, M.A., B.A. PENNANT, possibly also M.P.

POSSIBLY – M.I.A., B.A., A.I.O., QC.

POSSIBLY – STITT MT GAMBIA S.A.

NOTES It is possible that any one or more of the letters in LINE ONE could be initials as example say S. STITT, or even SAM STITT, or again T.M.STITT. It took me three hours to finish this study. If it should turn out fairly correct I could tell the story how it was done.

A New South Wales resident with a spy theory

After having read it, I am convinced that the corpse was a K.G.B. agent's, who outlived his usefulness and was liquidated by another K.G.B. agent. Several pointers suggest my theory; the man looks like a Russian or Baltic origin. All the trouble to make the body and clothes, belonging unidentifiable, the fact that he was not known in Adelaide points that he was sent there to be disposed. The book KGB The Secret Work of Soviet Agents, by John Barron, will give you some facts. As for the cipher in the Mirror, which goes as below.

(Capital Letters listed)

It is in German, the last line is Samstag, mittag (Saturday, noon) the rest I cannot decipher, but the rest must be the code for the address or person(s) he was ordered to meet. The local Soviet consulate could decipher the code but of course they won't talk. It is more convenient for them to dispose somebody who was no more use for them, than to return him to Moscow. I guess, he was a nuisance for them, discovered by his opposite agents like the C.I.A. so his superiors dispatched him to Adelaide and to his doom. He was probably disguised when he arrived from his last assignment, that's why no one recognized him. His executor must have taken his disguise just before he was doped, on a Saturday afternoon, then he was taken or directed to the beach, to die by a poison unknown to the (then) scientists of Adelaide. If November 30 1948 was a Saturday then the last line of the cipher strengthens my theory.

A complicated code theory
The following letter received by Len Brown is but one of the many complicated contributions towards solving the code sent to the SA Police.

May I refer to a BBC TV program, called Inside Story, about de (sic) socalled (sic) Sommerton (sic) Beach Mystery. This case was printed in the Sydney Daily Mirror in 1970 from the hand of journalist Mr Burgess.

I myself was so intrigued by that article that I spent weeks trying to solve the code. And till the day of writing this letter to you, I maintain that I found the right decoding. In 1970, as I remember well, I did send a letter to Det. Sgt K Moran and at the same time to the Sydney journalist. The latter never answered, from Adelaide Police I received a socalled (sic) cliché-letter that the case would be investigated. I must admit, that partly through my enthusiasm and partly through my not too perfect grasp of the English (written) language my argumentation was not very clear to read.

Senator (excluded) was willing to receive me and to listen to my explanation, and he considered my decoding important enough to address the Senate about this case, trying to prove that foreign agents were operating in Australia. You'll find his address to the Senate in the Weekly Hansard of ... (excluded) ... 1971.

May I assure you, Sir, that I am not a prankster, and not somebody who writes letters to everyone about everything. My only shortcoming is that I like to hear some judgment about my claim and following out of that, some satisfaction. I will enclose with this letter the complicated decoding, which is a combination of letters and figures.

To conclude this lettee (sic) may I assure You (sic) that I did not invent words in the decoding, on the contrary, they (the words) appeared quite unexpectedly.

If we look at Fig. A than (sic) we could say that the order in which the letters are placed is a remarkable coincidence, because the sum of each vertical row is 32 36 32 36 respectively. Let us see what the message is:

K	I	N	G
L	O	W	Y
A	R	D	U
M	E	D	T

One could say again that as Ardum is an old Latin work meaning KEEN this also is a remarkable coincidence, but I do not believe in two of these in a row.
I emphasize strongly that the word ARDUM was unknown to me, and also its meaning.
Let us go back to the message as mentioned at bottom of fol. 1:

When we leave out for awhile the already visible words than (sic) we have left:
NLNU/KILS/S/T/NAT

1 N	2 G	3 K	4 I
5 W	6 O	7 L	8 Y
9 A	10 R	11 D	12 U
13 M	14 T	15 S	16 E

Let us now have a closer look at the figures

5	9	4	3
1	6	2	12
7	8	11	10

and replace them with the letters of Fig. B, we find a macabre message:

W	A	I	K
N	O	G	U
L	Y	D	R

Lyon Drug WAIK.
I don't know what WAIK stands for. It could be a certain I.K. from W.A.
But that could have been a case for detectives, who are more clever than I am.

It is not very difficult to see that one letter S belongs to AD and making the word SAD (Glad News is not used in English). The message is now clear enough: NN KILLS T NAT (we will prove that the letter U is part of the word MORNING to make it MOURNING. (Note that the letter T fits in the evidence in suitcase).
But I think the most interesting part is still to follow.
Why did the "messenger" mutilate the message?

THE UNKNOWN MAN

A	MOURNIN	AS	SAD	NEWS	DAYLONG	NN	KILLS	AS	T	NAT	SONG
1	2	3	4	5	6	7	8	9	10	11	12

These 12 words must be placed in the right order. Is there some message in the "mutilation"? Let us find out and give each word a number.

5	9	4	3
1	6	2	12
7	8	11	10

We read then:

5	9	4	3	1	6	2	12	7	8	11	10
NEWS	AS	SAD	AS	A	DAYLONG	MOURNING	SONG	NN	KILLS	NAT	T

(GL could be the name of the murdered, I think of LOWY that could refer to the German LOWE, the English LION or LYON) and let us keep the word LYON for a while
Note how the sum of the first two rows of figures is always 21, e.g.:

```
5      9      4      3      =21
and    1      6      2      12     =21
       and    5      9      1      6      =21
              and    4      2      12     3      =21
                     and    9      4      6      2      =21
                            and    1      5      3      12     =21
```

A COINCIDENCE?

Although there is a difference in the fourth line of the code, it does not make any difference in the end result.
According the Sydney Daily Mirror of 1970 the fourth line is
        A W E T P
As in the last August TV program I think to have read
        A N E T P
But I repat, (sic) it does not make any difference.
If we program the computer so, that we slice the message in 22 netters (sic) lines and at the same time program the computer that

```
A.....................................N
B.....................................G
C.....................................K
D.....................................I
E.....................................W
G.....................................O
I......................................L
L.....................................Y
M ...................................A
O ...................................R
```

P .... D
Q .... U
R .... M
S .... T
T .... S
N .... E
O .... O (this crossed letter remains OO) but moves 4 places to left

the result will be: AMOR/NING/I/ASGL/AD/NEWS/DAY
LONG/NLNU/K/LSSA/ST/NATS/ONG

FIG.4

3 N	4 G	1 K	2 I
7 W	6 O	5 L	8 Y
9 A	10 R	11 D	12 U
13 M	14 T	15 S	16 E
32	36	32	36

1	2	3	4	5	6	7	8	9	10	11	12	13	14
			M	R	G	O	A	D	A	B	D		
			M	T	B	I	M	P	A	N	E	T	P
			M	L	I	A	B	O	A	I	A	Q	C
	T	T	M	T	S	A	M	S	S	T	G	A	B

Column 4 and 10 – M & A appear to be nulls

Therefore MESSAGE READS:-

			R	G	O	A	D	B	D			
			T	B	I	M	P	N	E	T	P	
			L	I	A	B	O	I	A	Q	C	
I	T	T	T	S	A	M	S	S	T	G	A	B

Extra M & A may be nulls

LINE 1	=	9	LETTERS
" 2	=	11	"
" 3	=	11	"
" 4	=	13	"
		TOTAL = 44	

CONSONNANTS   = 21} OUT OF PROPORTION :- PROBABLY A SUBSTITUTION
VOWELS   = 11} CIPHER OF MONO – ALPHABET TYPE

No OF	M	=	8
" "	A	=	4
= A	M	M	
A	M	M	
A	M	M	
A	M	M	

Therefore   ITT = (Probably) AMM
Therefore   I = A
              T = M

```
            R   G   O   A   D   B

            M       A               M
            T   B   I   M   P   N   E   T   P

                A           X   A
            L   I   A   B   O   I   A   Q   C
A   M   M   M                       M
I   T   T   T   S   A   M   S   S   T   G   A   B
```

IN MESSAGE NO OF LETTERS = 44
FREQUENTLY =

        CY   LETT
        M } SUSPECT NULLS OR SEMI NULLS
        A }

        X
        O   CHANGE OF READING METHOD
                OR
                END OF NULLS
                OR
                CHANGE OF CIPHER
                OR
                NO MEANING
                (X)
                R O (O) N E L Q C G D P S I T B

```
C.T.L  FREQ        PL LETTER
  R   =     1      I   =    A
  O   =     1      T   =    M
  X
  O   =     1      B   =    T
  N   =     1      S   =    I
  E   =     1      P   =    K
  L   =     1      D   =    ? *COMMON ERROR AMONGST UNSKILLED CRYPTOGRAPHERS.
  Q   =     1      G   =    O
  C   =     1      R   =    V or
  G   =     2      O }  =   W
  D   =     2      X }
  P   =     2      O }
  S   =     3      N   =    E
  I   =     4      E   =    N
  T   =     6      L   =    L*
  B   =     4      Q   =    ?
                   C   =    ?
                   A   =    S
```

MESSAGE READS NOW:-

```
V   D   W   S   ( )   T   ( )
R   G   O   A   (D)   B   (D)

M   T   A   ( )   K   E   N   M   K
T   B   I   (M)   P   N   E   T   P

L   A   S   T   W   A   S   (       )
                X
L   I   A   B   O   I   A   (Q   C)

A   M   M   M   I   S   ( )   I   I   M   O   S   T
I   T   T   T   S   A   (M)   S   S   T   G   A   B
```

VOWS DTD M TAMKEN M K LAST WAS Q C AMM IS M II MOST

AMM IS OUTSIDE BODY OF MESSAGE
THEREFORE = SIGNATURE OR NO MEANING

LINE 2 :-}   M   }   NULLS?
LINE 4 :-}   M   }

M IN LAST LINE COULD ALTER MEANING OF EXTRA I TO ORIGINAL S
LAST LINE READS:

SIGNATURE AMM : MISS I MOST
     X
     O LINE 3 DOES NOT SHOW END OF NULLS
     THEREFORE APPEARS TO BE CROSS OVER OR CROSSED WORD

THEREFORE LINE 4 READS
            I MISS MOST. AMM
OR   I MISS AMM MOST (IF AMMIS NOT A SIGNATURE)

SIMIL:-
        LINE 2 M ALTERS VALUE OF ONE OF TWO OUTSTANDING

LETTER M'S MOST & M=T
        THEREFORE LINE TWO READS:-
        T TAKEN M K OR M TAKEN T.K.
        T.K. COULD STAND FOR INITIALS FOUND ON SINGLET
        = T KEANE

FULL MESSAGE NOW READS:-
VOWS (D) T (D) M TAKEN T.KEAN(E)x
LAST WAS (QA)(C)

        I MISS MOST
                        AMM

D = ?   Q=?   C=?

ALTERNATIVES COULD READ=

        BOWS OUT/IN
        COWS IN
        DOWS OUT (NO MEANING UNLESS NAME)
        FOWS OUT (N MEAN)
        GOWS IN (NAME ONLY)
        HOWS IN (HOW IS) – NOT LIKELY
        POWS IN PRIS. OF. WAR\S
        QOWS OUT (N MEAN)
        SOWS IN (NOT LIKELY)
        VOWS IN   MOST LIKELY VOWS TAKEN
        XOWS OUT (N MEAN)
        YOWS OUT (N MEAN)
        ZOWS OUT (N MEAN)
        UOWS OUT (N MEAN)

D COULD EQUAL = D, C, Q, U, J, X, Y, Z, H
C COULD EQUAL = C, Q, D, U, J, X, Y, Z, H
Q COULD EQUAL = Q, D, C, U, J, X, Y, Z, H

SUPPOSITION

PL LETTER ALPHABET:- A B C D E F G H I J K L M N O P Q R S T U V W
CY   "   "   :- I T   N (W) S P L   E G K   VAB   R O

PL. L. A:- X Y Z

CY L. A.:-

     BECAUSE PL LETT M = NULL & ALSO CY LT
THEREFORE   "   "   L = (CY.L.)L

WE FIND THAT:-	A=I	E=N	K=P	L=LD=G	T=B	V=R
		I=S	N=E		B=T	
		S=A				
		W=O				
		O=G				
THEREFORE		G=W				

     THERFORE ELIMINATING XYZ WE HAVE LEFT
        C D F J Q U

THEREFORE AS J IS AN INITIAL LETTER COMMON IN AUSTRALIAN AND MANY EURO-
PEAN NAMES, IT IS MOST PROFLE THAT D IN FIRST LINE EQUALS J.

BECAUSE YOWS (SUCH AS MARR VOWS USUALLY TAKEN BETWEEN MALE & FE-
MALE). J AS AN INITIAL COMMON TO MALE AND FEMALE NAMES.

     THEREFORE FIRST LINE:-

     READS:-

     VOWS JT. JM   (M FROM 2ND LINE)

LINE 3 :- Q.C.

BY CALCULATION THERE ARE ABOUT 100 POSSIBLE TWO LETTER COMBINATIONS
LEFT TO EQUAL Q.C. MANY OF THESE CAN BE ELIMINATED AS UNLIKELY COMBINA-
TIONS.

BY CALCULATION OF SPARE INTERVAL EQUIVALENTS AND UNAVOIDABLE COMBINA-
TIONS THE CYPHER ALPHABET NOW READS

     LETT A B C D E F G H I J K L M N O P Q R S T U V W X Y Z
     LETT I C F J N K W Q S D P L T E G U H V A B X R O Y Z M=NULL

THEREFORE QC IN CYPHER = Q C, C Q (UNLIKELY)
                         H B, B H, (MOST LIKELY)
                         C F, F C, (POSSIBLY)
                         P J, J P, (POSSIBLE IF D DOES NOT = J)

FINAL PLAIN LANGUAGE MESSAGES NOW READ:-

1: <u>VOWS JT\JM TAKEN T.K . LAST WAS MB I MISS MOST.</u>
SIGNED   AMM.

OR

2:- <u>VOWS JT\JM TAKEN T.K . LAST WAS MB I MISS AMM MOST.</u>

IN ABOVE MESSAGES   T.K. MIGHT MEAN T. KEANN(E)
"   "   "   H.B.   "   "   HENLEY BEACH
"   "   "   AMM MAY BE DECEASED SIGNATURE

INFERENCES TO BE DRAWN FROM ABOVE MESSAGES:-
1. T.K. MAY HAVE BEEN A BIGAMIST
2. H.B. MAY HAVE BEEN AN EARLIER WIFE
OR
AMM
3. T.K. MAY HAVE BEEN AN ALIAS
        THEREFORE AMM MAY HAVE BEEN CORRECT NAME
 4. ORIGINAL MARRIAGE MAY HAVE BEEN H.B. TO AMM

IF QC IN LINE 3 EQUALS Q.C. :-
THEN Q.C. IS PROBABLY A GEAGRAPHICAL (sic) PLACE NAME SUCH AS:-

QUINCY }	CALIF. U.S.A.
QUICKSILVER }	
QUARRY	COLORADO U.S.A.
QUAKER HILL }	CORN U.S.A.
QUINEBAUG }	
QUEBEC	CANADA
QUEEN CHARLOTTE ISL	CANADA
QUEENS COUNTY	EIRE
QUEENSTOWN	CAPE PROVINCE
QUEENSTOWN	DOBH = CORK, EIRE

AND AUST. EQUIVS
ALSO REVERSED AS C.Q.
EG CAIRNS QUEENSLAND

READING THE ORIGINAL CIPHER FOR A SCRAMBLED WORD MESSAGE THE FOL-
LOWING UNSASISFACTORY (sic) MESSAGES ARE OBTAINED

(1)   MARGO BAD (D) BIT TEN PM (MAP) (PAM)
        MAIL BOX IQ AAC ITS MASS BAT G.M.T.
(2)   MARGO BAD (D) MAP TEN PM MAILBOX AAICQ
        IT MTS AM ST CAB
(3)   MARGO BADD   (X =O) OR (X=xO)
        PAM TEN PM
        MAIL BOAC QIA
(4)   MR BAGDAD

MI MAP TEN TBP
MAIL BOAC IAQ
ITS A SS MM TT BAG OR ITS A SM BAG SMT
(5) MR BAGDAD
MI MAP TBP
LAMB PO IAIQ
SS BAMMGITTA OR SS BIMMGATTA
                                                    ETC

MARGO DAPP BAD BIT
TEN MAIL BOX IQ AAC
ITS A STAB

Interview with Alfred Boxall continued

The ABC-TV interview with Alfred Boxall in 1978 referred to the code too.

Interviewer   Mr Boxall you had been working, hadn't you, in an intelligence unit before you met this young woman. Did you talk to her about that at all?

Boxall   No.

Interviewer   Was it not done, to speak about those things?

Boxall   Well it was not done to speak about any army affair.

Interviewer   So, she couldn't have known about your involvement with Intelligence?

Boxall   Unless someone else told her.

Interviewer   Because, you can see what I'm getting at, there are, there is a theory about this whole affair, that the man on the beach was a spy, of some kind?

Boxall   Um, it's a, quite a melodramatic thesis, isn't it?

Narration   For three decades people have tried to work out the meaning of these letters in the hope of cracking the so called code.

Interview with John Ruffels

The following interview is a conversation with John Ruffels in the same ABC television program in 1978.

Narration   One of the people who believes it is a code, linked with international espionage, is Sydney Postman, John Ruffels. The world political scene was far from stable in 1948 and the cold war was gaining momentum. With the blockading of Berlin, many people believed that World War III was not far off.

Ruffels   At the moment I'm doing research on foreign espionage in Australia from

1913 to 1963 with the intention of publishing a book about it because it's something that I didn't know about, but it was something in which I was interested.

Interviewer   Are you saying you see a link between the body on Somerton Beach and espionage, spy rings in Australia?

Ruffels   The atmosphere was right in Adelaide for a foreign power to have a spy in Australia.

Interviewer   Why in Adelaide in particular?

Ruffels   Well, the Woomera rocket range, the Eastern European refugee immigration to Australia was at its peak and quite a few of these Baltic migrants were being used in the construction of the Woomera rocket base. At that very time when the body was found on the beach, one of Britain's senior, research scientists was in Adelaide, whose name was Sir Henry Tizard and he was the man who was entrusted with Britain's greatest secrets in 1940 when Britain was trying to draw America in to the war.

Interviewer   Well historically you've painted the picture of the cold war and everything else, but why was the man here if he was a spy?

Ruffels   It's a very hard thing to say whether he was a Russian spy or a British Intelligence officer or a British Defence scientist who turned traitor to his country, or if he was an American Intelligence officer who'd been bumped off by the other side because this was the peak of the cold war, 1948, the days of the Berlin Blockade and so forth. Now my theory is that, and this is again only guess work, perhaps he'd been captured just after he discarded the book, taken to some place for interrogation, strong armed, not beaten but injected with some truth drug, Sodium Pentathol for instance which I gather would be some form of barbiturate in its form anyway. An overdose was administered. In either panic or as the sort of standard procedure or, you know, just something they decided to do, these people had to get rid of this man. They can't just leave him lying around, or he might have been related, or somebody might kick up some kind of scandal. So his body could have been thoroughly cleansed of labels, the labels might have been taken out after he had been captured, and also he might have, he might have given them some information and died after an overdose of this drug.

Interviewer   'Cause the difference between your approach and the police approach is that they assume that there is some kind of affair of the heart connected with it. You rule that out?

Ruffels   "Well not really, I have heard mention of this, in fact here's a clipping. Here from the Adelaide Advertiser of July the following year and this mention's the police interest in a woman in Adelaide through the fact that, can I read it?

(Reads article) 'Police located the woman from a telephone number, also written in pencil on the back of the book. (This is the book with the code writing on the back.) The woman, who wishes to remain anonymous, told police that when she was nursing at the North Shore Hospital, Sydney, about 3½ years ago, she gave a copy of the "Rubaiyat" to an Australian Army lieutenant who was serving in the water transport section.' The woman said that she subsequently went to Melbourne, she married and her mother received a letter from the fellow and some time in 1948 somebody called at the block of flats next door enquiring after a nurse that he once knew. She's not sure if it was the same man, and she's not sure if the man on the beach is the man she gave the book to but the police think that it's a bit coincidental that there is the link between the two you know. So there's possibly a good example of an affair of the heart there.

THE UNKNOWN MAN

CHAPTER 13

FRUSTRATING TIMES

The police investigators were becoming very frustrated. Their investigations of many promising leads were all dead ends. They had used the valuable services of law enforcement agencies throughout Australia to assist, and they knew that soon the future of the investigation would be in question. There were now strong indications that the deceased would not be identified as there were no fresh leads of any substance. Officers were being directed to other tasks and new priority investigations were impacting on their time and resources. Nevertheless, the police continued to clear up outstanding inquiries with the optimistic hope that a substantial lead would be forthcoming.

The final countdown
Replies to interstate reports requesting investigations were being returned, reports of missing people were still being received, the media continued to provide useful publicity and the public were still trying to crack the code. The following miscellaneous items were of some interest to the case.

Oleander bushes
A doctor living in Glenelg provided information about oleander bushes to the investigators. When he was a boy growing up in Angaston there were large numbers of oleander hedges and bushes growing in the town. His grandmother, who also lived in the town, had oleanders growing and from those bushes he would make smooth round spears. The bushes also had splendid forks for making a shanghai. His mother would not let her children and friends have shanghais at all, and warned them that the oleander was very poisonous. Also there was a story that the local butcher, years before, had used such sticks as skewers in his roast beef with a very serious, if not fatal, result. The doctor had looked up a book on poisonous plants used by the Indians but could not find any reference in it to oleanders. As the Indians walk about barefoot a great deal, any poisoning from the oleander might readily be attributed to snakebite. He believed that the death of *the Unknown Man* may have been caused by a very large double pink oleander.

In a subsequent letter to the police a short time later he wrote about his family's summer house at Brighton years before and how he remembered the oleander hedges around the blocks where people lived. He also referred to page 91 of Ellery Queen's Mystery magazine of June 1948 where Miriam Allen de Ford wrote:

An oleander tree grew in their garden and she was very fond of it. Her brother cut it down. She got a piece of the wood and whittled four meat skewers from it. The cook used them for joining the roast. That night she had salad. Her brother ate the veal and died half an hour afterwards. The doctor who attended said it was the heavy dinner of a roast on a hot night that caused it. The wood and every other portion of it is poisonous.

He also attached the reply from the Clerk of the District Council of Angaston to whom he had written to enquire about the incident involving the local butcher:

We have had to make numerous enquiries concerning the matter you mention.

So far as we can trace, there is no knowledge of any local butcher causing poisoning through using skewers made from Oleander bushes.

Possibly it may have been so, but the present residents have no recollection of it happening. Certainly the type of wood in the Oleander bushes would have been suitable for this purpose.

It has always been an understood thing that the bushes are poisonous and there are still quite a number of the Oleander bushes around the town.

Apart from this information we cannot help you much.

In our house in the main street of Angaston, we had several of these bushes, and my parents always impressed on me that they were poisonous.

A missing page of a stanza

A lengthy report was received from Senior Constable L Mason of Warragul Police Station in Victoria. It is a good example of the reach of the media, and the assistance provided by a member of an interstate police force.

> I have to report that, on even date, a man from Newborough called at this station and brought with him a copy of the "ARGUS" daily newspaper, on the front page of which is an article regarding the finding of a dead man on a beach in South Australia in 1948. The paper bore the date 22nd July 1949.
>
> The article referred to comments on the fact that a page torn from a book of poems was found in the possession of this person.
>
> Together with the newspaper, he produced a book of poems entitled "The Golden Treasury of Best Songs and Lyrical Poems in the English Language" and indicated where a page had been torn from the book. The coincidence regarding this missing page is that it is portion of Fitzgerald's interpretation of one of Omar Kyam's (sic) stanzas. The missing page would bear the page numbers 351 and 352. The page measures approximately 3½" x 5¾" and all except the bottom left hand corner is missing. The remaining piece measures 1" at the base by 2¾" in height.
>
> He informs me that he is an ardent reader of this volume and generally takes it with him on fishing trips during season. The first time he noticed the page was missing was following a trip with the Moe Angling Club to Glenmaggie Weir on 30th October 1948. On that occasion he made the trip with approximately 30 members of the Club. On the return from the trip he inadvertently left the volume in the bus, but recovered possession of it the day following the day of return.
>
> He does not remember noticing the page as missing prior to that date but it could possibly have been.

The missing 'Tamam Shud'

Constable R Dowling of the Melbourne Police submitted the following report relating to his inquiries to locate a copy of The Rubaiyat with a missing page:

> I have to report that I have made inquiries and a search of all likely places where the attached photographic sample of printing of the words "Tamam Shud" would apply in connection with the inquiry where it is desired to locate the book containing the poem RUBAIYAT, written by Omar Khyyam (sic) and which was thought to have

the words at the end of the particular poem torn from one of the large number of printed copies by some person in possession of the book.

I have been unable to find any copy of this particular book which has this page torn or damaged after inquiry at the Melbourne Public Lending Library, Robertson and Mullens Ltd, Booksellers, Elizabeth St. City, Handley's Book Depot, Bourke Street, W. Gaeppen, Little Collins Street and other places.

I have attached a clipping of the Melbourne Herald newspaper dated 23/7/49 which reports that the book containing the damaged page has been handed to the police in Adelaide who are conducting this inquiry.

Missing person reports continue
For years lengthy reports relating to missing husbands, fathers and friends continued to be received. Some reports related to husbands who had not been heard from for up to 17 years and fathers who had not been seen for at least 7 years. Although the person reporting them missing might have thought their relative could be the deceased, no positive identification was made. In each case the missing person was excluded because of description factors such as tattoos, scars and dental records. In some cases the nominated persons were located.

When police locate a reported missing person they can only encourage that person to contact the concerned person. There is no obligation on the missing person to do so. In reverse, the police can only advise the person who initiated the report that the nominated person has or has not been located, whatever the case may be.

A suitcase at the John Bull Hotel
At about 3.30 p.m. on 22 June 1950 Constable JJ Arthurson, acting under instructions of Detective Sergeant McGrath, went to the John Bull Hotel in Currie Street, Adelaide. He reported his conversation with the manager to Superintendent Sheridan:

> [Allan] Walters had taken over the management the previous day. Mick Richards who occupied a room at the hotel was leaving and he said there was a suitcase in his room that belonged to a man who stayed in the hotel in 1945. Richards thought the man was dead. The contents of the suitcase were examined. It contained private letters, writing paraphernalia, ration cards, etc. The name J. Carlin, Abminga via Marree, Central Australian Railways, appeared to be the name of the owner. The same name and address was shown on the ration cards. On a writing pad there was a number of writings under the heading 'OMAR KHAYYAM'.

Because the suitcase might have had some connection with *the Unknown Man*, Arthurson took possession of it and booked it into the MO Office.

A local newspaper published an article on this the next day.

SOMERTON MYSTERY REVIVED
The possibility of a suitcase and its contents, found in a city hotel bedroom on Wednesday, being connected with the Somerton body mystery, is to be investigated by detectives.

The Somerton mystery arose from the finding of the body of a man at Somerton on December 1, 1948.

Despite extensive police enquiries throughout all English speaking countries, the man's identity is still unknown.

Allan Roy Walters, who took over the management of the John Bull Hotel, Currie street, city, on Wednesday, told police yesterday that a former employee had handed him a suitcase which had been in his bedroom.

"Omar Khayyam"

The employee told Mr. Walters that the suitcase belonged to a man who stayed at the hotel in 1945. The case contained letters, writing papers and ration cards.

Papers in the case bore the name J. Carlin, Abminga, via Marree, Central Australian Railways.

Among the contents of the case was a pad on which there was some writing and the words "Omar Khayyam."

A piece of paper bearing the words "Tamam Shud" was found in the trouser pocket of the dead man. The words are from the Rubaiyat of Omar Khayyam, a copy of which was found in a motor car at Glenelg, shortly before the discovery of the body.

The words "Tamam Shud" had been cut from the book, the pages of which were the same in colour and texture as the piece of paper found in the dead man's trouser pocket.

On 26 June 1950 William Allan Jaeschke, a grower of Winkie via Berri, advised police that he was staying at the John Bull Hotel at the same time that Carlin stayed there. Carlin spoke of the North and said he was a ganger on the Railways around Katherine. He had two sons who were working a gold claim somewhere. He came from Sydney, and his wife was still living there. He thought Carlin's Christian name was Jim or James. He believed Carlin also had stayed at the Ambassadors Hotel before 1945. He remembered the first name of the manager of the John Bull in 1945 was Bill and he lived at Payneham. He and Clarrie Thomas would know Carlin. He described Carlin as about 58 to 60 years, 5'10" (178 cm), medium build, dark complexion and medium coloured hair thinning on top. He wore glasses to read.

On that day the following article was published in the local newspaper.

Not linked with body on beach

Following information received today, police do not now link the case found in a city hotel bedroom on Wednesday with the Somerton body mystery.

The suitcase had been left at the John Bull Hotel, Currie Street, City, in 1945.

Papers in it bore the name J. Carlin, Abminga, via Marree.

Among the contents was a pad on which was written verses from Omar Khayyam.

Today police received a report from a man who knew the "J. Carlin" referred to when he was at Katherine.

The informant said Carlin had "queer tastes in literature."

His description of Carlin was in no way similar to that of the Somerton victim, whose body was found against the seawall on the morning of December 1, 1948.

The final inquisition

Coroners Act, 1935
SOUTH AUSTRALIA
(TO WIT)

AN INQUISITION taken for our Sovereign Lady the Queen at Coroner's Court Adelaide, in the State of South Australia, on the 17th & 21st June, 1949, & 14th day of March, 1958, before THOMAS ERSKINE CLELAND, a Justice of the Peace and a Coroner for the said State, concerning the body found on the shore at Somerton on the 1st December, 1948;

AND I, the said Justice of the Peace and Coroner, do say that I am unable to say who the deceased was. He died on the shore at Somerton on the 1st December, 1948. I am unable to say how he died or what was the cause of death.

In witness whereof the said Coroner has hereunto set and subscribed his hand and seal

The fourteenth day of March, 1958.

Signed: T.E. Cleland J.P., Coroner

Media bonanza – the New Zealand story

In November 1959 Edward Bonner Collins (alias Thomas James Hunter), who was serving a sentence in Wanganui Prison in New Zealand, concocted an unbelievable story that produced some of the largest headlines available to the print media. One example, the Sunday Mirror of 22 November reproduced here, but excluding previously reported material.

THE MAN WHO FORETOLD HIS DOOM
A STORY THAT MAY SOLVE ONE OF GREATEST RIDDLES THAT EVER BAFFLED POLICE

Amazing clue to mystery death

A New Zealand convict is certain he can solve one of Australia's greatest mysteries – an unidentif ed body found on a South Australian beach 11 years ago.
He says he talked with the unknown man whose body was found on Adelaide's fashionable Somerton beach on December 1, 1948.
The convict, E.B. Collins, Wanganui Prison, says that the man:
Was an American born Ship's steward named Titus Kean, who deserted in Australia in 1918.
Was illegitimate and went to extraordinary lengths to cover his true identity.
Predicted 10 years before he died the time and manner of his death.
Gave him the "key" to a code said to have been written by the dead man.
Collins has made extensive protestations to the Sunday Mirror this week, claiming he can

solve the riddle that has baff ed all Australia.

His story, sent to the Sunday Mirror with the permission of prison off cials, is a fantastic development in a world-wide search which to date has failed to uncover any trace of the man's identity.

The article then covers in detail the background to the Somerton story.

Now from Wanganui Prison, E.B. Collins says he met the dead man on a Saturday morning in 1938, in Christchurch.

This is his story:

We met in a bar. He asked if he could join me. He said his name was Titus Kean, but he used the name Tom Kean. He was well-dressed, pleasantly spoken and well-mannered.

He asked me to join him in a drive to Timaru and ordered a taxi.

He said he had been waiting for three days to meet me – because he knew the meeting was pre-ordained.

I told him this was nonsense because I had never seen him before.

But he said: "Nonetheless, it's true. Just as true as life for me will be Tamam Shud in 10 years."

He explained the meaning of the words, and said he was 36 and would be dead in 10 years.

He said he was born an illegitimate on September 6, 1902, in the United States. In 1908, his mother gave him into the care of distant relatives named Kitto, an itinerant labouring couple. While working on a Texas Ranch in 1917, Mrs. Kitto told him that his mother had died.

His father was a man named Goodman. The name Kean was his mother's surname.

Kean told me he drifted to Wyoming, worked on another ranch, but could not settle down.

He moved to San Francisco and became a steward on a ship to South America.

He worked on four ships, but not under the name of Kean, and got good discharges from all of them.

He told me that in San Francisco in 1918 he switched identities with an English Steward.

This steward looked like him, wanted to live in the United States, and had missed his ship to England because he was getting treatment.

They practiced writing each other's signature and they changed papers and names. Kean told me he sailed for England, and in 1919 was engaged as a steward on a ship to Australia.

He had deserted and had not been to sea since. He worked in different jobs in New South Wales and gambled. One night, he said, he won a large amount at two-up.

He had not worked since that night, but had continued gambling.

He told me: I have always looked after myself. I keep fit by doing a lot of bike-riding.

"Also I've kept on the move and I suppose I could say I've enjoyed life. But from time to time I worry about my birth."

Kean told me that he attended a séance in Melbourne in 1928, and had seen his mother materialize.

He did not claim to be a spiritualist, but said: "Life goes on after death and in 10 years I will live in a spirit world, which goes on for all eternity."

He said that he attended another séance in Auckland in 1933, and the medium told him he would die near the end of 1948 and his death "would be something of a mystery to all."

I asked him why he was telling me all this and he replied: "Because I rarely use my correct name."

"When I die I will not be known to any person, and more than a decade after my body has been found you'll establish my identity."

I asked him how and he told me: "You will draw my likeness and submit it to an

Australian paper and my hand will guide your effort." He then gave me a card with capital letters on it – the same as those found and which I have seen published. But on the other side of the card were more of the cryptic letters:

MRGOADBAD
AMLLANSNN
NWOOKEDA
LLKEIMNAY

The first line was the same as the first line in the other set but two of the letters were transposed.

He said he could not tell me the meaning, but added that I would write his story after seeing the first lot of letters in print.

I do not know how he knew I would ever see those letters; I thought he was mad.

"When I die," he told me, "a man will find my body on the beach and thinking that I am drunk he will rob my body of more than 600 pounds. He will also steal this pair of scissors."

Kean showed me a beautiful pair of small scissors engraved with a most unusual design.

"I'll know when I am going to die," he said, "and I will remove all clues from my personal effects that could establish my identity. I will do this about two days before I die."

"Why do such a thing?" I asked.

"Because," he said, "by doing so I will be helping my mother attain spiritual bliss. At the moment my mother is in the second circle – there are four circles before one reaches the highest spiritual sphere."

He told me that the steward with whom he exchanged identities would be dead before I told this story.

I pointed out to Kean that the authorities would discover his identity even if he removed clues.

"No, they won't," he said. "I never travel under my own name. When I book into a hotel I never use my correct name.

"In a few days I'll be returning to Australia. Here's my ticket. See – it's not under the name of Kean. As a matter of fact, I bought this from a chap who changed his mind about going to Sydney."

"My death will seem strange to many people. Some will assert that I was murdered. Others will say natural causes will be right.

"When you write my story Ted, what I have told you will be investigated and my death will no longer be a mystery.

"Everything will be proved beyond all doubt, and people will come forward after reading the story and support what you write."

He told me that the second set of cryptic letters he gave me held the key to the first set, which would be found after his death.

I asked him: "What makes you so sure that I'm the person you thought you had to meet to tell your story?"

He replied: "Because I have seen you in my mind for months.

He said he didn't care what people thought. He had told me the truth, and his prophecy would be fulfilled.

He had with him a copy of the Rubaiyat and he quoted some passages from it.

He told me he would meet me in Wellington a couple of days later. He did, although at the time I had no intention of visiting Wellington.

He was sailing for Sydney in a couple of days and said that he would never see me again.

His story was so fantastic that I thought he was mad. But I have related it as he told it to me.

The article featured prominently in other newspapers throughout Australia. The following is a part of an article that appeared in an Adelaide newspaper.

A New Zealand convict is reported to have claimed he can solve the 11-year-old Somerton body mystery.

He says he can identify the unknown man.

Adelaide police said today the convict could have seen the story and the man's photograph in a number of national publications.

"But we will study this fantastic report," said the acting Chief of the CIB, Senior Insp. G.L. Gully.

"It will be investigated in the same way as all other matters that come to hand."

INTERVIEW

The mystery body was found propped against the seaway at Somerton on December 1, 1948. Homicide detectives already have been assigned to explore the report.

It appears certain arrangements will be made for police to question the convict, E.B. Collins, who is at present at Wanganui Prison.

Adelaide homicide detectives have never pigeon holed the mystery. As detectives have been promoted and taken off the case it has been handed on to other men.

"It is not as though publicity of the mystery has been conf ned to SA," one detective said.

"The story has appeared many times in national and interstate publications and the facts and the death mask have been circulated throughout the world."

Detective Senior Constable 'Charlie' Hopkins, who was attached to the Homicide Squad, was assigned to compile a comprehensive report of all the relevant details about the circumstances and events surrounding the death of *the Unknown Man*. His report to Senior Inspector Gully was forwarded to the Commissioner of Police on 30 November:

Attached hereto is a report from Detective Hopkins setting out the circumstances of the finding of an unidentified body of a male person at Somerton Beach on the 1st December, 1948.

Also attached is a cutting from the newspaper called the 'Sunday Mirror' (Sydney) of a statement made to their paper by a man named E.B. Collins, a prisoner in the Wanganui Prison, New Zealand.

Collins claims knowledge of the identity of the unknown man and gives a detailed article in this newspaper of his association and conversations with the dead man.

I have read this article and it appears to me that Collins has had some contact with a person who may have had knowledge of the articles appearing in newspapers at the time of the finding of the unknown man. It seems strange that Collins did not come to light with this information until about 11 years after the finding of the body. Collins has gone into much detail and the article given by him to the newspaper tallies with reports in various newspapers who from time to time published articles on this particular case.

I would suggest that this report, together with the newspaper cutting, be forwarded to the Commissioner of Police, New Zealand, with a view to having Collins interviewed and assessing the truthfulness, or otherwise, of this man's statement.

Collins interview – New Zealand Police
Detective Senior Sergeant Bevege of Wanganui CIB reported on 12 December 1959:

Collins stated that he had read an article published in the February 1959 issue of "The "Parade", published in Australia, and on reading the article immediately associated this person with Titus Kean whom he had met in Christchurch in 1938, and the circumstances of his death were identical to what Kean had stated would happen to him.

Having read the article in "The Parade", he wrote to the Editor of the Publication, and was then communicated with by letter from the Sunday Mirror asking for information. Collins replied asking what would be the fees for the manuscript. The Sunday Mirror wrote to him twice to hurry the manuscript through, and told him that the fee would be 20 guineas. Collins stated that he expected at least 50 pounds, but was annoyed when he received a cheque through Truth N.Z. Ltd, Wellington, for 15 guineas in New Zealand currency. (Confirmed he received a cheque for 14 pounds 10 shillings on 8th December 1959 from Truth N.Z. Ltd for this article)

Collins stated the details of the code published in the newspaper, and stated that when he met Kean he was shown the cryptic letters on a piece of very thin paper and he doubted it would be the same piece of paper that was found on the deceased. He (Collins) never forgot these cryptic letters, and made a note of them in the back of his prayer book. From then on Collins claimed "Kean's conversation passed into the limber of forgotten things until reading The Parade". All the letters had been written on a card given to him by Kean.

When pressed for further information, Collins replied, "I'm not making any statement to the Police or giving any further information. I'm not putting my eggs into one basket and no one is getting the story until I get the money."

He stated that he was going to write another article of about 1,500 to 2,000 words and if the publishers are interested and like to pay the price, then the Police can have it after publication, as Collins is only interested in what he can get for the article. He claimed all the Newspapers were syndicated and that they would make money out of his article and that they were worth more than what he had been paid for the first article. Collins could not identify the photograph of the deceased as he was a much younger man, and 20 years had elapsed since he saw him. Nothing further could be obtained from Collins.

Collins has 81 previous convictions since 1918, mostly for false pretences. He was first declared an Habitual Criminal at Christchurch, New Zealand on 11th October 1924, vide P.G. 1924/702. Since then he has spent most of his time in Gaol, and was last convicted at Christchurch on 6th June, 1956, vide P.G. 1956/780, when he was sentenced on a number of charges to Preventive Detention. It appears that at the time of his alleged meeting with Titus Kean, Collins was discharged from Gaol.

While in Prison over a number of years Collins has written articles for newspapers and magazines, and at the present time he is in possession of a typewriter assigned to him by the Education Department. Collins is the chairman of the Literary Group and his main hobby consists of writing articles with a view to publication. He has had one or two published.

Collins has written 38 letters to persons outside the Prison during the period 16/5/59 to 4/12/59, some of which are to the Auckland Weekly News, Taranaki Sports News, Truth N.Z. Ltd, Parade Magazine (Sydney) and the Sunday Mirror (Sydney) and other outside organizations.

From the information obtained concerning the activities of Collins in writing articles for magazines and Newspapers over the past few years, and the knowledge of his reputation, it is reasonable to presume that this story is a fabrication by Collins for monetary gain, and is without substance. This view is shared by others.

Visitors to the grave
There were periodic reports of flowers suddenly appearing on the grave of *the Unknown Man*. They were placed at the site at no predictable time and on no known anniversary. On occasions police attempted to predict visitors to the site but without success. It has been said that immediately after unsuccessful 'stake outs' by police, a bunch of flowers would appear again. It has also been said that a certain amount of suspicion was attached to the flowers appearing because they were quickly located and the fact reported.

The West Terrace Cemetery staff on one occasion reported seeing violets growing at the gravesite: it appeared that someone had deliberately planted them.

Police at one time spoke with an elderly woman who seemed to be showing an unusual interest in the gravesite. They spoke with her and formed the opinion that she was slightly eccentric, and did not appear to have any association with *the Unknown Man*. Indeed, it is not uncommon for people to place flowers on the graves of people not known to them. Some people often become attached to a lonely and neglected grave that they see when visiting the graves of their own loved ones.

CHAPTER 14

A FINAL TWIST

The following information causes some concern and throws some theories into turmoil. There is no evidence that the information was placed before the coroner, but if it had been it may have impacted on his findings.

A new witness

The author knew the late 'Don' O'Doherty during most of his police career and in his years of retirement. O'Doherty retired as a Detective Sergeant and then took up employment with the South Australian Jockey Club as the Racecourse Detective. Although he was not directly involved in any of the investigations, he maintained a general interest in *the Unknown Man*.

In 2003 O'Doherty produced a copy of a report he had submitted to the Officer-in-Charge of the CIB more than four decades earlier. On 5 December 1959 Detective Don O'Doherty received information from a businessman in relation to the Somerton body. The witness, who wished to remain anonymous, revealed the following:

He stated that at about 10pm on the evening prior to the body being found on Somerton Beach the following day, he saw a man carrying another man on his shoulders along the foreshore. At the time he was single and in company with another man, and two girls. He cannot remember the name of the man but he did nominate the name of the girls who were two sisters. He believed the two sisters later went interstate. They were all walking along Somerton Beach towards or near a location known as the 'dugouts'. They saw a man carrying another on his shoulder, walking south, near the water's edge. He could not describe the man.

The author identified and located the businessman in the latter part of 2003. A lengthy conversation took place and he supplied this information:

He had not received a visit from police since his initial contact. He was now retired and living in the area of Somerton Beach. He can vividly remember the incident he reported and recalls that it was definitely on the evening prior to the body being reported in the newspaper. The next day the two sisters discussed the incident with him and they thought the police should be advised. They did not advise the police because they believed that the police would have already been advised by others. When he was young and later as a teenager he was living in a suburb east of Somerton Beach. He and friends always walked or rode their bikes to Somerton Beach. They would cross over Brighton Road, travel west along Whyte Street to the beach and then travel north along the beach as far as Glenelg. He was in his early 20's during the night he saw the incident. They were somewhere near a location that was commonly known as the 'dugouts', walking north towards Glenelg. His attention was drawn to the person carrying the man because it was unusual. The man appeared to be well dressed and walking south in the wet sand because it was harder and easier to walk on. He thought the person being carried must have been drunk and couldn't walk. He cannot remember the name of the other man in the group as he had only met him that day and he appeared to be a friend of one of the sisters. His own sister may know the name of the man. He could not nominate the time of the incident. He later married and after reading various stories about the 'Somerton Body' he thought it may be of interest to the police so he decided to advise them.

In company with the witness I went for a drive in the area. He showed me the route he travelled and he believed the position he saw the man carrying the other man was in the vicinity of The Broadway or thereabouts. He did say that it was not at the 'dugouts' but they were walking along Somerton Beach towards them. He was not able to walk along the foreshore with me to get his bearings.

This information caused me to re-examine the evidence given at the inquest. Obviously, the medical experts were having difficulties supporting their opinions based on the suggestion that the deceased had remained in the same position from 7 p.m. until the following morning. The lividity above the neck and ears raised questions about the position of the deceased when he died. Concerns were also expressed about the absence of vomit on the body or at the scene.

Revisiting that evidence leaves the finding of the inquest open still.

Dr John Dwyer – 'The post mortem rigidity was intense, and there was deep lividity behind particularly above the ears and neck'.

Professor John Cleland –'The lividity around the ears and neck was perhaps surprising in view of his position, but it was explainable'.

Professor Sir Stanton Hicks – 'I have been proceeding on the assumption that this was self-administered. If it had not been self-administered, and the body brought there, that would remove any doubts as to the time at which death took place, as well as any other difficulties'.

Remarks by Coroner Cleland
Coroner Cleland's findings also questioned issues similar to those raised by the medical experts. He also referred to facts that questioned the identification of the deceased.

On 21 June 1949 the inquest was adjourned sine die with the coroner commenting:

It was thought that the deceased must have arrived by train at the Adelaide Railway Station, left his case at the luggage room, purchased a ticket for Henley Beach but missed his train, and then travelled to Somerton by bus. Neither the luggage room attendant, nor the officer who issued the Henley Beach ticket, nor the bus conductor can remember seeing him. No one has come forward to say that he was seen at Somerton between the arrival of the bus and 7 p.m.

I have been discussing the circumstances on the footing that the body found on the morning of the 1st December was that of the man seen in the evening of the 30th November. But there is really no proof that this was the case. None of the three witnesses who speak of the evening of the 30th saw the man's face, or indeed any part of his body that they can identify. If the body of the deceased was not that of the man mentioned and if the body had been taken to the place where it was found, the difficulties disappear. If this speculation, for it is nothing more, should prove to be correct, the original assumption that it was the deceased who left the suitcase at the luggage room, bought the rail and bus tickets, removed the clothing tabs, and put the printed words "Tamam Shud" in a pocket, would require revision.

Although he died during the night of the 30 November – 1st December, I cannot say where he died.

The question of 'lividity' was an issue with the experts, in particular the observations of blood that had gravitated behind the ears of the deceased. This observation in some way suggested the possibility that the deceased had died lying on his back. Did he die elsewhere? Did he die of natural causes? If he was poisoned, who administered the poison? Why was he killed? Who was *the Unknown Man*?

Edameh daarad
(It continues)

APPENDICES

Though this story finishes with 'A Final Twist', there is an obvious need to supply additional information so the reader is fully apprised of some topics of direct relevance that have not been addressed in the text. The subject in Appendix 4 'Poison – Cause of Death' for completeness is fully covered in Chapter 10 (The Coronial Inquest). The evidence is somewhat fragmented and difficult to comprehend. As a result I have extracted and collated relevant information on this subject to provide a convenient reference point. Wherever it is applicable I will comment or give an opinion. I have refrained from making many corrections to transcripts, statements, media reports and other documents.

APPENDIX 1 – WEATHER CONDITIONS

Detective Sergeant Leane supplied information on the weather from 23 to 30 November 1948. The maximum temperature and general conditions for that period were:

23 November – 79.9°F (26.6°C), clear day and clear night

24 November – 91.7°F (33.1°C), clear during the morning, afternoon overcast

25 November – 70°F (21.1°C), overcast during the day and evening

26 November –70.1°F (21.2°C), overcast early morning, clear during the afternoon and evening

27 November – 79°F (26.1°C), clear during day and evening

28 November – 69°F (20.6°C), clear during the morning, cloudy during the afternoon and evening

29 November – 67.4°F (19.7°C), cloudy during the morning, clear during the day and evening

30 November – 72°F (22.2°C), cloudy during the day and visibility fair to good. During the early evening, it was cloudy and at about 8 p.m. it was hazy.

The Unknown Man was wearing brown fawn trousers, a white shirt with collar, a red, white and blue tie, a brown knitted pullover and a grey-brown matching double-breasted coat. He was also wearing clean brown lace-up shoes and heavy knitted socks.

The young couple who were on the beach in the evening of 30 November said they went there to cool off from the warm weather. They both stated that the usual common attire today would be shorts, a light top and thongs. At the time they saw the man lying on the sand the mosquitoes were plentiful and very annoying.

Because there was a theory that the body may have been substituted, I made inquiries with medical people to establish if mosquitoes attack dying people or the bodies of the recently deceased. I have not been able to obtain any information on this subject. Although there was no autopsy evidence produced at the inquest I am aware that ants do attack and leave prominent marks on the bodies of deceased persons.

APPENDIX 2 – TRANSPORT

Trains

William West was employed by the South Australian Railways as a Recorder. Part of his duties were to be aware of the arrival and departure times of trains. He supplied the arrival time information in relation to the country South Australian and interstate trains at Adelaide Railway Station during the morning of 30 November 1948:

Bowmans – 8.20 a.m.
Robertstown – 8.47 a.m.
Willunga – 8.49 a.m.
Angaston – 9.05 a.m.
Melbourne Express – 9.15 a.m.
Broken Hill Express – 9.17 a.m.
Mt Pleasant – 9.20 a.m.
Angaston – 10.00 a.m.
South East – 10.54 a.m.

The scheduled departures to Henley Beach that morning were at 5.13, 5.23, 6.03, 6.38, 6.59, 7.11, 7.27, 8.02, 8.15, 8.53, 9.30, 10.50 and 11.51. All of the trains were on schedule except for the last train which departed one minute late.

Did *the Unknown Man* arrive from Melbourne or from Sydney via Broken Hill?

On 10 September 2002 I visited 'Tiny' Eddlington and I am satisfied that he is an expert in his field. He was a very friendly man who oozes enthusiasm about his past occupation with the South Australian Railways. He joined the Railways in 1942 and I have no doubt he enjoyed his work and would have stayed longer if he did not have to retire at the specified age.

I showed him a copy of the ticket found on *the Unknown Man* and without hesitation he said,

> That is a single ticket from the Adelaide Railway Station to Henley Beach and it
> has not been validated. It is Second Class because there were no First Class tickets
> issued to Henley Beach. If it was a return ticket in would be different and would
> have a perforated section that could be torn off. It cost 7 pence to purchase a single
> ticket and a return ticket would cost 12 pence. It would be 2 pence cheaper to buy
> a return ticket and it would cost 14 pence to buy two 7 pence single tickets to travel
> there and return.

He made the following observations:

> There is no way anyone could walk through the barrier gate and onto the platform
> without having the ticket validated. To get onto the platform you had to either have
> a train ticket or a platform ticket and it would be 'clipped' by a Barrier Porter. The
> Barrier Porters were injured or disabled SAR employees, and they were noted for
> being very officious and they were very, very strict. No ticket to validate, there was no
> way you would be allowed onto the platform. Also if they allowed anyone onto the
> platform or onto a train without a ticket being validated, and an inspector checked it
> and found that it had not been validated, they would be in serious trouble.

All the Port Line railway stations were manned and when you got to Woodville the guard would collect and retain all the validated tickets to Henley Beach. At Woodville the train branched off the Port Line and travelled through to Henley Beach. From Woodville a passenger could purchase a ticket at the railway stations of Albert Park, Seaton Park and Grange. As soon as the passenger got on the train and sat down the guard would collect and retain your ticket.

I asked him, 'Because of Railway Regulations would someone be prevented from entering the platform area if they were carrying a suitcase?' Tiny said, 'No, you could take a suitcase on the train. You could put it in the Guard Van and the guard would get it off for you, or you could store it in the racks above the seats'.

On 15 September Tiny spoke with me again to reiterate and confirm his previous information. He spoke of the route and the railway stations that the Henley Beach train passed through. He advised me that when the train reached Henley Beach it turned around and returned on the same line to Woodville. He also said that the Henley Beach train was very popular and large numbers of people travelled that route to the beach in the summer.

I believe that whoever purchased the ticket to Henley Beach did not use that ticket to enter the platform area of the Adelaide Railway Station.

Cloak Room

The Cloak Room at the rear of the Adelaide Railway Station was a convenient place to store bicycles, parcels and suitcases on a short or long-term basis depending on the needs of the person.

On 30 November 1948 an unknown person deposited a suitcase in the Cloak Room and was issued with luggage ticket number G52703. The top section of the ticket was attached to the suitcase, and the bottom portion was handed to the depositor to produce when collecting the article. A set daily fee was charged, and each additional day it remained in storage a further daily fee was incurred. Full payment was required before the item was released. It was quite common that many articles remained unclaimed.

Ralph Craig was on duty that day and he issued ticket G52703. He was on holidays during the inquest and no statement from him is available. (There is a South Australian Railways record of an RGR Craig, a packer, being at Mt Bryan on 15 January 1923 and passing an exam in 1924. This person is listed as working at various stations.)

Harold Rolfe North gave a statement and evidence at the inquest. He was a Senior Porter with the Railways employed in the Cloak Room. He examined ticket G52703 and said it was issued by Craig on 30 November and that the stamp on the rear indicated it was issued after 11 a.m. (The clock stamp shows the date and time of issue, in this case between 11 a.m. and noon.) The suitcase remained unclaimed but North was contacted by police and he produced the suitcase for them. He checked the records: no overcoat was deposited on the same day but there were other articles deposited that day that remained unclaimed. The depositor's half of the luggage ticket was never located but items in the suitcase have been linked to *the Unknown Man*.

North stated that there were no facilities at the Railway Station where a person could bathe, shower or shave. Anyone requiring those facilities could go to the nearby City Baths or elsewhere.

One speculation is that the person who purchased the Henley Beach ticket did not get on the train at 10.50 a.m. or missed it. It is also possible that the person may have purchased the Henley Beach ticket prior to 11 a.m. and then discovered that the train did not go near his intended destination. In 1948 the train travelled west from the Adelaide Railway

Station to the beach suburb of Grange. The train line then branched sharply to the south and ran parallel to the sea to the adjoining suburb of Henley Beach where the line ended. The beach suburb of Glenelg is further south from Henley Beach.

The spy theory associated with this mystery speculates that *the Unknown Man* walked onto the platform and did not get on the train because he noticed someone following him. It is also possible that someone else may have purchased the ticket and placed it in his clothing at a later time to add confusion. I have no way of confirming the facts in relation to the ticket. The theorising will continue.

Whoever deposited *the Unknown Man*'s suitcase at the Cloak Room of the Adelaide Railway Station did so at or shortly after 11 a.m. on 30 November 1948.

Bus information

The bus ticket found in the clothing of *the Unknown Man* was shown to Edmund Leslie Hall, a Claims Officer's Assistant employed by the Municipal Tramways Trust. He examined the ticket and stated that it was issued by Conductor Arthur Anzac Holdernesse on 30 November 1948. His running journal shows that the 7d ticket numbered CB88708 was sold by Holdernesse somewhere between the Adelaide Railway Station on North Terrace and the intersection of West and South Terraces while the bus was en route to St Leonards. The ticket shows that it was issued on a bus that departed from North Terrace at 11.15 a.m. The area mentioned was the only section where 7d tickets were sold. After passing the intersection of South and West Terraces the cost fell to 6d. The ticket in question was the sixth of the nine 7d tickets sold on that trip. The total number of passengers on the whole trip was 40, but how many of those people were on the bus at a given time could not be established. The St Leonards bus ran at intervals of about 30 minutes. This was the first bus to leave for St Leonards after the 10.50 a.m. train departed to Henley Beach.

Arthur Holdernesse, who sold the ticket, heard what Hall had said in the inquest. He had no recollection of the trip and had seen the logs for that trip. He could not remember whether the bus was heavily loaded or not. He could not remember seeing a man similar to the plaster cast shown at the inquest.

On 29 July 2002 I had a conversation with Ed Hall and he told me of his knowledge of the relevant bus routes. The area west of Moseley Street, Glenelg linked with Worthley's Buses, a private company which had routes in the South Glenelg and Somerton areas. The St Leonards bus did not travel into the main area of Glenelg but went west along Anzac Highway and when a short distance from the sea turned to the north and traversed streets in St Leonards before returning to Adelaide via Anzac Highway. The route of the St Leonards bus from August 1947 to 1949 was:

West on North Terrace from opposite the Adelaide Railway Station, south on West Terrace

and then southwest on Anzac Highway.

North (right) into Osmond Terrace, St Leonards.

West (left) into St Ann's Terrace.

North (right) into Todd Street.

East (right) into McFarlane Street.

South (right) into Osmond Terrace.

To the terminal on the east side of Osmond Terrace just south of McFarlane Street.

East (left) into Anzac Highway and return to Adelaide Railway Station via West and North Terraces.

Re-naming and re-arrangements of this area now changes Osmond Terrace to Old Tapleys Hill Road and the suburb of St Leonards is now Glenelg North.

There was once a train service from Adelaide to Moseley Square, Glenelg. In 1948 a tram service using the dedicated double railway line provided a direct link from the centre of Adelaide to Glenelg. The tram crossed over Brighton Road and travelled down the centre of Jetty Road to Moseley Square, stopping before the Glenelg jetty. The return to Adelaide was on the up track. The tram travels the same route today.

For those not familiar with the geography of Adelaide, the relevant beach suburbs commence in the north at Grange where the train travelled south to terminate at Henley Beach (the unused train ticket). The next suburb south, West Beach, joins Glenelg (bus ticket used; book discarded). South of Glenelg is Somerton Beach (body found).

There was then a strong argument to extend the train service from Henley Beach to Glenelg. Unconfirmed reports suggest that maps showing a proposed route from Henley Beach to Glenelg were displayed in the Adelaide Railway Station in 1948.

I suppose the question will remain unanswered as to why *the Unknown Man* embarked on a confusing journey to the destination where his body was found. Was he a recent arrival confused by the alternative routes to his destination? Henley Beach was a popular seaside location. There were boarding houses in that area and it had direct train access. Did he originally intend to travel there but changed his plans and intend to go there later? Why did he purchase a one-way ticket? These and other speculations brought to the fore a theory that he was a spy. It has been established that he did not enter the platform area because the ticket had not been validated at the entrance gate. Did he know his destination, and was there a planned meeting? Did he walk into an unexpected situation? Did he or another party deliberately present a false trail to confuse others or was he murdered? Perhaps he just wished to die in peace and remain unknown.

APPENDIX 3 – DESCRIPTIONS

Like many people interested in *the Unknown Man* I have struggled to compile a full description of him, his property and his activities. So, new and additional information from the various sources is included in this appendix which focuses on descriptions of him, the clothing he was wearing, his suitcase and its contents.

The deceased

Detective Sergeant Leane's report and his evidence at the inquest provide a description of and details about *the Unknown Man*.

5' 11", well built, broad shoulders and square, well developed limbs, large hands, hair slightly receding in front, gingery coloured hair, fairly coarse turning slightly grey at the sides, back of neck and behind ears, slight wave in hair, no distinct part, about 45 years, grey eyes, clean shaven, natural teeth. Scars on the body were three small scars inside left wrist, one scar inside left elbow, curved and about 1" long, one scar or boil mark 1" in length upper left forearm. [The last mentioned scar was on the left upper arm.]

Natural teeth, I think there were 16 missing, 8 on top and 8 on the bottom.

… this man was an inveterate smoker, because of the stain on his fingers. This man's hands were hard, but were not rough from performing manual work …

The shoes now are roughly in the same condition as they were when found. They are practically new, and very clean. They look as though they had been polished that morning or later.

Dr John Dwyer described his post-mortem examination to the inquest;

> The body was that of a tallish man, I thought about 45 years of age, with greying hair, and he was in good physical condition. There was every sign of his having taken care of himself in the way that his fingernails and feet were looked after. There was no exterior markings of note. The nails I thought just carefully trimmed, probably with scissors, not with a file or nail clippers.

> The general impression I gained was that he was a man whose bearing you would take notice of, by reason of his general appearance. There was the expression about his face as though he might have been an educated man. The post mortem rigidity was intense, and there was deep lividity behind particularly above the ears and neck.

> I later handed a chart of the missing teeth to Constable Sutherland. It would be similar to say that there were more of the central teeth remaining. Those remaining were the central teeth in each jaw. Anyone looking at him in the ordinary way, if he were to laugh, would notice the teeth were missing. If he were speaking, the missing teeth were not noticeable.

> The legs were sunburned right up to the crutch. The trunk was not sunburned. It appeared that he had gone about with a shirt on, and his bathing trunks. The sunburn was definitely the previous season's sunburn or earlier. If he had been burned on this summer it would have been more pronounced. If he had been sunbathing I would have expected the trunk to have been sunburned as well. It is possible that the browning of his skin was due to his occupation, but he had not been indulging in that occupation for some time if that was the case. I would say that the skin had not been burned by the sun for some months. If he had been burned in October or

November, the sunburn would have been darker. It might have been even further back than the previous summer when the sunburn was sustained. It would have been the previous summer or longer when he sustained the sunburn.

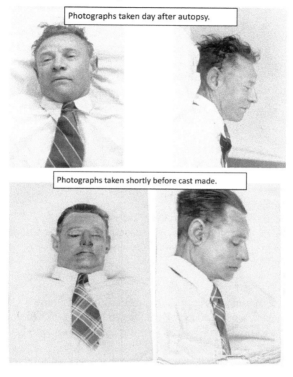

Photographs taken day after autopsy.

Photographs taken shortly before cast made.

Professor John Cleland's evidence at the inquest emphasised the man's attention to detail:

I could not say if it were possible that the deceased had been in the habit of wearing a beard and moustache, and had recently shaved. I consider the fingernails and toenails very well cared for. They were clean, and many people who find their way to the morgue have toenails which are dirty and unattended to. His were clean. I saw indications that the deceased took some trouble about his cleanliness and appearance.

Paul Lawson and cast.

Paul Lawson, taxidermist, provided a statement and evidence to the inquest:

I made a mould of the head and shoulders of the body. On looking at the deceased's legs I am of the opinion that he was used to wearing high heel boots. I form that opinion because the muscles of his legs were formed high up behind the knee, similar to the muscles of a woman who wears high heeled shoes.

I have no doubt that Lawson produced a perfect cast of the deceased at that time. I believe that the body was very bloated at that stage and does not produce a likeness comparable to the original photographs.

Teeth

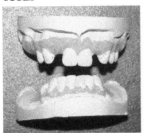

During the initial stages of the investigation standard forms for indicating dental records were not available. The format in which the teeth of the deceased were depicted and circulated was somewhat confusing and caused some further inquiries over time. I have known Dr Kenneth A Brown for many years. He is a respected expert in the field of odontology, and prior to his retirement was a Senior Lecturer in Forensic Odontology at the University of Adelaide. He has main-

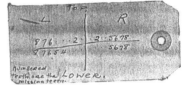

tained a keen interest in *the Unknown Man* mystery. Indeed, he recounts that when he participated in the University's annual Prosh Day parade, he and his fellow students were on the last float, which they had entitled 'Tamam Shud'. As a result of our lengthy discussions on *the Unknown Man*, in July 2003 he obligingly produced for me dental casts with some approximate replications of the man's upper and lower teeth.

Clothing and items

The Unknown Man was wearing brown fawn trousers (Stamina Brand – Crusader cloth), a white shirt with collar, a red, white and blue tie, a brown knitted pullover and a grey-brown matching double-breasted coat. He was also wearing clean brown lace-up shoes and heavy knitted socks.

It was later established that the following items were located with the deceased: a handkerchief, a pair of underpants (Jockey type), a singlet, a train ticket, a bus ticket, a part packet of Juicy Fruit chewing gum, two combs, a quarter-full box of Bryant & May's matches and an Army Club Cigarette Packet, containing seven 'Kensitas' cigarettes, which was a different brand.

A hat and overcoat were accepted as common attire for men to either wear or carry in 1948. Constable Moss when giving evidence at the inquest specifically referred to not seeing a hat at the scene. That was unusual. It was expected that the deceased would have sufficient means of support (money or bank passbook), but he appeared to have none. Besides, the deposit section from the Cloak Room ticket was missing.

Lionel Leane – 'I did not find an overcoat. I have checked at the railways, but there is no numbers 02 or 04 which were for overcoats ... The luggage ticket could have been in the overcoat, if he had had an overcoat and discarded it somewhere'.

Harold North – 'I have already looked at the records, but there was no overcoat on this particular day lodged at the cloak room'.

In a recent newspaper article (1 August 2009) in part the following information was printed:

In the past six months (name excluded) has researched the police evidence and source material such as the inquest report. He is fascinated by the details, like the fact the slip of paper on which "tamam shud" was written was so carefully concealed in the man's trousers. "The pathologist, Sir John Cleland, struggled to find it a second time, even though he had found it before, because it was in a very, very secret pocket," (name excluded) says. "It was a very special pocket that you don't find on any old pair of trousers."

The piece of paper bearing the words 'Tamam Shud' was rolled very tightly and was found in the fob pocket of the man's trousers. The pocket was referred to as a fob pocket because it was designed to hold a fob watch as a pocket watch. This style of pocket was very common. In fact, my police uniform trousers until 1970 had such a pocket. People in the clothing trade have advised that the pocket was normal in 1948 and is still available. Professor Sir John Cleland did not infer that he could not locate the paper on the second occasion because it was in a secret pocket. He was stating that he could not find the paper on the second occasion because it was so small.

Suitcase

Detective Sergeant Leane took possession of an ordinary brown suitcase at the Adelaide Railway Station on 19 January 1949. It was in good condition with no stickers or travel identification attached. It contained:

1 dressing gown and cord
1 laundry bag (word 'Keane' on it)
1 scissors in sheath
1 knife in sheath
(The scissors and knife were covered with a scabbard made of zinc tin and bound with sticking plaster.)
1 stencil brush
4 singlets (1 with name torn off and 1 bearing the word 'Kean')
4 pairs of underpants (2 Jockey type and 2 ordinary type)
2 ties (one bearing 'T Keane')
1 pair of slippers (size 8)
1 pair of trousers (Marco Brand – Crusader Cloth) with dry cleaning or laundry marks
1 sports coat
1 coat shirt
1 pair of pyjamas
I yellow coat shirt
1 shirt (name tag gone)
6 handkerchiefs
1 scarf
1 piece light cord
1 cigarette lighter
8 large and 1 small envelopes
2 coat hangers
1 razor strop
1 razor
1 shaving brush
1 small screwdriver
6 pencils
6d in cash (found in trousers pocket)

1 toothbrush and paste
1 glass dish
1 soap dish containing 1 hairpin, 3 safety pins, 1 front and 1 back stud, 1 button
(brown), 1 tea spoon, 1 pair of broken scissors, 1 card of thread (tan)
1 tin of tan boot polish (Kiwi brand)
2 air mail stickers
1 rubber

Leane measured the trousers in the suitcase: they were the same size as the trousers worn
by *the Unknown Man*.
At the inquest Leane referred to the items in the suitcase:
'Two pair of underpants (ordinary type)'
'It is possible that the 'e' on 'Kean' might have been washed or rubbed off'.
'6d in cash was found in the trousers pocket'.
'One front and one back collar stud' (The studs were used to attach a separate collar to
a collarless shirt. This was common attire then.)
'One brown button'.
'One card of tan thread'. [Barbour's cards of cotton were very common during this
period.]
'One scarf'.
'One bath towel'.
'The case is practically new. Wherever it came from has been taken off the end of it; the
luggage label has been removed, I mean'.
'The clothes in the case were well kept and tidy'.
'The dressing gown is of reasonable quality, and there is a pair of slippers to match.
They have been worn fairly well'.
'Most of the pencils are Royal Sovereign, 3 of them are H type, which would be drafting
pencils'.

Comparisons of items
During the inquest Leane and Cleland gave evidence comparing the items found on the
body and in the suitcase. They referred to stitching repairs and the size of clothing that
linked the deceased to the suitcase.
There were references to tags having been removed from clothing. It is difficult to as-
sess whether or not the references were to name tags specifically or to the clothing labels
that may have borne the name of a recent owner. During this period individuals commonly
wrote their name in waterproof Indian ink on the maker's labels, made new name tags
and sewed them on or wrote directly on an item of clothing. Clothing items were not easily
procured and charitable institutions and other organisations were established to supply
second-hand products. I am confident that the majority of clothing supplied by these outlets would have had the previous owner's name attached somewhere. I would also expect
that the purchaser would remove these names for obvious reasons. To show the difficulties
in analysing *the Unknown Man*'s clothing I pose the questions:
How many and which items of clothing had the tags/labels removed?
How many and which items of clothing did not have the tags/labels removed?
How many and which items of clothing indicated that a name tag had been removed but a
label was still attached?
Did either of the two pairs of trousers indicate the removal of a label or name tag?
In what position was the name 'Kean' written on the singlet?

THE UNKNOWN MAN

There are too many unknowns to give an opinion on this subject. It was not uncommon to write a name on the thick neck binding or the bottom hem of a singlet. I have no doubt

that the name 'Keane' on the laundry bag and the 'T Keane' on the tie were both written directly onto those items, and it would cause unnecessary damage to remove them. I do accept that if they caused any concern they could easily be 'blocked out' by applying Indian ink. I cannot give a reasonable explanation as to why the only name tags located on the items displayed the same or a similar name. Were they originally part of a deceased estate or were they meant to confuse? I am inclined to suspect that the labels on some of the items of clothing had been removed by the deceased because they contained names other than his.

There are also a number of unknowns in respect to the trousers. Both pairs were easily sourced to their places of production in Australia. The pair of trousers that were located in the suitcase had the pocket label attached and written on it were three individual laundry or dry cleaning reference numbers. Despite extensive inquiries they were not identified to an Australian source. It was suggested that the numbers were similar to those used in the United Kingdom. Does this suggest that after the trousers were purchased in Australia they were cleaned somewhere in the United Kingdom, and later returned to Australia?

APPENDIX 4 – POISON – CAUSE OF DEATH

The cause of the death of *the Unknown Man* is probably the most contentious subject in the story. Experts gave very detailed evidence at the inquest but because the information is somewhat fragmented in the story I have selected passages of the relevant evidence for this appendix as a convenient reference point.

Dr John Bennett examined the body in a police ambulance outside the Royal Adelaide Hospital at 9.40 a.m. on 1 December 1948:

> Life was extinct when I examined the body. I thought death could have occurred up to 8 hours before my examination, not more than 8 hours. I would put the time of death at 2 o'clock at the earliest. I based the opinion on the rigor mortis but I did not make a note of the extent of it at the time. I formed the opinion as to the cause of death from just a cursory look at him, from the cyanosis. There is nothing else about the body which I noticed.

Dr John Dwyer made a post-mortem examination at the City Mortuary at 7.30 a.m. on 2 December 1948.

> The post mortem rigidity was intense, and there was a deep lividity behind particularly above the ears and neck.

> There was a small patch of dried saliva at the right of the mouth. The impression was that it ran out of his mouth some time before death when he was probably unable to swallow it, probably when his head was hanging to the side. It would run vertically. It had run diagonally down the right cheek.

> There was blood mixed with the food in the stomach. There was food in the stomach. I would say that the food had been in the stomach for up to three or four hours before death. It is difficult to give an opinion on that, because if the person is in a state of anxiety, that digestion may be suspended. (*Experts advise it is almost impossible to gauge time when items were eaten from the digestion of food.*)

> I have made microscopic examination of the disease, and there was pigment in it, although I cannot say of what disease. It does not resemble malarial pigment, and I can only keep an open mind on the matter.

> The blood in the stomach suggested to me some irritant poison, but on the other hand there was nothing detectible in the food to my naked eye to make a finding, so I sent specimens of the stomach and contents, blood and urine for analysis.

> I am quite convinced that the death could not have been natural, as there is such a conflict of findings with the normal heart. Some factor must have influenced the heart to bring about that state of affairs, or alternatively the centre which controls breathing. I feel quite certain that death was not natural. I think the immediate cause of death was heart failure, but I am unable to say what factor caused heart failure. Something stopped the blood from being pushed along, because of the cyanosis.

If the man was alive at 7 o'clock and dead by midnight, if it were a carefully judged dose of barbiturate – there are records of barbiturates, in one case 72 grams of sodium amytal, which is quiet a heavy dose and one would expect it to leave signs, and the patient recovered. Nembutal has been stated to cause death in cases of 7.5 and 6.7 grams, another one is a name which I will not mention, and it has caused six cases of death in doses of 30 to 38 grains.

On the whole, I think it is probably correct that barbiturate is not the cause of death, except that as I said earlier it is a possible explanation. It is my opinion that in view of the chemist's finding it is unlikely that barbiturates are responsible for death. On the other hand, being driven as far as one can possibly go, I find that the cause might be the cause which I originally suspected.

I think that from the food that it was probably a pie or pasty which he had eaten as his last meal.

I think the question is still open, but in view of the congestion I think failure of the heart is more likely than failure of the respiratory centre.

I saw no obvious sign of a hypodermic needle having been used. I considered the possibility of one having been used, especially if it were used in an unusual place.

If a man had access to diphtheria toxin, that certainly could be a possible explanation, but it would be very unusual. He would have to have access to a place where diphtheria toxin were being manufactured. A very small amount of that would cause the haemorrhages.

There are possibilities of the aconite or aconitine being used, and there are chemical difficulties about their isolation. Knowing how reliable Mr. Cowan is in his analysis, I have to think along the lines that poison was the cause of death, which cannot be found on analysis.

Robert Cowan, the Deputy Government Analyst, received various samples from the autopsy on 2 December 1948:

I carried out analysis of those specimens, but was unable to find signs of any common poison in any of them. I tested for common poisons. Cyanides, alkaloids, barbiturates, carbolic acid, are the most common poisons. If any of the poisons for which I tested were the cause of the death, they would not be absent from the body after death if they were taken by mouth.

There are cases of which I heard in which barbiturates are the cause of death and yet are absent on analysis. I think it is unlikely if they were taken by mouth that they would not be detected in the stomach contents. I cannot say if a man were alive at 7 o'clock in the evening and dead about midnight, it would need a massive dose to cause death.

I found no common poison present, and I do not think any common poison caused death. I cannot suggest anything, other than I think it is most unlikely that a common poison caused his death.

Off hand I am not aware of poisons which can cause death but decompose in the body so that they are not discernible on analysis. I would say that it would be highly probable that any poison causing death would be discoverable on analysis. I am still speaking of poisons taken orally, as distinguished from poisons injected.

I feel quite satisfied that if death were caused by any common poison, my examination would have revealed its nature. If he did die from poison, I think it would be a very rare poison. I mean something rarely used for suicidal or homicidal purposes.

When I spoke of rarity of poisons, I was speaking of rarity of their being used as poisons, not the rarity of their existence.

Professor Sir John Cleland gave his evidence on 21 June 1949:

I saw the body after it was embalmed. I have considered the circumstances disclosed in the evidence, and I came to the opinion, taking all the circumstances into account, that death was almost certainly not natural, and in all probability that some poison had been taken, with suicidal intent.

I have read the account of the post-mortem, and there is nothing to indicate death from natural causes.

I think if he did commit suicide whatever he took commenced to have a soporific effect on him before he had made his way as far along the beach as he had intended, that he had only time to descend the steps, found he was becoming drowsy and lay down with his head and shoulders resting against the seawall, in a position which is within a yard of the steps, on a summer evening, which would be frequented by several people at least.

I do not remember if there was any post-mortem evidence of lividity of the neck and shoulders. Supposing the respiration was failing, his face might get dusky, and the blood might gravitate down to the ears after death. The lividity around the ears and neck was perhaps surprising in view of his position, but it was explainable. It would depend on how much his head was supported, it may have been slightly supported, perhaps no more than one's head supported on a pillow. My opinion is that not only was death not natural, but was probably caused by some poison.

It is possible for certain poisons to be excreted from the body before death so that they are not noticeable on analysis. Barbiturates and Alkaloids may not be detected on analysis. On the other hand, such negative findings must be rare, and if they had been taken, it would be a very remarkable coincidence that common poisons of that nature should have given that difficulty in detection, and at the same time the person concerned seemed to have taken undue trouble to hide his identity.

It makes one rather think that he may have gone to equal trouble to use something which caused a quiet death, something unusual, which was unlikely to be found. It would presuppose some knowledge, either a medical man or someone associated with a laboratory, or possibly as Sir Stanton Hicks suggested, an illness in the family for which some drug had been prescribed which would achieve the result intended.

If a common poison were used and not found, even in the presence of ordinary circumstances, the dose must have been enough, and just enough, to cause death. As far as I can estimate he probably died at or before midnight, and that is a comparatively quick death from poisoning, barbiturate and so on, and one would infer that to produce death so quickly a large dose had been taken, and that would be readily detected. Every poison we have suggested seems to be discounted.

We found no evidence of vomiting. A possible stain on his trousers did not look like vomit, and we did not detect any evidence of potato, and he had been eating potato.

Barbiturates are the things which could have caused death, if only they could have been found. If a barbiturate, it would probably be a sodium compound, which are absorbed faster and broken down more rapidly, but even in such a case it would appear that 50% would remain and be detectible.

A drug which had been prescribed medically, as I have mentioned, would be difficult for the ordinary person to obtain. Of course, the man may have been a chemist or pharmacist. There was no sign of vomiting, and any trace of those substances would be difficult to detect.

It is difficult to find any poison which fits the circumstances. There always seems to be some little point which prevents us from accepting any particular poison as being the cause of death. It is impossible to be certain, but in my mind there is very little doubt but that the death was unnatural.

The evidence of Sir Cedric Stanton Hicks, Professor of Physiology and Pharmacology, was detailed:

I have become aware of various facts in connection with the death of this unknown man. I have formed an opinion as to whether death was natural or not. I think it was not a natural death.

I am in agreement with the other medical evidence with regard to that. Being no signs of violence about the body, first of all I accept the findings of Mr. Cowan, who is a very competent and conscientious chemist, and then acting on the possibility of there still being an undiscovered barbiturate, I would expect to find death from respiratory failure and an enlarged left ventricle of the heart, which was not the case. The postmortem findings exclude the possibility of barbiturate being the cause of death, in my opinion.

I accept the evidence that the man probably died at 2 o'clock at the earliest, and that he was seen to move at 7 o'clock the previous evening.

In cases where death is said to be due to barbiturates, and in which barbiturates have not been found, in cases mentioned, the poison is sulphonal. It is a possibility, but not in this case because of the condition of the heart, and I might add because of the viscera.

There have been cases where death has known to be from barbiturates, but such has not been found on analysis. In the case of sulphonal, it is possible that the dose was the bare minimum sufficient to cause death and to leave no trace on analysis. It is my opinion that to cause death in seven hours the dose would have to be massive.

I could perhaps give my reason for suspecting a possible group, they are, one, that the heart was contracted, and two, that the lungs and in particular the liver and spleen were engorged, and three, that the wall of the stomach was not engorged but there had been blood extravasated into the cavity of the stomach. These facts, because they are facts, suggest to me the action of a poison which caused the heart ultimately not to relax and fill in the normal way, and that prior to its stopping in the unfilled condition, there must have been some time during which its filling was getting less and less. If the heart were filling less and less as time went by, that would mean that more and more blood would be remaining on the input side of the heart, and that would explain the engorgement of the viscera found at the post-mortem.

The fact that there was blood in the gastric contents suggests to me that there had been some violent contractions of that organ, or that there had been some inflammation of the organ. No inflammatory agents were detected by Mr. Cowan, nor did the post-mortem examination suggest that some irritant metallic poison might have been involved, or an acid. Therefore I am inclined to conclude that a member of a group of drugs causing the heart to stop systole might have been used. The first word in the exhibit is the name of the group, and the other words are members of the group.

Of the members of the group, I would say that there are several variants of number 1, and I had in mind more particularly number 2, which would be extremely toxic in a relatively small dose, I mean even in an oral dose, and would be completely missed by any of the tests applied and would in fact be extremely difficult if not impossible to identify even if it had been suspected in the first instance. I mean it would not be identified in ordinary chemical tests. Such a substance would be quite easily procurable by the ordinary individual, I do not think even special circumstances would be required.

They might even have been procured from a case under treatment, but I think you would have to prove that to a chemist. It would imply intelligence and shrewd observation, but not necessarily a knowledge of the way in which it would cause death because that might have been unpleasant. The only missing fact which would have made me confident is the absence of signs of vomiting, but there is sufficient variation between individuals to account for it or he may have vomited before he took up his position by the seawall, but I confess that I would have been more confident in drawing a frank conclusion had there been signs of vomit somewhere about him.

I have been proceeding on the assumption that this was self-administered. If it had not been self-administered, and the body brought there, that would remove any doubts as to the time at which death took place, as well as any other difficulties. If death had occurred seven hours after the man was seen to move, it would imply a massive dose. The drug which I have mentioned in a massive dose could have caused death in that time, and could still have been undiscoverable. The circumstances are consistent with its administration, and some of them even suggestive of it. Nothing is inconsistent with it.

There would have been convulsions with the poisoning in the group mentioned. I understand there was no sign of disturbance in the sand, and I can only assume that so many people walked in the sand that there was no evidence that there had not been convulsions. I am only going by what I was told, that there had been a lot of people around the body, and sand being what it is it would be impossible to draw any conclusion. That is something as well as the vomiting about which I would have liked further evidence. There must have been convulsions, which of course does not mean that there would be violent movements of the body, but there must have been convulsions.

If told that he was in the same position at seven o'clock the night before he was found, and still in the same position when found, I could not draw any inference from that because he could have had convulsions without changing his position. Convulsions may precede death, they do not necessarily precede death, but I would expect them to. The question of whether or not convulsions precede death would relate to the physical state of the individual. If he were in a dilapidated condition, I would expect convulsions, but in this case I would expect some. Convulsions are mainly of the arm. I suppose you could call the movements which you described to me as a convulsive movement. The popular idea of a convulsion is that it is violent, but it does not necessarily mean movements of the arm, although they can be strong movements. The convulsion is a movement, not just a stiffening. This movement at seven o'clock could well have been the last convulsive movement.

A very factual description was given by Dr. Bennett, who said the man appeared to be just like a person who had had a coronary seizure, and that is also in keeping with the conclusion that I have come to. The substance could have been taken orally. Had it been taken by injection it would have acted more rapidly.

Coroner Thomas Cleland remarked in his report at the adjournment of the inquest in June 1949:

Three medical witnesses are of the opinion on the postmortem findings that death was not natural. The words "Tamam Shud" support this conclusion, and indeed put its accuracy beyond reasonable doubt. There was no indication of violence, and I am compelled to the finding that death resulted from poison. But what poison?

No doubt minimal doses of certain common poisons could have caused death and have been eliminated from the body before death. But on the expert evidence no such minimal dose could have caused death so quickly, and a more massive dose would certainly have left traces which would have been detected on analysis.

The only poison which Sir Stanton Hicks can think of, and which is consistent with the postmortem findings, is one of the group he mentioned. But here again there are difficulties. There was no vomit, although there was some evidence of convulsion.

I have been discussing the circumstances on the footing that the body found on the morning of the 1st December was that of the man seen in the evening of the 30th November. But there is really no proof that this was the case. None of the three witnesses who speak of the evening of the 30th saw the man's face, or indeed any part of his body that they can identify. If the body of the deceased was not that of the man mentioned and if the body had been taken to the place where it was found, the difficulties disappear. If this speculation, for it is nothing more, should prove to be correct, the original assumption that it was the deceased who left the suitcase at the luggage room, bought the rail and bus tickets, removed the clothing tabs, and put the printed words "Tamam Shud" in a pocket, would require revision.

The evidence is too inconclusive to warrant a finding. There is no evidence as to who the deceased was. Although he died during the night of the 30 November – 1st December, I cannot say where he died. I would be prepared to find that he died from poison, that the poison was probably a glycoside and that it was not accidently administered; but I cannot say whether it was administered by the deceased himself or by some other person.

During the past few years I have particularly noted documentaries and articles on various poisons. One documentary related to a husband staging the death of his wife by providing circumstances that indicated she died as a result of falling off a horse and hitting her head. Eventually evidence was forthcoming that proved he had administered Ricin to her. I have read numerous articles on poisons including Thallium, Ricin (Castor Beans), Digitalis (Witches' Gloves and Dead Man's Bells), Strophanthus (Kombe arrow-poison), strophanthin, oleander bushes, Hemlock, Diphtheria toxin and many others. I also read with interest that cows can eat the deadly Nightshade with no effect, and pigeons are unaffected by opium. I will rely on far more learned people than I to provide the evidence of what poison caused the death of *the Unknown Man*.

I am of the opinion that a poison eventually caused his death. The absence of any vomiting at the scene and the time of death being put at 2 a.m. causes some concern. Does this suggest that the poison was administered at another location? I have reservations as to the identity of the poison, the source, how it was procured and who administered it.

APPENDIX 5 – THE RUBAIYAT

In my childhood I read and learnt many lengthy poems but they were in a format that told a simple story that was easy to interpret, such as:

> With my saddle for a pillow,
> and the dewy grass a bed.
> Not a roof to form a shelter,
> but the starry sky o'head.

Introduction to The Rubaiyat

When I first read the words 'Tamum Shud' they meant absolutely nothing to me, and I had no idea what type of book The Rubaiyat was. I eventually located an old newspaper article which mentioned Omar Khayyam, Edward FitzGerald and showed the last page of a Rubaiyat with a verse and the words 'Tamam Shud' at the bottom. I was none the wiser. I read the verse:

> And when Thyself with shining Foot shall pass
> Among the Guests Star-scatter'd on the Grass,
> And in thy joyous Errand reach the Spot
> Where I made one – turn down an empty Glass!
> TAMAM SHUD

Verse 75 had me stumped but I decided to at least try and interpret what it meant. I thought that 'Thyself' may be the moon with a shining foot, passing over a group of guests (scattered like stars in the sky and obviously drinking) on the lawn. After passing further the rays of the moon reached a spot where someone, obviously drunk, finished his final drink and turned down an empty glass.

I had to find a copy of The Rubaiyat. I eventually purchased a copy that contained the first, second and fifth editions that had been rendered into English by Edward FitzGerald. I read the verses with interest but I could not interpret them. I did notice that 'Tamam Shud' in the book I purchased was a different font to that I had read in the article. I also noticed that verse 75 in the first edition became verse 110 in the second edition and verse 101 in the fifth edition. To add to my confusion the first line of verse 75 in the first edition changed to 'And when Yourself with silver Foot shall pass' in the second edition and changed again to 'And when like her, oh Saki, you shall pass' in the fifth edition. The word 'thy' in the third line of verse 75 in the first edition became 'your' in the second and fifth editions. Also, where the words 'Tamam Shud' appeared at the end of verse 75 in the first edition, the single word 'Tamam' was written at the end of the corresponding verses in the second and fifth editions.

I obtained a newspaper article with a photograph of the piece of paper bearing the words 'Tamam Shud' in an unusual font that had been found in the pocket of *the Unknown Man*. I was aware that a copy of The Rubaiyat found in a vehicle at Glenelg in 1948 had the portion with the words 'Tamam Shud' removed.

Despite numerous inquiries I was not able to establish the whereabouts of the original copy of The Rubaiyat. So I then attempted to purchase a duplicate of the book. I had no alternative but to review the documentation submitted by Detective Len Brown who had originally attempted to trace the piece of paper to a particular copy of The Rubaiyat. Brown was not involved with the inquiries relating to The Rubaiyat handed to police by the Glenelg businessman.

Brown's information

The following information relates to the investigations made by Detective Brown prior to the copy of The Rubaiyat being located in the vehicle at Glenelg. The following is part of his statement:

On Wednesday 8th June, 1949 I went to Beck's bookshop in Pulteney St., Adelaide and made a search of a number of copies of a poem named RUBAIYAT and written by Omar Khayyam. This poem has been translated to English by a man named Fitzgerald and is a very popular poem and can be found in practically every library and a large number of homes. In one particular copy by Collins Press, England I examined the printing on the slip of paper with the print at the end of the poem, namely Tamam Shud and found that the lettering in each came from the same font of print.

Brown's evidence at the inquest elaborated on his statement:

I went to Beck's Book shop in Pulteney St., Adelaide where I looked through a number of copies of the poem, until I found one copy at the end of which appeared the words "Tamam Shud" in the same font of type as the words on the slip of paper I possessed. I held that copy up to the light, and passed this slip of paper over the words "Tamam Shud" in that copy, and they are identical in size and length. That copy was published by Collins Press of England, and is distributed to Australian distributors although printed in England.

The paper on which the words are written is known as coated wood free art paper, substance of 28 X 36, 56 lbs to the 500 sheets. That is the paper which is before me. I did not compare this paper with that in the Collins Book. If this is a Collins impression, the one which I saw would be a different impression. The type of paper I have is the type used in book manufacture. It appeared to be much the same sort of paper as appeared in the Collins Book. Different impressions of the same book might be printed on different paper. These words appear at the end of the first edition, at the end of the second edition the word "Tamam" appears.

On 10 June 1949 the detective submitted a lengthy report to be forwarded to all States:

I beg to report that on the 1st. December, 1948, the body of a man was found on the beach at Somerton S.A. All efforts to date have failed to establish the identity of this man.

On making a search of the clothing on the deceased, a small slip of paper bearing the words "TAMAM SHUD" was found. Until recently the meaning of these words could not be found, but it has now been established that these words mean "To Finish" or "To End" and is found in the conclusion of the Poem RUBAIYAT written by Omar KHYYAM a Persian Philosopher. This work has been revised by Fitzgerald and it has been found that the lettering as per attached photographic copy comes from a font of print used by the Collins Press, England, for whom W. Cooppen of 527 Little Collins St., Melbourne, Victoria and Australian Publishing Co. Pty Ltd., Bradbury House 55 York St., Sydney, N.S.W. are the Australian distributors.

As the slip of paper bearing these words was in good condition, and was in the fob pocket, it suggests that the slip was torn from one of these copies in circulation shortly before death.

All States replied with a negative result. On 20 June Constable AH Southern of Sydney CIB wrote:

> I have to report having interviewed Mr. Pentelow, Deputy Principal Librarian, Mitchell Library, McQuarie Street, Sydney, this date, in connection with the within mentioned matter, and he informed me that hundreds of copies of the Fitzgerald edition of the "Rubaiyat" had been obtained in the past, both for use in the Sydney Library, and also for disposal per the Country Order Branch of same, and as the volumes are not minutely examined for damage or deletion after use by readers, it would be an impossibility to identify any particular reader who might be responsible for the deletion of the portion of the volume containing the phrase referred to in this file.
>
> I also interviewed Mr. W. Goodchild, Secretary, Australasian Publishing Company, 55 York Street, Sydney, and was informed by him that the copies of the poem referred to edited by his company would number in the thousands and would be distributed throughout the Commonwealth.

After *The Rubaiyat* found in the vehicle at Glenelg was handed in, the police made a greater effort to find an identical copy of the book because the words 'Tamam Shud 'had been torn from that copy. Considerable publicity was given to this subject and I can only presume that a photograph of the actual Rubaiyat was made available to the media as a photograph with details appeared in numerous newspapers throughout the country.

The following is part of an article that appeared in the media.

During the same period a photograph of the page torn from The Rubaiyat also appeared in newspapers.

> All efforts yesterday to obtain a similar copy of the book from city book shops failed. If police could obtain a similar copy, they would be able to check on the print used in the words "Tamam Shud."

My search for a Rubaiyat

As I could not find confirmation that the two photographs were of The Rubaiyat handed to police, I was somewhat sceptical about their authenticity. But in the absence of evidence to the contrary I had to accept that they were what they purported to be.

Combining the information supplied by Detective Brown and all of the available photographs I commenced my search to find a duplicate copy of The Rubaiyat. I was in a slight dilemma. Were there Whitcombe & Tombs and Collins editions of the book, and both with the words 'Tamam Shud' in the same font? What a search! I not only realised how popular the book was, but the number of different versions also astounded me. For years I searched the country, looking through bookshops, stalls, markets and libraries in most States. I even donned the 'white gloves' and perused copies in the National Library of Australia. I was not successful in locating an identical copy, and I did not view a copy where the words 'Tamam Shud' matched the font on the piece of paper found on *the Unknown Man*. I also enlisted the help of experts in the field of books to obtain the particular copy but this was unsuccessful too.

Although I did not locate what I was searching for, I could not resist purchasing many of the copies of The Rubaiyat that appealed to me. Eventually I had to restrict my purchasing because too many copies appealed to me. Nevertheless, an enlightening read was obtained on an interesting subject.

Rubaiyat: Plural of the Arabic word Rubaiyat, a quatrain or stanza.
Quatrain: The verse or verse number.
Stanza: A verse.
Tamam: The End.
Tamam Shud: The Very End.
Saki: The 'cup-bearer' of Persian poetry.

Boxall's copy

During a television interview on the Somerton mystery in 1978 Alf Boxall produced a copy of The Rubaiyat that had been presented to him by the nurse in the Second World War. Quatrain 70 in her handwriting was shown and quoted during the interview. For obvious reasons the nurse's signature was blacked out, and she was referred to as either 'Jestin' or 'Jestine'. In a recent newspaper article her signature was revealed, but I have difficulty in comprehending the reasoning why this was done. As it has been revealed elsewhere, I have inserted the details in the body of this story.

In 2004 I travelled interstate and located the current owners of the particular copy of the book in question. After speaking with a very obliging person I was shown the actual copy of The Rubaiyat.

SHA'IR OMAR
KHAYYAM

By
A.W. HAMILTON

and the
RUBAIYAT

EDWARD FITZGERALD
Illustrated by
G.W. STIRLING

The book was printed by the Australian Publishing Company in Sydney and had been purchased from the Craftsman Bookshop at 10 Hosking Place, Sydney. I also read and noted the inscription and saw the nurse's signature.

A few months later I went to the address of the Craftsman Bookshop but the shop no longer existed.

Recent searching

If the copy depicting the actual Rubaiyat is correct, then it could not be carried in the pocket of the clothing worn by *the Unknown Man*.

I continued searching for a copy of *The Rubaiyat*, and in recent times I was successful in purchasing two first edition copies from an overseas source that were both first editions printed and published by Whitcombe & Tombs Ltd. One copy was of no assistance because it was printed in a different font and there was no 'Tamam Shud' at the end. The other copy was more promising but, unfortunately, it was not an exact copy of that shown in the photograph. The front cover was an identical design but was slightly smaller than the one in the photograph. Quatrain 75 was in the same font, as was the 'Tamam Shud'. The photograph of the copy had 'Quatrain 75' typed under the bottom right corner of the stanza, and the page positioning differed. The photograph depicting the actual copy had a larger border with a very significant watermark. Although I have finally found The Rubaiyat with 'Tamam Shud' in the identical font to that found on the deceased, I am yet to find an identical copy. During the course of my search, I have conversed with hundreds of well-meaning people who have tried to assist me. Maybe the photographs herein will help me!

Left: Copy printed in media
Right: Copy purchased by author

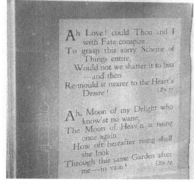

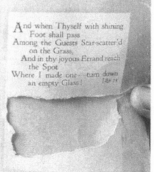

Copy produced in media depicting actual copy of Rubiayat

Extracts from a copy of The Rubaiyat of Omar Khayyam translated by Edward FitzGerald and edited and introduced by Dick Davis.

Omar Khayyam

Despite the fact that Khayyam was a relatively famous man in his own lifetime, very little is known about him for certain. He was born in 1048, in Naishapur, and died in the same town in 1131. Naishapur was at that time the capital of Khorassan, the north-eastern province of modern Iran.

In 1074 the ruler of Iran, Sultan Malek Shah, and his chief minister Nizam ul-Mulk, appointed Khayyam the head of a group of astronomers and mathematicians brought together to reform the calendar. The brilliance of this reform, which resulted in a far more accurate system than that used hitherto, made Khayyam famous throughout the Islamic world – as an astronomer and mathematician.

His recorded writings are in prose, on mathematics (algebra, the theorems of Euclid) and philosophy (free will and predestination, the problems of universals), and virtually all of them in Arabic, whereas the quatrains that have made his name known throughout the Western world are, of course in Persian.

Edward FitzGerald

Edward was the seventh of eight children: by the time he was born (on 31 March 1809) his parent's marriage, at first cordial enough, had degenerated to a state of barely tolerant distance between the two.

From 1837 to 1853 he lived in 'Boulge Cottage', a small lodge on one of his family's estates, his possessions crammed into the building's two habitable rooms. Then for a while he took rooms in Woodbridge itself, until in 1864 he bought a dilapidated farmhouse just outside the town; he was to live here until his death in 1883. With his retiring nature, he wanted nothing better than to shut himself up 'in the remotest corner of Suffolk'. His circle of acquaintances gradually narrowed – though it did include George Crabbe (in whose house he was to die), son of the poet Crabbe, whose work he greatly admired; his last literary project was a selection of Crabbe's poems that he published at his own expense.

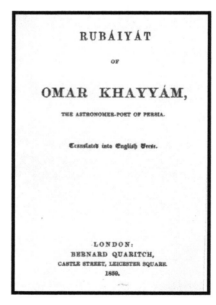

RUBÁIYÁT

OF

OMAR KHAYYÁM,

THE ASTRONOMER-POET OF PERSIA.

Translated into English Verse.

LONDON:
BERNARD QUARITCH,
CASTLE STREET, LEICESTER SQUARE.
1859.

FitzGerald's Rubaiyat

His version of the Rubaiyat is, then, an attempt to reproduce in English what he took to be the essentials of Khayyam's poetry.

The saki – the cup-bearer – of Persian poetry can be of either sex, and the fact that Persian does not distinguish the gender of pronouns leaves the ambiguity unresolved.

It is true that he does select drastically among the quatrains, seeking out those he can make into what he would call 'readable' English. It is also true that he fundamentally alters the formal status of the quatrains. In the Persian each quatrain is an entirely separate, discrete entity, and the order is that all collections of Persian Poetry – the poems are arranged alphabetically according to the last letter of the first line (according to the rhyme therefore). FitzGerald has arranged his selection as a continuous poem, describing the day of a disillusioned, agnostic dilettante who has turned to wine as an antidote to his broodings on fate and death; it begins at dawn with an admonitory flourish and ends with the dying fall of dusk and the rising of the moon.

Perhaps the single most important formal element in the success of FitzGerald's subsequent versions was the substitution of the Persian rhyme scheme (a,a,b,a and very occasionally a,a,a,a,) for Jones's two heroic couplets. The change may seem slight, but it was crucial to the creation of the tone Fitzgerald was looking for. The returning final rhyme is what gives that sense of emphatic certainty, of inescapable truth, almost of a kind of intellectual trap, which characterizes the Rubaiyat.

The story of the 'discovery' of FitzGerald's translation after it had languished unregarded for a year or so became for a time an archetypal tale of neglected genius winning through at last to deserved recognition. But if Fitzgerald was neglected, it was largely his own fault: he published the poem anonymously and in an extremely obscure fashion. And only two years were to elapse between publication and the work's becoming a resounding success.

He first offered a selection of the quatrains to Fraser's Magazine, though he was afraid that the work's impiety would make it unsuitable for a 'family' journal and did not send the stanzas he considered most likely to give offence. John Parker, the editor of Fraser's, kept the poem for a year without either rejecting or accepting it. FitzGerald finally lost patience and withdrew it. He then had a privately printed edition of 250 copies made – anonymously – of which he gave 210 to the bookseller Bernard Quaritch.

The pamphlet appeared in 1859, by coincidence the year in which Charles Darwin's The Origin of Species also appeared, and the two works together can be said to have largely defined the intellectual climate of late Victorian Britain.

It is doubtful whether Quaritch sold a single copy of the Rubaiyat between 1859 and 1861. To get rid of his pile of unsold pamphlets, he reduced the price (from one shilling to one penny) and placed them in a bargain box outside his shop.

By 1868 Quaritch was suggesting a second edition to FitzGerald, who agreed and considerably expanded the original work (from 75 to 110 quatrains), as well as making numerous minor revisions. A third edition came out in 1872, and again FitzGerald made considerable changes, this time leaving out some of the quatrains he had added in 1868. In order to help sell another translation by FitzGerald – of Aeschylus' Agamemnon – Quaritch identified him as the translator of Omar Khayyam in 1875. This infuriated FitzGerald, but it did mean that he enjoyed a modest fame during the last years of his life; his translation was particularly popular in America, where pirated editions appeared. Despite his retiring nature, it must have been of some satisfaction to him, as he had numerous well-known literary figures among his friends, to be able to point to a respectable literary success. In 1879 a fourth edition, again with revisions, appeared. This was the last edition to appear in FitzGerald's lifetime, but when he died, in 1883, a marked-up copy of this fourth edition was found among his papers, and this was used as the text of the fifth, posthumous edition that appeared in 1889; it therefore represents FitzGerald's last thoughts on the text.

What one might call the Khayyam cult only began in earnest after the translator's death, and it is doubtful whether even in his most extravagant fantasies FitzGerald ever foresaw the extraordinary popularity that the Rubaiyat would eventually achieve. His innate diffidence could never have allowed him to imagine himself as the author of what was to become probably the single bestselling book of poetry ever to appear in English.

A well-known Australian bookseller who is an avid collector of the Rubaiyat related a story in the 'Australian Country Style' of a trip to England. A dealer showed him a copy of the first edition of the Rubaiyat by Edward FitzGerald. Even at a penny a copy the publisher Quaritch had been unable to make any money out of it and the first edition was pulped. The number of surviving copies was miniscule. Some years later the collector purchased an actual first edition for 15,000 English pounds.

I had discussions with two reliable sources who viewed the original copy of the Rubaiyat found with 'Tamam Shud' torn from the last page. I am now of the opinion that the photograph appearing in newspapers was not that of the original Rubaiyat but a similar copy with a portion torn out for distribution as an example. *(Refer to the photograph 'Copy produced in media depicting actual copy of Rubaiyat' Pg 169)* That particular version needs to be viewed to establish if the words 'Tamam Shud' or similar were printed on that page.

I was also advised that the area torn from the actual copy was smaller than that shown in the newspaper photograph, and that the piece of paper with the words 'Tamam Shud' found on *the Unknown Man* fitted into the torn area perfectly. I also established that the relevant copy of the Rubaiyat was either the same size or slightly larger than the photograph titled; ('*Copy purchased by Author' Pg 169*). If this information is correct then that pocket edition could easily fit into the coat pocket of *the Unknown Man*.

Some sources have suggested that there were indents on the rear of the Rubaiyat and were possibly caused when the book was used as a support to write on another piece of paper. The letters were exposed when police rubbed a lead pencil across the indents. The information is hearsay and cannot be confirmed.

Another reliable source has stated that there was a name on the rear of the Rubaiyat. Some evidence tends to support this.

APPENDIX 6 – THE NURSE

Over the years a lot of speculation has been made in regard to the fact that there is no reference to the identity of the nurse. I have been unable to locate any references to her in any official documentation or file in respect to the investigation of *the Unknown Man*. There is certainly no evidence that she ever made an official statement about what she knew. This fact alone has placed an aura of mystery around her and has caused some to raise the subject of conspiracy, without identifying their reasoning or who they believe is involved.

She first came to the notice of the police when a telephone number was found written on the discarded copy of *The Rubaiyat* at Glenelg. Detective Errol Canney was assigned the tasks of identifying the telephone subscriber and interviewing the person. The details that he obtained steered the investigation in a new direction.

In very broad terms there is no obligation on any person to provide a statement or even speak with the police. Often some people will provide information to assist an investigation, but for many and varied reasons they are reluctant to become involved further or to have their identities revealed. Under these circumstances the police have no alternative but to accept and honour the terms or to walk away without the assistance. There can be no doubt that the nurse had many reasons to protect her identity, and that was most certainly protected and honoured by the police. She did provide information regarding *The Rubaiyat* she gave to Lieutenant Boxall and sufficient details to identify where he worked and lived. Unfortunately, some peripheral aspects of this information will forever be in question.

Apart from a few minor discrepancies the information did identify Boxall, and the police could be forgiven for believing that further investigations would soon establish that he was *the Unknown Man*. How wrong they were! Not only was he alive, but he produced *The Rubaiyat* the nurse had given him and also corroborated her version of the events. That leaves a serious question. What was the connection between her telephone number, the discarded copy of *The Rubaiyat* and *the Unknown Man*?

What else did she pass to the police? There is no official evidence to establish what further information she gave, but it does not necessarily follow that the police did not deliberately, unintentionally, confidentially or otherwise pass details to the media. It is necessary to make an assessment of some of the specific details that appeared in a number of newspapers.

BODY MYSTERY DEEPENS

Police have discovered also that the woman gave a similar copy of the book to an Army lieutenant in Sydney about three and a half years ago, and that the lieutenant later tried to contact her in Melbourne, when she wrote back saying she was now married.
Police have also discovered that the Somerton body was found within a quarter of a mile of the woman's home.

Woman's story

The woman whose telephone number appears in pencil on the cover of the book told police that when she was nursing at North Shore Hospital in Sydney about three and a half years ago, she gave a similar copy to a lieutenant who served in the Water Transport section of the Army.
Later, she said, the lieutenant wrote to her mother's home in Melbourne. She replied to his

letter, telling him she was married. Subsequently, the woman told police, she and her husband settled in Adelaide. Last year a man called at the house of a neighbour, inquiring for a nurse he once knew.

Army Off cer Sought to Help Solve Somerton Body Case

Detectives investigating the Somerton body mystery yesterday interviewed a woman who had given an Australian Army lieutenant a copy of the "Rubaiyat of Omar Khayyam," which she believed could be identical with the book found in a motor car at Glenelg last year.

The woman who wishes to remain anonymous, told police that when she was nursing at the North Shore Hospital, Sydney, about 3½ years ago, she gave a copy of the "Rubaiyat of Omar Khayyam" to an Australian Army lieutenant who was serving in the water transport section.

The woman said that she subsequently went to live in Melbourne, where she was afterwards married. After her marriage she received a letter from the man. She replied telling him that she was now married.

Sometime last year, she could not remember the month, she was told that a man had come to some flats next door to her home and enquired for a nurse. She did not know, however whether this was the same man.

After seeing a plaster cast of the head and shoulders of the dead man, the woman said she could not say whether the dead man was the lieutenant she had known.

EX-OFFICER FOUND – AND HIS "RUBAIYAT"

The clue was given by a former army nurse, now married and living in Adelaide, who told police that about three years ago she had given the man, Lieut. Alfred Boxall, a copy of Omar Khayyam's "Rubaiyat" when he was in hospital.

She thought the book might have been identical with one found in a car at Glenelg.

Boxall said he had given the book to his wife in June, 1945, and it has been in her possession ever since.

Mystery may be unsolved

Three and a half years ago an Adelaide woman gave a former Army lieutenant a copy of the "Rubaiyat of Omar Khayyam" similar to the one from which the Somerton victim tore the last words "Tamam Shud" meaning "The End." The copy of the "Rubaiyat" given to him by the Adelaide woman was shown to the police. Boxall said he had given the book to his wife in June, 1945.

Boxall's wife yesterday showed a Sydney newspaper reporter her husband's copy of the "Rubaiyat." The book was completely intact and undamaged. There was no writing in any of the pages. *This could not be true because the actual copy had an inscription inside the front cover.*

Mrs. Boxall said her husband gave her the book at Christmas, 1944, and she had had it ever since.

Points for analysis

I make the following points in relation to the information above in an attempt to establish what is possibly true and what may be speculation.

'The woman told police that when she was nursing at North Shore Hospital in Sydney'.

This is true and could possibly have been supplied by a police source.

'…about three and a half years ago, she gave a similar copy to a lieutenant who served in the Water Transport section of the Army'.

This is true and could possibly have been supplied by a police source.

'Later, she said, the lieutenant wrote to her mother's home in Melbourne. She replied to his letter, telling him she was married'.

It is true that her mother lived in Melbourne. It is true that she had moved from Sydney and lived with her parents in Melbourne. Is it speculation that the lieutenant wrote, and she replied to his letter? I don't think so. I suspect that she did mention this fact to the police and this also may have been supplied to the media by a police source. She was certainly not married at that time. At the time of her interview by police she was using the name of her future husband but she was definitely not married. The police obviously believed that she was married and that was her correct name.

'…the woman told police, she and her husband settled in Adelaide'.

At the time of her interview with the police she was not married and there is no evidence she was living with her future husband. There is a strong possibility she did mention this to police and that information was supplied to the media. There is no evidence that the police were aware that she was not married.

'Last year a man called at the house of a neighbour, inquiring for a nurse he once knew'.

Is this speculation? I don't know, but it does seem unusual taking into consideration the fact that there is a connection between her telephone number and *the Unknown Man*. If he had her telephone number he also had access to her address through the Adelaide telephone directory. She was a nurse, and the deceased was in the vicinity of her home on 30 November 1948.

'The woman who wishes to remain anonymous'.

This is true. There is no evidence that the police ever revealed her identity or her address. It may also be true that the police accepted her account that she was married and her correct name was Teresa Johnson. There is no evidence to suggest that the police were aware of her maiden name.

'The woman said that she subsequently went to live in Melbourne, where she was afterwards married'.

She did live in Melbourne, but she did not marry in that State.

'After her marriage she received a letter from the man'.

'The man' infers she is referring to Alf Boxall who was the man in question at that time. Was this journalistic licence? I do not know.

'the lieutenant later tried to contact her in Melbourne'.

As above.

'She replied telling him that she was now married'.

'She replied' infers that she knew the address of 'The man'. She certainly gave police the name Alf Boxall, comprehensive service details and the part address of 'Para (sic) Street, Maroubra', which was more than sufficient to identify and locate him.

'she wrote back saying she was now married'.

As above.

'Sometime last year, she could not remember the month, she was told that a man had come to some flats next door to her home and enquired for a nurse. She did not know whether this was the same man'.

She did live next door to some flats. This information was possibly supplied to the media by a police source. The last part of the above quote infers that she had no personal contact with the man who allegedly called at her home.

'the Somerton body was found within a quarter of a mile of the woman's home'.

This is a reasonable estimate. Possibly supplied to the media by a police source.

'The clue was given by a former army nurse, now married and living in Adelaide'.

There is no evidence that she was an army nurse. Possibly misinterpretation by the media.

'about three years ago she had given the man, Lieut. Alfred Boxall, a copy of Omar Khayyam's "Rubaiyat" when he was in hospital'.

There is no evidence that Alf Boxall was in any hospital during the period that the nurse resided in Sydney. This is possibly a misinterpretation by the journalist.

'Boxall said he had given the book to his wife in June, 1945, and it has been in her possession ever since'.

THE UNKNOWN MAN

Boxall departed for active overseas service in June 1945. He did not return to Australia until the latter part of 1946. (This would have made his quoted time about 4 years before the time allegedly quoted by the nurse)

'Mrs. Boxall said her husband gave her the book at Christmas, 1944, and she had had it ever since'.

Her husband was based in Sydney as an instructor at that time. (This would have made her quoted time about 4½ years before the time allegedly quoted by the nurse)

'Boxall's wife yesterday showed a Sydney newspaper reporter her husband's copy of the "Rubaiyat." The book was completely intact and undamaged. There was no writing in any of the pages'.

The book was produced and shown during the 1978 television interview with Boxall. I have also viewed the book with the obvious inscription inside the cover. If the above quote is correct Mrs Boxall must have produced a different copy of The Rubaiyat.

Questions raised
There certainly is an element of truth in the majority of the information quoted in the items above, but there are other events which require further consideration. It also raises the more important question, 'Did she lull the police into a false sense of security by providing correct information about Boxall, or was there also some other information interposed about another person?'. This raises the following points:

Did Boxall know she moved from Sydney in 1946, and did he know her Melbourne address?

There is no evidence to suggest that he had any contact with her after she gave him the copy of The Rubaiyat.

Did she write back to Boxall or to someone else?

There is no evidence that Boxall ever received a letter from her.

Why would she allegedly state that she was now married?

She was certainly not married at that stage.

Was her mother, who was living in Melbourne ever interviewed?

There is no evidence that her mother was ever interviewed.

Who was the man who called at her home seeking a nurse?

There is no evidence that Boxall ever visited Adelaide.

Who would know her Adelaide address?

There is evidence that *The Unknown Man* did. There is no evidence to suggest that Boxall knew her address.

Who would know she was using the surname of her future husband in Adelaide?

There is no evidence that Boxall possessed this information.

Who would not only know her current Adelaide telephone number, but also know that it was listed under the surname of her future husband?

There is no evidence that Boxall possessed this information.

Why was her telephone number found in the discarded copy of The Rubaiyat that was linked to *the Unknown Man*?

There is no satisfactory explanation to this question.

Was it *the Unknown Man* who called at her home enquiring for a nurse during the time frame quoted?

The Unknown Man was in the area on 30 November 1948, and his body was located in the vicinity of her home.

Did she know the identity of *the Unknown Man*?

I have my opinion.

Police contact with the nurse

It has been alleged that Detective Canney believed that the woman knew the deceased and that it was thought she would later contact the police and pass on more information.

During the afternoon of 26 July 1949 Detective Sergeant Leane conveyed the nurse to the South Australian Museum in Adelaide where he showed her the plaster cast of the deceased. Her reaction to seeing the bust was described as, 'Completely taken aback, to the point of giving the appearance that she was about to faint'. She did not identify the bust as anyone she knew.

Detective Brown is quoted as stating that:

On the back cover of the 'Rubaiyat' were a number of phone numbers ... In one case, I still feel the person might be able to help ... might have some clues to the dead man's identity. It's only my suspicion but, with the effluxion of time ... when one member of the household dies that person may come forward ... or the person may let the clue die.

At one stage I was fortunate to receive old scraps of paper, some of which had a few old telephone numbers written on them. They were meaningless to me. I became aware of a forthcoming auction where old items were listed and I purchased an old Adelaide telephone directory. In my spare time I read through the directory checking the list of telephone numbers I had against those in the directory. I set myself the laborious task of checking a certain number of pages each spare night and I eventually located a number that was significant. This number allowed me to obtain a name that eventually led to sufficient details for me to identify the nurse.

In 2002 I had a lengthy conversation with the woman. She continually diverted the topic from the subject in question. I formed the opinion she was either very evasive or just did not wish to talk about it. On the subject of The Rubaiyat she did say there were many versions then. She did not have a copy, but they were a book of love poems. She then asked me why it was significant. She could not remember Alf Boxall. I mentioned that she gave police his name and address when they first spoke with her. Other aspects and events were discussed. She did say that about 20 years ago at another address she had a visit from the police. She said she did not know anything then, and she did not know anything now. She gave me information about her family and said that they were not aware of the incident as she had not discussed it with them. At a later date I had a further discussion with her that produced no information of any significance. She nominated some ailments and said she was unwell.

Shalom to the nurse

Since I first took an investigative interest in this mystery one of the most often asked questions has related to the identity of the nurse. The majority of people were genuine inquirers who required peripheral details, and accepted the reasoning why her identity was not public information. Some ridiculously asked for details so they could speak with her and get her to 'talk', and apply various means of harassment to achieve a result. Others I classify as either gossipers or egotists who only wanted the information for the selfish purposes of knowing the details or revealing them to others. They cannot accept that the woman's family are unaware of her involvement, and that nothing can be gained by revealing her identity. I am aware that some trails that lead to her identity are available; unfortunately, in recent times a certain item of information was publicly released for the first time.

Sometime after the birth of her child Prestige Johnson moved to the same address as the nurse at Glenelg.

In early 1950 the dissolution of the marriage (Decree Nisi) of Prestige Johnson became absolute.

A few months later Prestige Johnson and the nurse married.

In 1995 Prestige died.

In 2007 Teresa died – Rest in Peace.

It is my opinion that the nurse knew the identity of *the Unknown Man*.

APPENDIX 7 – ALFRED BOXALL

When I first took an interest in *the Unknown Man* there was nothing apart from very basic information available in relation to Alfred Boxall. I was able to obtain a small amount of information in Canberra. I commenced a computer file with the intention of meeting him in the future.

Alfred Boxall was born in London, England on 14 April 1906. I have no other information as to other members of his family or when he migrated to Australia. On 12 January 1942 he enlisted in the Australian Military Forces (2nd AIF) at Paddington, New South Wales. At that time he was 35 years of age, married to Susie Isabelle and had one child (gender unknown). He was a motor mechanic by occupation and lived with his family at 19 Parer Street, Maroubra.

His Army number was NX83331. His description was 5' 7" (170 cm) tall, grey eyes, dark brown hair, dark complexion and scattered linear scars over the outer surface of his left arm.

In early 2004 I was in Sydney with my family, and after climbing the Sydney Harbour Bridge I decided I would visit Maroubra. The taxi driver and I were not a good combination – he got completely lost and I did not have a clue where we were. Eventually the driver worked out where we were and with me navigating by his street directory, $40 later I arrived at my intended destination.

I visited a neat little home at Number 19 and spoke with an obliging gentleman who had owned and lived in the house for some years. He did not know Alf Boxall but he did show me the renovations he had made. After taking a photograph of the front of the house he took me to a lady down the street who had lived there for many years. She knew the Boxall family but she could not assist as to their whereabouts. She did, however, indicate a bus terminal where I could catch a bus that would drop me in front of my hotel for $2.50.

Later in Canberra I obtained comprehensive details of the service record of Alfred Boxall. The following details show his service record.

Service Record

12/01/42 Marched to General Details Depot, Sydney

17/01/42 Taken on strength, Cowra

23/06/42 Transferred to North Australia Observation Unit

10/08/42 Operational Area of the Northern Territory, North of Parallel 14.5 degrees South latitude from 10 August 1942 to 7 September 1942. On 06/06/43 he was transferred to Australian Water Transport Coy. (small craft) RAE. Served with 4 Australian Water Transport Company from 6 June 1943, and was detached to Northern Australia Observer Unit until 7 September 1943.

He wrote of his experience with the NAOU:

"...apart from normal intelligence duties on the main land was required to carry out special operations under the direct orders of G.O.C. Warforce. These included small craft operations in the Timor Sea during the Timor campaign, which were carried out by Capt. David Herbert O.C. 'A' Co. NAOU, his brother Sgt. Herbert and myself (Alfred Boxall)."

Stationed Small Ships, Larrakeyan, NT. Served NT Coast from Darwin to Victoria River. Arnhem Land and East Coast Waters. Two journeys north from Darwin into the Timor Sea. Activity in area at time included air raids on Darwin Harbour and air raid at Winnellie during stay there. Duties M.T. mechanic – Small Ships Engineer. Primary function – Coastal observation. Travelled to NT per road and returned by air.

06/12/43 Appointed Lieut. Posted to 12 Aust. Water Transport Op. Coy (Small Craft) (AIF) (Seconded – Instructor Water Transport Wing SME)

14/06/44 Another child Lesley was born.

20/06/45 Appointed Engineer of Craft – 13 Aust. Small Ship Coy (AIF) from Instr. Water Transport Wing L.H.Q. S.M.E.

06/08/45 Trans. To AATC (Water Trans)

12/09/45 Cairns to Port Moresby

17/09/45 Port Moresby to Bougainville.

15/10/46 Depart for Rabual. Arrived Brisbane 18/10/46

(12/09/45 to 18/10/46 – Overseas area of service – Solomon Islands)

29/12/46 Appointed First Engineer, 1 Aust. Cargo Vessel from Engr of Craft, HQ 3 Aust WT Gp (AIF). M/In from leave ex Services Trg Centre Ingleburn.

20/01/47 M/Out to 1 Cargo vessel "Crusader". In absentia on cessation of Det Services Trg Centre.

16/05/47 Allotted Regt Duties 12 Aust Small Ships Coy from First Engr, 1 Aust Cargo Vessel.

31/05/47 With 1 Aust Cargo Vessel "Crusader".

14/06/47 M/I from A.C.V "Crusader".

25/06/47 M/I from HQ 12 Small Ships Coy. Emb Ambon on Water Transport Duties. Departed Brisbane for Ambon.

20/10/47 Arrived Darwin from W/T Duties.

15/01/48 D/Emb Sydney from W/T Duties.

12/04/48 Army Service terminated. (Two dependants under 16 years of age)

Entitled to Defence Medal, War Medal and Australian Service Medal.

I also learnt, unfortunately, that Alfred Boxall had died in 1995.
I incorporated some of the details in the sequence I wrote on 'The war years'. I originally used a fictitious name to prevent any embarrassment to the Boxall family, but since then many articles have been produced that have identified him.

I read a number of informative books on the subjects of the North Australia Observation Unit and the Australian Small Ships Company.

In June 2004 I met with some of Boxall's family, including his daughter Lesley. We had a very comfortable meeting that included a comprehensive discussion and exchange of considerable information. I was able to view the copy of The Rubaiyat given to Alf by the nurse at the Clifton Gardens Hotel. After the visit we maintained contact and exchanged information that left me feeling that I had actually met Alfred Boxall. He had lived an interesting life and I was sorry that I had never had the opportunity to sit down and have a chat with him.

Additional background
The following information was supplied by Boxall's family.

Alfred Boxall was born in Hammersmith, London, and came to Australia as an infant with his parents and older brother Fred. They lived in Sydney, initially in the suburb of Canterbury, and later in Ashfield. In 1914 the family, now with baby Louise, returned to England to visit relatives. Their return to Australia was delayed by the outbreak of the First World War.

In July 1915 the family obtained berths on the Benalla, and they commenced their return journey. After travelling 800 km into the Indian Ocean, a fire developed in the hold of the vessel, leaving no alternative but to return to South Africa. With smoke billowing from the hold they arrived in Durban two days later. After the cover of the hold was removed the vessel burst into flames. It was with great difficulty that the fire was eventually contained and extinguished by land appliances.

Alf and Fred enjoyed the freedom of the town, but their mother fell down a gangway and was confined to the hospital for the 6 weeks they remained in the port. With no further hitches they eventually arrived in Australia.

In May 1916 Alf's father enlisted in the AIF, and the family went to live with his mother's sister in Fairfield, where the children apparently lived in a tent near the chicken yard, until his mother eventually purchased a house in the nearby ti-tree scrub. His father returned to Australia in March 1919. Then they lived briefly in Chatswood, Neutral Bay and Blakehurst before moving into their house which was built in Forest Road, Peakhurst.

Alf attended various primary schools, but a bout of chicken pox prevented him from sitting for his Qualifying Certificate examination, thus preventing him from entry into high school. Instead, he studied mechanical engineering at a technical college and worked as an assistant mechanic for 4 years with Garratts Ltd in Elizabeth Street, Sydney. He assembled Fiat and Overland cars, and in his spare time developed his passion for riding motorcycles. In 1925 Alf sat for the first motor mechanics examination held by the NRMA which resulted in him obtaining a job in Braidwood.

In 1927, as a result of the accidental death of the NRMA's Queanbeyan-based patrolman, Alf was called in to act as official NRMA duty patrolman during the opening of Parliament House in Canberra. He was subsequently employed by the NRMA as a road patrolman based in Goulburn, riding a Harley Davidson motorcycle with sidecar. Alf joined the Goulburn Motor Club and when a competition was held on the completely dry Lake George he created a land speed record of 100 mph (160 km).

In May 1930 the Great Depression forced the NRMA to withdraw their rural services and so Alf returned to Sydney. He obtained employment in charge of the Turramurra branch of NW Brain & Co., Ford dealers, but after 6 months he was 'laid off' in January 1932 due to the 'slump in trade'. The next few years were difficult but somehow he managed to pursue motorcycle racing at the speedway. It was not until 1936 that he was able to obtain permanent employment with R Crealy Pty Ltd, cartage contractors in Haymarket, where he was responsible for maintaining their fleet of 24 trucks.

In 1937 Alf married his 'Black-eyed Susan', Dulcie Smith from Goulburn, who he had been courting for 10 years. In 1940 Alf was employed by the NSW Department of Public Transport, a wartime protected occupation, which meant that he was not able to enlist in the services until he could prove that his skills were essential to the war effort.

He enlisted in January 1942 and after basic training at Cowra joined the 19th Field Regiment. In June he transferred to the 2/1 NAOU, which had been raised to patrol the coast, watching for an expected Japanese invasion. This commando-style unit succeeded the Darwin Mobile Force, a small elite combat force that had been formed prior to the outbreak of the Second World War, and was based at Larrakeyah Barracks in the expectation they could be rushed to any point from the Kimberley's to the Gulf of Carpentaria to contain any enemy incursion. Most of the 'Nackeroos' were from the Outback as the unit was originally horse mounted; using saddles from the First World War that had been stored at Singleton. They were stationed at strategic points in small groups. Liberally supplied with automatic weapons and powerful radios, they were to move across the front of any landing force, pouring on heavy fire but falling back and sending signals to HQ until the main force was deployed to resist the landing. In June 1943 Alf was transferred to 4 Australian Water Transport Company (Small Craft) RAE, which had been given the task of supplying and maintaining the 'Nackeroos'.

Alf often mentioned events during his service, in particular working with an aboriginal friend named Mordecai, substituting butter for oil in the engine of a boat and taking a 31' boat down river to Timber Creek with brothers David and Xavier Herbert. After his retirement Alf visited Mordecai in the Northern Territory. He also intended to find a large tree which marked as far as they had been able to travel on the river to Timber Creek. However, he became ill and had to return home without reaching the tree.

APPENDIX 8 – THE CODE

When the list of letters in the back of The Rubaiyat were released to the media, their purpose or meaning was not obvious to anyone. The newspapers describe them as a 'code'. Since that time the letters have captured the attention and imagination of hundreds of people from all walks of life devoting thousands of hours attempting to provide a reasonable explanation of their meaning.

Codes and ciphers are a subject in themselves and they have been in existence since people first communicated with each other. They can be transmitted by the use of signals or by the use of the written or spoken word. Clever people have devised them and they have been decoded by cleverer people. Many books and articles written on the subject are available to people who have an interest in that field. Some years ago I read with interest The Man who broke Napoleon's Codes, the story of George Scovell by Mark Urban.

During the Second World War Germany devised and used the sophisticated Enigma Machine but its code was eventually 'cracked' by the Allies. Germany suspected it may have been cracked and placed another cog in the complex machine. This too was broken eventually. The Japanese code was broken prior to the war. When they changed it during the war, it too was broken.

People have used written or verbal 'keys' to transmit and transcribe codes. Interesting articles have been written about the Second World War armed merchant raider Kormoran and the sinking of HMAS Sydney. Detmers, the German captain, allegedly used a dictionary as a 'key' to record the events in his personal diary. Interesting references are also made to the 'Vigenere' and 'Playfair' codes.

It was not uncommon for servicemen about to be posted to undisclosed destinations to discuss and develop codes with loved ones to advise them of their eventual location. It was also not difficult to bypass the censors by constructing a letter home with six sentences that commenced with letters that spelt 'DARWIN'.

First part of Zodiac cipher that was solved by a local high school teacher

In the late 1960s a serial murderer in California known as 'Zodiak' taunted authorities by delivering a cryptic note written in a series of symbols and stated that they would reveal his identity. Government authorities could not decipher the message. A school teacher and his wife saw the cipher in a newspaper, and thought they had solved it in a very short time. Assuming that the killer's ego might cause him to begin the message with 'I' and also use the words 'kill' and 'killing' they matched the characters/symbols to letters of the alphabet.

The message was revealed but it did not contain his name. In a second note, known as the '340 Cipher' because of the 340 characters that it contained, the killer increased the number of different characters to represent each letter of the alphabet. The murders continued, and the killer delivered further notes, but despite the efforts of experts in this field neither the crimes nor the ciphers have been solved.

Comments attributed to Gerry Feltus
No-one can deny the power of the press, and the media can be a valuable ally in police investigations by their far-reaching promotion of detail to the public, which in turn generates useful responses. At times a little 'journalistic licence' is used and sometimes a few 'flowers' are thrown in for good measure. I have always gone out of my way to assist the media and to ensure that the information is correct. I have met and dealt with some very credible journalists over the years and I respect and accept the way they are obliged to present a particular article. I have never sought to promote myself and sometimes it has been quite embarrassing for me to read items associated to me that have been obtained from other sources or remarks I have made off the cuff.

In respect to *the Unknown Man* I refer to the following two lengthy newspaper articles that dealt with the subject. I am including this information because the articles are on the record and several people have made reference to me specifically and to the articles generally.

The first article was published in The Weekend Australian Magazine of 15–16 September 2001. Selected passages are included here because the bulk of the article is similar to other material.

The mystery of a dead stranger found on an Adelaide beach 50 years ago continues to haunt two generations of police

THE MAN WITH NO NAME STORY JANET FIFE-YEOMANS

The case of the Somerton Man landed on Feltus's desk at the South Australian major crime squad about ten years ago and it could not have found a better home. Feltus is a patient detective who misses nothing. He speaks with the economy of a bloke from the country – his family are farmers from Streaky Bay in South Australia. He also has a keen interest in the history of outback towns and the local police, a history in which the Somerton Man plays a starring role. "When I first got the file, I just flicked through it but it sucks you in." says Feltus, 58, a senior sergeant.

"Those letters have to mean something," says Feltus. "I try to keep away from it because I know that the more you look at it, the more you can become obsessed with it. I'm not obsessed with it. I vowed and declared not to have anything to do with the code but I doodle away and wonder if I can come up with something that has anything to do with it. Then I come back to reality."

"I often wander around and jot down little things that could be checked out even now. It's good to have a fresh eye on cases because you can get tunnel vision," says Feltus. Sometimes he takes the file home to read and re-read. He pulls out a neat A4 pad full of tidy writing in black pen. "I'm just trying to complete a full story on it and go back through it and see if there's anything we can do to resolve some of the issues. You keep wondering: did someone miss something?"

Feltus believes it is more sinister, although he does not subscribe to the theory that the stranger was a spy. But then again: "Why would he go to the elaborate lengths he did and create this mystery if he wanted to kill himself, unless there's something we have missed? And to me it's very, very unusual that this particular copy of The Rubaiyat was found with the two phone numbers that link the nurse and Boxall. How come?" It seems the only two people who knew the nurse's identity – Boxall and Detective Canney – are now dead.

"Why screw up that piece of paper into the fob pocket of his trousers and throw the rest of the book into someone's car instead of a rubbish bin – if indeed it was the dead man who cast the book away? Perhaps someone gave him the piece of paper and says, 'Go to the beach to meet a guy who has the rest of the book and that's how you will recognize him.' Did he meet him? Or perhaps the book was thrown into the car because he knew it would be found and get publicity and the person for whom the code letters were meant would read them in the press," wonders Feltus.

But Feltus's work continues to raise more questions than answers.

On 7 November 2004 a very lengthy article appeared in the Sunday Mail. It is a lengthy article and only the following selected passages are included.

'Poisoned' in SA – was he a Red Spy?
Matt Clemow

It is the start of the Cold War and Australia is gripped by paranoia about communism and the spread of Soviet Power.

Wounds still raw from World War II and memories fresh from the awesome power of the atomic bomb, the country sees Opposition Leader Robert Menzies launch his campaign against the Red Menace.

At the same time, the British are moving into Woomera to start the controversial "Blue Streak" missile program, heightening Australia's perception of its important role in world affairs.

In Adelaide, the body of a man, without identifcation and apparently poisoned – is found on a suburban beach.

Before long, as the case becomes more confused, speculation starts that he is a Soviet spy.

Hard-nosed detectives initially treat the case as just another body; illness or suicide are the first suspicions.

"Someone will turn up and identify him in a couple of days," they say.

Wrong. Almost 56 years later, nobody has.

The case develops into one of the most intriguing deaths in the history of South Australia Crime.

Soon to be retired Detective Senior Sergeant Gerry Feltus has been delving into the mysterious circumstances of the Somerton man for more than a decade, mostly in his spare time.

One day, the 61-year-old says he may even write a book outlining the facts of a case he first learnt about as a young detective working in Major Crime.

But it's hard work; all the evidence has been destroyed or lost over the years and most witnesses have died. Only a plaster cast of the man and a few photos remain. That, and hundreds of newspaper clippings.

But his eyes light up when he talks about the case. He speaks of the conspiracy theories, the logic and the unknowns.

Each option is packed with possibilities.

"I first became interested in the case when I was at boarding school at Somerton Park in 1956," he said. "During winter it was too cold to swim, so walks were arranged and we often walked past the location where the body was found and the older people would tell us about 'the guy who

was murdered there',"
It was also suggested the soldier was involved in intelligence work during World War II – adding to the intrigue of their coincidental involvement. Detective Senior Sergeant Feltus said the "spy theory was often raised".
"It is one of the most intriguing subjects I have dealt with," he said.
"It is a complete mystery and because there is so much unknown detail many theories come into play.
"One branch-off is the 'Spy Theory' and this in itself cannot be excluded. The link between the location where the body was found, the contact number of the nurse and the link between the two copies of the book are also a mystery.
"The so-called code in the book also opens up another can of worms."
Throughout all the twists and turns of this remarkable story, the code has proven the most intriguing. It has been passed on to thousands of people – but no one can shed any real light on it. Leading mathematicians, astrologers and code-breakers have tried to crack it using their own theories. The note even was given to Naval Intelligence in the 1990s.
A Tasmanian man has spent most of the last year trying to match the letters to numbers in the scene reminiscent of Russell Crowe in the movie A Beautiful Mind. And a New South Wales man believes the answer is in lining up the letters to musical notes.
But while many have their own theories, none makes more sense than the case itself. All the lingering questions remain: Was it suicide or murder? Was he a spy or a jilted lover? Was the mystery nurse involved in any way? How did he die? Where did the poison and/or the luggage ticket go?
After 56 years, police are no closer to answering any of these questions.

CRACKING THE CODE

THE letters scrawled on the back of the Rubaiyat of Omar Khayyam which the mystery man threw away a short time before his death have long fascinated code breakers.

RENOWNED code breaker Jim Gillogly, a Californian computer scientist, believes the letters are just as likely to be his actual thoughts.

Rather than spell them out, the man may simply have used the first letters of words.

FOR example, MLIABO could represent "My Life Is A Bundle Of…"

ITTM could be "I Think That My…."

"THIS is credible for a suicide note," Mr Gillogly says.

ANOTHER code-breaking guru, British scientist and maths whiz Simon Singh, concurs with Mr Gillogly's theory, saying the note "doesn't appear to be too complicated" and the letters are likely to be acronyms from a message to himself or an association.

DETECTIVE Senior Sergeant Gerry Feltus, who has been involved in the case in recent years, says if this theory were applied, the last line could be "It's Time To Move To South Australia Moseley Street Glenelg …"

My attempt at code cracking

The list of letters located on the rear of The Rubaiyat raise two questions in particular. Is it a code? What is the 'key'? Apart from a couple of names changed to protect identities, the majority of the information known to me is presented to you. Over the years I have attempted to convert the letters to the old alpha-numeral numbers on the telephone dial and many other conversions without success.

In about 2002 I came to the conclusion that the so-called code was possibly a simple message. I worked on the theory that it was some form of 'shorthand' which was written in such a way that only the individual could read it or others if they knew certain facts. I have seen many people taught and trained in the subject of shorthand who could not only write and read their own notes, but also those of other trained people, and vice a versa. I have also seen people use their own form of shorthand by writing words and excluding the 'vowels'.

I then considered that maybe the letters in the left column represented some form of a 'key' leading into a sentence of information. I studied the first 'key' letter and I could see the letters W, M & N and found that if I excluded the vowels O and A, maybe it was a reference to WOMAN. I went to the second line and studied the 'key' letter and I could see the letters M and N. If I excluded the vowel A, it could be a reference to MAN. Using the same principle this would make the 'key' in the third line WOMAN and the 'key' in the fourth line MAN. I could not make any sense of the 'key' letter in the fifth line, if it was a 'key'.

If I accepted that the 'key' in the first line was WOMAN, were the following letters the first letter of words that provided some information relevant to a woman? Using the first line of letters as an exercise I wrote 'Roger Go Over And Buy A Beer Darling', knowing full well that it was meaningless.

I then compiled a list of all the letters (excluding the 'keys') and then listed all the words that were relevant to the investigation e.g. M = Melbourne, married, Moseley, moved etc. By applying the words to the lines of letters some interesting results were forthcoming.

Looking at the lines of letters I was of the opinion they had been written on three separate occasions. The first three lines of letters were written on the first occasion and when it was found that the five letters on the second line needed correcting, they were crossed out and re-written on the fourth line on the second occasion. The re-written five letters were again incorrect hence the 'X' over the 'O'. Maybe the five new letters (AIAQC) refers to the correct information. This means that the first three letters of 'LIA' = Living In Adelaide, could have changed to 'AIA' = Also In Adelaide Q? – C? I also believe that the last line of letters was written on the third occasion, at a later time or under different circumstances.

In respect to the line 'It's Time To Move To South Australia Moseley Street Glenelg' attributed to me in the preceding newspaper article, I quoted it as an example of the formula I was using. The sentence does have relevance to the circumstances but I do have slight variations in words that have the same relevance. Also, some people confuse Moseley Square and Moseley Street as both are in Glenelg.

I now believe that I know what the letters represent, but I will gladly stand corrected if my interpretation is incorrect. It is now your turn to join the many people before you who have attempted to solve the mystery of the 'Letters' (see back cover). Have fun!

Recent material

The following was printed in a newspaper article on 1 August 2009:

(name excluded) read about the Somerton Man 15 years ago in a list of the top 10 un-solved crimes in Australia that also included the disappearance of Harold Holt and the Beaumont Children. The Somerton Man struck him as a potentially fascinating project for his cipher-cracking engineering students.

"I tried to ring up the cops and get copies of the code, drew a blank, they wouldn't return my calls," says (name excluded), who has developed a broad knowledge and passion for solving the case. "Eventually I found one in The Advertiser and that was the start of my real interest."

A bit of a rash statement! I also obtained my first copy of the 'code' from The Advertiser. From the day I first become involved in this matter I held the view that the letters printed in the newspapers throughout the country were quite misleading. To fully appreciate the factors it was necessary to view a copy of the writing. Since that time I have provided hundreds of people throughout the country with a copy of the writing. I have never refused anyone who requested a copy, and as a result of people requesting particular clarifications I have also provided them with a copy of the writing if they did not possess one.

In respect to the comments by (name excluded) I point out that when the project he makes reference to commenced, I attended meetings and discussions with both him and his students. I contributed specifically to their project and generally to *the Unknown Man* subject, excluding matters of a confidential nature. I also responded to a request from (name excluded) and supplied him with a scanned copy of my reproduction of the writing.

I do have some reservations as to why the original concept was extended from the initial code-cracking exercise, to claims of solving a murder and wanting to exhume the deceased. I admire the enthusiasm of the students and I support and wish them every success in their specific project. I will be most disappointed if after all their efforts they only produce evidence that 'He could have just been a crazy man writing down letters'.

———————◆◆———————

APPENDIX 9 – CIGARETTES

During and after the Second World War cigarettes were rationed. When they were eventually taken off the ration list they were still in short supply. In 1948 shops and other outlets only stocked a small range of the more common brands, which often sold out very quickly. It would have been more common for a smoker to purchase a packet of tobacco and papers and roll their own cigarettes. It was not only cheaper but depending on how thick they were rolled, in excess of 50 cigarettes could be obtained. Packets of 'Tailor made' or 'Ready rolled' cigarettes, as they were commonly referred to, were considered a luxury and as a result were often smoked sparingly. Cigarettes could be purchased in packets of 10s or 20s, and shopkeepers sold them singularly some times. Packets of 20s ranged in price from 2s (20 cents) to 3s (30 cents) depending on the brand.

Detective Sergeant Leane made the following references:

This man was an inveterate smoker, because of the stain on his fingers.

The cigarette packet was 'Army Club' but the contents were Kensitas', a different brand, there was also found a box of Bryant and May's matches, quarter full ...."

In a statement he referred to the list of the man's property which, in part, reads:

On body: 1 packet of Army Club Cigarettes containing 7 Kensitas Extra Size Cigarettes.

In Suitcase: 1 cig. lighter

The cigarette lighter was similar to that issued to USA service personnel during the war. It was readily available post-war. A spark was created from a flint which ignited a wick that was inserted into cotton wool soaked in petrol, shellite or some other inflammable spirit.

Constable Moss, who attended the scene at the beach on 1 December 1948, observed a partly smoked cigarette lying near the right ear of the body.

Army Club was a popular and common brand of cigarettes during and after the war. The Kensitas cigarettes being in the Army Club packet could indicate that the man could not purchase Army Club. He either purchased or borrowed the Kensitas brand and placed them in the empty packet.

On 6 August 2002 I went to a well-established tobacconist in Adelaide where I had a conversation with Mr Tunney. He stated that Kensitas was a reasonably common brand of cigarette. They were a plain cigarette (no cork tip or filter) and were sold in packets of 20s. He located an invoice that showed his shop had last imported the Kensitas brand in February 1956 from the manufacturer, Alfred Field & Co. Ltd of Birmingham, England.

I was later advised by a lady that during or just after the war Kensitas cigarettes were sold with a small pack containing four cigarettes attached to the main packet. They were an advertising gimmick which stated 'Give this pack to a friend'. She also said the packet had a picture of a valet on the front.

On 14 November 2002 I was finally able to purchase a Kensitas cigarette tin in a second-hand shop. The lid shows a white background and the trade mark is a small circle containing the upper half of a valet dressed in a black tuxedo, with a white shirt and bow tie. He is carrying a tray in his left hand on which there is a packet of cigarettes, no doubt Kensitas. The background to the circle is coloured red. Underneath the circle is the word Kensitas, and under that is the word Cigarettes. Not that it means too much but it was a tin I found and not a cigarette packet. On the tin it states 'Made in England. J.WIX & SONS LTD., 210 OLD STREET, LONDON. E.C.L.'.

On Sunday 17 November 2002 I had a conversation with Pete at Cambrai. He loaned me an old 'Army Club' cigarette packet so I could photograph of it. The packet is described as follows: 'Army Club' in large cursive writing across the top, and crossed swords with the crest directly underneath. On the left of the crest is written, 'The crest is, the mark of, Distinction'. On the right of the crest is 'The Firm, of three, Centuries'. Under the crest are the words 'Sandhurst Size', and under that is 'Cavanders Limited'. On the rear of the packet is a photograph of an army officer with a cigarette in his mouth. He is wearing a cap and great coat. Under the picture is 'Army Club', again in cursive writing. On the right side of the packet are the words 'Army Club Cigarettes' in cursive. On the left side is the same writing with the following words in very small print: 'Manufactured by Godfrey Phillips (Aust) Pty. Ltd. Melbourne, Victoria'. On the top and bottom is the same cursive 'Army Club' with the words 'Corked Tipped' underneath. (I have been advised that it is a newer packet because cork tipped cigarettes were made much later than 1948.)

Poison and cigarettes

I have been contacted by people who have asked many questions relating to the subject of cigarettes generally and specifically to the involvement of poison. The following extract is from a lengthy newspaper article:

Many readers believe that the man was murdered – by poison
There was no phial found beside the body, no container of any sort.
But an analysis of dust from the pockets showed no chemical.
There was no needle marks on the body, no trace of poison in the stomach contents.

> But he could have died from poison.
> A Birrell Street, Bondi Junction reader wrote:
> "The packet of cigarettes in his pocket was Army and Navy Club.
> "But the cigarettes left in it were Kensitas. Why?
> "Poison, perhaps, in a cigarette?"
> Pharmacologists said:
> "Not only possible but not very terribly diff cult."

I have seen no reference or evidence that the dust from the pockets of the deceased or the cigarettes were ever subjected to any analysis. I have no idea what happened to the cigarettes or of their current whereabouts. I believe that the partly smoked cigarette was left at the scene.

Other queries

Yes, there was a brand of cigarettes named 'Kensitas'. After the war there were dozens of different brands of cigarettes, but the majority of those brands have since disappeared from the market. I am familiar with most of the brands, including Army Club, but I cannot recall Kensitas.

Nicotine stains are caused by the continual direct smoke from a burning cigarette passing over the skin. Staining is caused by the position a cigarette is held in the hand, allowing the smoke to pass over the fingers or the cup of the hand. Some smokers, particularly shearers or people using both hands, will often smoke a cigarette by leaving it between their lips. This method often shows heavy nicotine staining to the mouth area. The amount of nicotine does not necessarily indicate that a person is a heavy smoker. I have seen many smokers from European countries, particularly Russia, holding cigarettes in a position that no smoke passes over the hand. Also, it does not follow that a smoker will hold the cigarette in the predominant hand, thereby revealing either right or left handedness.

Some current brands of cigarettes have had some of the chemicals removed, and the cigarettes will often stop burning if left for some time in an ash tray. During the period in question cigarettes contained chemicals, including saltpetre, and this caused them to burn continually. They have been used as a timing device by inserting a fuse through a hole in a burning cigarette at the required position. They have also been used as an incendiary device by inserting the unlit end of a lighted cigarette into the appropriate end of a box of matches. When the cigarette burnt to the match heads they all ignited causing a substantial flame.

I believe *the Unknown Man* could have purposely extinguished his partly smoked cigarette, but not with the intention of discarding it. Due to the availability and cost of 'tailor made' cigarettes in the latter part of the 1940s, it was not uncommon for a smoker to extinguish a half-smoked cigarette and save it for later. It was also not uncommon to return it to the cigarette packet or retain it behind an ear, similar to a pencil. Some smokers also retained their 'butts' and after obtaining sufficient tobacco used a cigarette paper to roll an additional cigarette.

Update

I thought I had made sufficient references to the habits of smokers but perhaps I should include the following information to clarify a further point.
In the newspaper article of 1 August 2009 it was stated:

> (Name excluded) inquiries have led him to question some of the police's assumptions. The discovery of Kensitas cigarettes in an Army Club packet was assumed to have been the common practice of putting cheaper cigarettes in a more expensive packet. (name excluded) tracked down an old gazette that showed it was Army Club cigarettes that were cheaper. "So what was he doing with more expensive cigarettes in a cheaper packet?" he asks."

Firstly, it was not 'some of the police's assumptions' but used in part of an example of a possible explanation I had given to not only (name excluded) but many other people who posed the same question.

Secondly, the price comparison has no relevance because it is an unknown factor as to why he had the small number of Kensitas in an Army Club packet. Maybe his alternative brand was Kensitas, and he may have either purchased eight loose cigarettes or a packet of ten, until he could obtain a packet of Army Club. Who knows?

To expand on the above comment attributed to me I will include the full content of my possible explanation. I made reference to people who normally rolled their own cigarettes, when attending public events, for convenience purposes, would sometimes take or purchase a packet of tailor-made cigarettes. It was also not uncommon for people to purchase a packet of cheaper Turf cigarettes and put them in an empty, more expensive Craven A packet. For all intents and purposes then a tailor-made Craven A cigarette is being smoked.

APPENDIX 10 – DNA – EXHUMATION

Since the inception of DNA analysis becoming available as a valuable tool in the investigation process I have been fully aware of the capabilities associated with it. I have attended many courses, lectures, meetings and discussions to keep abreast of the considerable progress being made in this field. During my work in the Major Crime Investigation Section investigating homicides I gained considerable knowledge and experience in using the facilities associated with DNA to identify victims, offenders and linking both to a crime scene and associated exhibits. I am also aware of the giant leaps that have been made in this field in recent years, including isotope testing on bone samples. There is considerable documentation available to those who wish to pursue this very interesting subject.

Some visible human hairs are imbedded in the plaster cast of *the Unknown Man*, which is currently housed in the Police Historical Museum. I often considered the possibility that sufficient DNA could perhaps be obtained from samples of these hairs. I was also approached by others who held the same view, and others who were convinced that the protruding end of the hair would contain the actual root, which would be suitable for obtaining DNA. This is not so because a mould was first made of the body by Paul Lawson, and the protruding hairs that imbedded in the mould would have been plucked from the body with the root or a broken hair protruding from it when the mould was removed. This process was reversed when the plaster was poured into the mould. Therefore, any hairs in the cast of *the Unknown Man* may have root material imbedded in it.

I discussed this subject with experts in the field of DNA and the hair sample idea was dismissed. Even if DNA could be obtained it was not going to produce a name, and who could it be matched to. Unfortunately, the best prospect for obtaining DNA was lost when the original samples taken at the post-mortem disappeared, and also when the clothing, suitcase and contents were destroyed.

Considering the possibility that something may happen to the cast of *the Unknown Man* or some serious contamination could occur, I decided to obtain random hair samples for future reference. In 2006 I was fortunate to make contact with a past acquaintance who was an expert in hair samples and DNA in the forensic science field. This person agreed to examine the hair samples. In the same year I was advised:

No suitable DNA could be obtained, possibly due to formalin and other contamination. There was noticeable insect damage to the hair shaft. One hair looked like it had a putrid root, which is common to see when the hair is attached to a dead person. (There is not much literature on how long it takes for a root to get putrid following death) it is around 8 hours. Other than the above observation – not too much more – looked like caucasian hair.

Witnesses have made reference to *the Unknown Man* having a red tinge to his hair. From my own observation of the cast I agree. In a Special Report by journalist Pat Burgess a Litchfield reader responded: 'Burgess found pale ginger hair ahering (sic) to the plaster cast. How many men are there of 45 years of age who have pale ginger hair?'

That is a very interesting question! It would require an expert statistician to provide the answer.

In the early 1980s I attended a course in Sydney. One of the subjects covered was 'probabilities'. A professor from the University of Sydney presented a lengthy lecture. There was a lot of apprehension regarding the subject but in the end everyone agreed that it was probably one of the most informative lectures in the course, and it was presented with perfection. The professor finished by saying, 'You can make statistics tell you whatever you want them to tell you'. Another participant attributed this quotation, 'You don't need

THE UNKNOWN MAN

statistics to tell you that most people (excluding wars and other disasters) die in bed', to Mark Twain.

It would be an interesting exercise just to follow the path of 'Eric the Red' and his Viking hordes during their ventures, and then establish how many genes containing red hair were left behind. Their descendants over the years have no doubt taken those genes to places throughout the world, and continue to do so.

DNA testing has produced interesting statistics that claim that 1 in 5 children are not the product of their presumed father. Does this mean that if 25 children walk past you every fifth one is illegitimate, or is it the first five or maybe the last five? It has also been claimed that if a person submits to a DNA test the results will produce a large number of names that they may be descendants of. There has been extensive migration over the years where it is possible a family with a surname of Thorvaldson could have migrated to a number of different countries. A brother could have migrated to England and changed his name to Thorson, and a sister could have migrated to America, changed her name to Valdson, and then married a person with the surname of Smith. Was the Unknown Man a descendant of 'Eric the Red'? Possibly, but does it really matter?

A recent documentary about an unidentified child, who died as a result of the sinking of the Titanic and was buried in Canada, was of great interest to me. Using available records, DNA samples and other known information the child was eventually identified as being from a family living in Europe. This was a great result and was done for a legitimate reason and supported by facts.

Exhumations do take place upon application to the appropriate authority normally by the police to further criminal investigations, and in recent times by other parties to obtain DNA evidence to support civil proceedings. These applications are supported by factual evidence.

For many years mummies have been exhumed in Egypt for scientific purposes. DNA has also been a valuable tool in identifying the lineage of the Pharaohs.

The subject of exhumation could easily extend into war graves and ancient Aboriginal burial sites. I am sure that legitimate objections would be raised if actions proceeded without appropriate consideration, consultancy and the required authority.

I am aware that there are private moves afoot to apply for the exhumation of the Unknown Man for the purpose of obtaining DNA. I object to this course of action most strongly. There is no legitimate evidence to support this application and it would be wrong to allow it to happen. I believe this application will only satisfy curiosities, personal interests or promote exciting publicity for other purposes. There is no evidence to suggest that he was murdered, there is evidence that he possibly died from an unknown poison and there are circumstances and evidence to suggest that he may have committed suicide.

The police have not requested that an exhumation should take place, and this is the appropriate authority to submit such an application. In 2001 I contemplated submitting an application to have the body of the Unknown Man exhumed. The only grounds to support this application was that maybe with current forensic advances, specimens could be obtained that would identify poisons that could have resulted in his death, and at the same time DNA could possibly be obtained. I arranged a comprehensive discussion with Ross James, John Gilbert and Roger Byard, forensic pathologists at the Forensic Science Centre. I produced background information and copies of the relevant evidence from the inquest. I quote from the comprehensive reply I received from Dr Ross James:

The toxicology issues are interesting. While their methods were rather primitive their chemists were good at finding both the limited (much more so than nowadays) drugs available for therapeutic purposes. Poisons were much more widespread and widely used and it is fair to say that their chemists would be more adept at finding them than our present chemists. Of course they were quite unable to identify organic poisons (the 'exotic poisons') and we wouldn't be much better now. There simply isn't any evidence supporting drugs or poisons and it is unlikely that a contemporary examination (given that he was embalmed and presumably buried) of exhumed material would provide the answer.

In view of the above and with no other supporting evidence I did not proceed with the application.

If an exhumation of *the Unknown Man* is contemplated for the purpose of testing the effects of formalin on DNA, I would suggest that the experiment be performed on the body of Linda Agostini (the Pyjama Girl). She was preserved in formalin for many years and if DNA can be extracted, her heritage and place of birth are known for further testing of the capabilities of DNA identification.

I have no objections to exhumations but I do believe they should be approved for the right reasons. If a person came forward with substantial evidence that supported a view that *the Unknown Man* was their great-grandfather, grandfather, father or close relative and they were prepared to supply their own DNA for a comparison test there could be no objection.

Although he has no name, for many years people have taken a personal interest in him, some travelling from interstate to visit his grave and others have adopted him as a real person. He was buried as a real person in a proper grave site with an appropriate headstone, by a group of people who cared. He was buried as *the Unknown Man*. Why change it to 'Mister X'.

I believe that if an exhumation is approved for the wrong reasons it would amount not only to the desecration of the grave site but also of the body of the deceased.

APPENDIX 11 – ADDITIONAL INFORMATION

The following information either has been generated through the media or it relates to subjects that may have already have been covered. I have included items for completeness.

Woomera – Baltic migrants
I recently located an undated letter from a woman who supplied the following information:

> In reference to the unidentified man found on [the] beach.
>
> My husband was working at the Rocket Range for a while until a few weeks ago, and I thought he may have seen this man up there, as I remarked that he looked like a Balt, and my husband said he looked faintly familiar to him.
>
> Some of these Balts often came on leave with large sums of money on them.
>
> His mates wouldn't probably hear of his death as they wouldn't be interested in the newspapers, not being able to read English, and would probably think he was taking longer leave.

Strathmore Hotel – Elliott
On 1 December 1982, The News published the first of a very comprehensive and detailed 2-part series by Tom Loftus. I only include details relevant to this new issue. The second part was published the next day.

The Somerton body mystery

Was he a war spy hounded to his death, a victim of the criminal underworld, a seaman, a professional man, a musician, a gambler, a horseman?

Did someone kill him with an exotic untraceable poison, did he end his own life by the same means.

Or was he simply a lovelorn man who died of a broken heart?

Such questions have baffed police and tantalized the public since the Somerton Body Mystery began on this day (December 1) in 1948. Today the News interviews a mystery witness casting a new light on this mystifying case.

'I won't be seeing you'

There was something about him that commanded immediate attention. It wasn't exactly his physique – though he looked strong and fit for a middle - aged man.

Good looking he wasn't – but there was an air of distinction about him.

Receptionist Mrs Ina Harvey took it all in as he walked into Adelaide's Strathmore Hotel.

Then as he signed the register, Mrs Harvey – she cannot remember the name he used and the hotel register for the period has been destroyed – noted two other unusual features about the stranger.

"He had no baggage, except for a small black case – such as a doctor or a musician who played the flute might carry," she said.

"And he looked distraught – a beaten man.

"He spoke very quietly almost in a murmur – as if he was so tired he could hardly talk."

After 34 years, Mrs Harvey spoke publicly for the first time of her possible connection with the mystery.

Black case

She still vividly remembers the stranger she believes could have been the Unknown Man.

She revealed also a curious sidelight to the man who stayed at the Strathmore

Hotel for a few days before December 1, 1948.

And in the process she may have cast new light on a mystery which has baffled local, interstate and international police forces.

Despite the best efforts of police and medical experts, neither the identity or the manner in which the Unknown Man died has been established.

Mrs Harvey's suspicions about the new guest led her to instruct a male employee to search his room while the guest was out.

"The employee – I cannot remember his name now – told me the only thing in the room was the little black case.

"And the only item in the case was a needle.

"From his description I got the impression it could have been a hypodermic syringe. That has stuck in my mind all these years."

One of the more fascinating aspects of the mystery was the inability to reach a conclusion on the death. The bulk of the medical testimony leaned towards the belief that the Unknown Man had been poisoned – whether self administered or not, nobody could say. Ten years after finding the body, the Coroner, Mr T. E. Cleland – now deceased – was forced to conclude: "I am unable to say how he died or what was the cause of death."

During the stranger's stay at the Strathmore Hotel he stayed in Room 21 or 23.

"I don't think he ever went into the bar," Mrs Harvey said. We had a couple of conversations but he never talked about himself. They were only superficial exchanges.

"He had a general air of refinement. I thought he was a professional man. When he spoke, his grammar was correct and lucid. He certainly didn't murder the Queen's English.

"If he knew the term 'Tamam Shud' – the last line of Omar Khayyam's The Rubaiyat, meaning 'the end', he certainly wasn't a peasant."

On the last occasion they met, the stranger gave Mrs Harvey a present – "just a little gift, a box of powder with blue markings, I don't think I ever used it."

"He mumbled something to the effect that I had shown him compassion. And then he said, 'I won't be seeing you again'."

The way in which he said it convinced her "that man is no longer with us."

The terminus for the Glenelg bus was right outside the Strathmore Hotel. Did the stranger walk out the front door and catch a bus to Somerton and a place in history as the Unknown Man?

One of the very few items found in his clothing from which all labels were removed, was a bus ticket to Glenelg.

Across the road from the Strathmore Hotel is Adelaide Railway Station where police later found his unclaimed luggage.

Coincidence or not?

When publicity started flowing on the mystery of the unidentified body, Mrs Harvey's thoughts kept returning to the stranger who had stayed at the Strathmore Hotel.

She approached her brother, Mr Laurie Elliott, the funeral director who embalmed the Unknown Man's body, with a request to see a picture.

"I was struck by the distinct resemblance with the man I had met," she said.

Why had she not gone to the Police? "I had no conclusive proof and hotel receptionists had to be discreet," she said.

Seeking

Mrs Harvey emphasized there was no romantic liaison between her and the stranger.

"I was just sorry for him. Anyway I was a married woman. I felt he was a person in deep trouble seeking support but too far gone to ask for it."

She concluded: "I am still of the opinion that the man I met was the Unknown Man – but it wouldn't stand up in court. Now I will never know if it was the same man."

Detective Sergeant R. Thomas of the Major Crime Squad said the new evidence would be assessed, just as all information was checked.

Was a vital clue missed?

Was a vital clue missed by medical experts who examined the body of the Unknown Man 34 years ago? The body, which was found propped up against the seawall at Somerton Beach on December 1, 1948, has never been identified.

There was no identification of any kind on the body. The clothes contained a railway ticket, a bus ticket and a piece torn from a book containing the words Tamam Shud (meaning The End). And 10 years after ... (repetition omitted) ... without reaching any conclusion on the cause of death.

But the balance of expert evidence leaned towards the view that the Unknown Man had been poisoned.

Adelaide funeral director, Mr Laurie Elliott, who embalmed the body, recalled this week how he had seen a puncture or tiny scar near the tip of the right index finger. "The scar did not show up until I pumped embalming fluid into the arm," he said. He could not recall if he had informed the police of his find but he had informed them of other scars he had discovered just above the left wrist.

Scar

Mr Elliott's revelation is particularly tantalizing in view of the "stranger" who stayed at the Strathmore Hotel for several days prior to December 1.

A search of his room revealed only a small black case containing a piece of medical equipment. Hotel receptionist Mrs Ina Harvey said that from the description given by the hotel employee it appeared to be a hypodermic syringe. Yet Dr J. M. Dwyer, then pathologist at the Royal Adelaide Hospital, who carried out a post-mortem on the body, told the inquest he had seen no evidence of a hypodermic needle having been used.

And when I raised the issue of the scar at a recent meeting with Dr Dwyer and Mr Elliott, the doctor said: "I must have missed it. I don't remember seeing it. I would have examined the fingers. It must have been a very tiny mark."

But he was emphatic he had not specifically looked for a scar or a puncture mark on the fingers. Even if he accepted that scar had been there he rejected its significance.

"It doesn't make sense to use a hypodermic syringe on the side of the finger," he said.

But Dr Dwyer is still convinced the Unknown Man died of poisoning – even though no trace of poison was found in the body.

During the inquest the names of two kinds of poison – suppressed by the Coroner – were suggested as the cause of death.

The late Sir Stanton Hicks, then professor of human physiology and pharmacology at Adelaide University, suspected one of the poisons because of the condition of some of the organs.

One of these, he explained, would be particularly toxic in relation to small doses by the mouth, would be completely missed by any of the tests applied, and would in fact be extremely difficult if not impossible, to identify even if it had been suspected in the first instance.

Weed

Only one expert, Deputy Government Analyst Robert James Cowan, who examined organs from the body, asserted that death was more than likely to have occurred from natural causes than through poison because of failure to detect any poison.

But Dr Dwyer, now medical officer with the Country Board of Health and Hindmarsh City Council, backs up his claim of poisoning because he saw signs of asphyxiation and there was "absolutely nothing wrong with the heart."

[John Burton Cleland] ... Professor of pathology at Adelaide University, had discussed the possibility of the poisonous weed, hemlock, being used.

Professor Cleland had probably raised the possibility because he was a great botanist and he would have said it was available along the Hackney Rd, near the Botanic Gardens, Dr Dwyer said.

"It is a well-known weed – they poisoned the Greek philosopher Socrates with it," he said.
Dr Dwyer acknowledged that such a substance would have been found if looked for.
"The ordinary substances would have been assessed by Mr Cowan but a thing like this would have escaped him," he said.

Humble
Dr Dwyer believes the mystery will never be solved.
"Who's going to identify him. Most of the people who would have known him would be dead by now," he said.
Standing by the neglected graveside of the Unknown Man in West Terrace Cemetery this week, Mr Elliott recalled the humble burial

service, attended by a handful of people, 34 years ago.
As the service concluded, Captain E. J. Webb of the Salvation Army said: "Yes, this man has someone to love him. He is known only to God."
If such is the case then that's "Tamam Shud" (The End)

Dr Dwyer's evidence to the inquest included:

I saw no obvious [signs] of a hypodermic needle having been used. I considered the possibility of one having been used, especially if it were used in an unusual place. There were two marks between the knuckles and the back of the right hand, they appeared to be recent abrasions just before death, they were in the hollow of the knuckles, but they did not appear to be significant.

On 7 December 1998 the following article was published in The Advertiser. A very small portion that is relevant to this section has been selected.

Fifty years ago last week, on December 1, 1948, the body of a fully clothed man was found on the beach at Somerton. It was to become one of the most baffling cases in the State's history and today remains unsolved. Jeff Turner reports.

Beach keeps its grim secret

Years later, the man in Room 21 at the Strathmore Hotel on North Tce became the centre of attention. The hotel's receptionist at the time was puzzled by a well-dressed, well spoken guest.
Her suspicions saw her order a search of his room. It contained only a black medical case, containing what seemed like a hypodermic syringe. The mysterious guest checked out the day before the body at Somerton was discovered.
Why had she not come forward at the time, when police were crying out for clues?
"I had no conclusive proof," she said in a newspaper interview in 1982. "And hotel receptionists had to be discreet."
Mysteries thrive behind such discretions – much to the frustration of police, unable to close the bulging file on just one body at Somerton beach.

Other witnesses also gave evidence of their examinations of the deceased, and made references to scars. There is no evidence or references to needle marks.
I do not place much credence on this information. I am more than satisfied that every hotel, boarding house and other similar establishments in Adelaide and other areas were checked by police during the relevant period. Also, during the relevant period and consistently thereafter there was sufficient information and photographs published to prompt credible witnesses to come forward.

Robert 'Nugget' Walsh – still missing

On 25 May 1987 a well-meaning family sent the following letter to the police in regard to a person who was suspected of being *the Unknown Man*.

After 39 years we were amazed to see the Case of *the Unknown Man*, coming up again, the body on the Somerton Beach. He was boarding two doors away from our house with Mr & Mrs Dolly Thompson when Mr Thompson died he still stayed there. Our children were ... (ages excluded)....years old at the time. They can remember the case & the man. He was known as Bob Walsh a respectable clean dressed & likeable fellow. He did not speak much of himself only he had been on sea boats & mending sails. He went from Mrs Thompsons & when it came up in the paper 39 years ago & showed the body all around Morgan knew it was him. Mrs Thompson was most concerned & with Mrs S. Runholm from Morgan as well went to Adelaide to identify the body. Apparently they did not get anywhere. It was stated at the time he died of natural causes. Since then Mrs Thompson & Mrs Runholm have passed on. If this can be of any help to you. We would be very pleased.

I am satisfied that Walsh was not *the Unknown Man* because he does not match the description and he allegedly had a tattoo. The last known information relative to his whereabouts makes reference to his possible travel to an interstate location.

Missing person – Adam Wren

In September 2001 I received a letter from a man living in Victoria who was making inquiries on behalf of the family of Adam William Corrie Wren, who was born in Cumberland, UK in 1908. Wren came to Australia as a sponsored migrant and landed in Melbourne in 1927. He was involved in a farming accident and had a substantial scar down his left shin. For the past five years the man had been trying to locate Corrie Wren on behalf of his brother who was 91 years of age and still living in Cumberland. He had a photograph of Wren taken when he left the UK for Australia. His family lost touch with him in about 1939 when he worked on several properties in the Murray River area. The person thought there may be a possibility that Wren could be *the Unknown Man*.

On 26 September 2001, I contacted this man and after a discussion we came to the conclusion that Wren was not *the Unknown Man*. If any information of substance becomes available it will be passed to the inquirer.

Forensic opinion sought

On 20 July 2001 I compiled an overview of the circumstances surrounding the death of *the Unknown Man*. I attached statements and copies of the evidence in respect to the cause of death and poisons by the medical people who appeared at the inquest. These were used in my discussion with the three forensic pathologists at the Forensic Science Centre.

A few days later I received the following letter from Dr Ross James MB BS FRCPA: Thanks for the opportunity to read this material. I enjoyed seeing some views from more than 50 years ago which makes strange reading today.

Dr. Dwyer looked at over 10,000 cases before he retired although I am unsure when he started. He was not a trained pathologist and knew almost no histology but nevertheless he was very experienced at post mortems. He was rarely caught short of a cause of death, almost never did any histology and would only do toxicology if he couldn't avoid it. On the other hand the publicity given this case meant that he would have given it his best shot. He has done histology on the spleen because of its enlarged size (although he didn't either weigh or measure it) but admits he couldn't make sense of the appearance of the pigment. I wouldn't exclude a natural death on the basis of Dr Dwyer's post mortem. All kinds of diagnosis from undiagnosed leukaemia to myocarditis could have been present. Even with much better facilities these days we still have about 5% of our cases where we can't find the cause of death.

The toxicology issues are interesting. While their methods were rather primitive their chemists were good at finding both the limited (much more so than nowadays) drugs available for therapeutic purposes. Poisons were much more widespread and widely used and it is fair to say that their chemists would be more adept at finding them than our present chemists. Of course they were quite unable to identify organic poisons (the 'exotic poisons') and we wouldn't be much better now. There simply isn't any evidence supporting drugs or poisons and it is unlikely that a contemporary examination (given that he was embalmed and presumably buried) of exhumed material would provide the answer.

The only people to emerge well are the investigating police and it is no fault of theirs that we are no wiser as to the identity or cause of death. In 1948 the cultural diversity so common now was beginning and displaced Europeans arrived from all over.

Prof JB Cleland, the professor of pathology, was the brother of Tom Cleland who became Coroner before KB Ahern. Prof Cleland was actually a microbiologist with a particular interest in botany but he did go down to West Tce and do a few post mortems. He used to stretch out the removed intestine and go along sniffing for poisons.

I hesitate to say it but if the same case turned up on Somerton Beach today we may well achieve precisely the same results as they did 50 years ago.

Sulphur dioxide – poisoning

The following information was received in November 2004 from a man with expert qualifications and experience in the field of food preservation (food safety and nutrition). The following selected passages are from that information:

> As I said, I may be way off base with my idea, but on reading Sunday's article and that his last meal was a pasty and that he died of cardiac arrest, it made me think of my days as a senior ... (excluded – personal details) ... Some concerned the misuse or overuse of the preservative sulphur-dioxide. This salt is found in several forms, sulphite, bisulphite and meta-disulphite. When mixed with water (moisture) the gas sulphur-dioxide is liberated ... (excluded lengthy details relating to school and rotten egg gas) ... and this gas assists in the inhibition of micro-organisms, can be used as a bleaching agent (e.g. pickled onions) and as an anti-enzymic agent (prevention of oxidative browning of certain fruits and vegetables), so it was and still is, widely used in the food industry for the above reasons. When one cuts up potatoes and if they are then exposed to air, a blackening occurs, which makes them unacceptable to consumers, hence it was common practice of smallgoods bakers to use sulphur-dioxide in diced potatoes and other vegetables for pasty manufacture and was referred to in the trade as 'chip whitener'. It is still used in sausage manufacture and until a few years ago was still allowed in minced-meat in SA. In minute amounts, it is relatively harmless, particularly as cooking of foods tended to dissipate the gas. However, certain individuals, such as asthmatics, can be sensitive to it and react slightly when others do not even notice it themselves. In larger amounts, especially for we sensitive ones, it can be highly dangerous, the symptoms of such an intoxication being respiratory distress, cardiac arrest and death. I remember several cases we investigated which concerned excessive levels in cooked pastys, one which resulted in hospitalisation of 2 people, the amount present being so great that dissipation did not fully take place ... (excluded confidential details re prosecution) ...

Later, the SA Food & Drugs Act Regulations permitted the addition of this preservative to diced potatoes for the purpose of further processing and I think that the limit was in the vicinity of 50 ppm.

... and I may be leading you up a garden path. However, I am sure that the salt would have been used in 1948 and therefore the likelihood exists that your man may have been an unfortunate victim. If it was a weekday, the pasty may have been fresh indeed and the levels of the preservative quite high. Whether or not the pathologist would have suspected this or whether analytical techniques of the time might have divined it from his stomach contents is beyond my competency.

Every contribution is appreciated.

EPILOGUE

I will briefly summarise selected items that are relevant to this investigation:

The police investigation
Some parties have levelled a number of criticisms towards the police investigation generally and to individuals specifically. The case management of a file in 1948 cannot be compared to the facilities that are currently available to capture, record, index and archive files. Today the case management facilities are structured to ensure that every step of an investigation is recorded in the format of delegated inquiries and individual results, miscellaneous information, listings of all exhibits, every statement and any other snippet of information that is obtained, irrespective of the relevance to the investigation. Under the 'discovery rules' that currently apply the file is made available to relevant bodies. To make a comparison of 1948 to current times one only has to compare the request from the Coroner shown in the section relating to 'Coronial Inquest', where he specifically nominated the witnesses he required to appear before him. Apart from those statements no others are available today. This does not indicate that other statements were not taken and available at the time. It is quite possible that certain information has been culled, separated or lost from the file during the time it has floated through the system. This problem is experienced by other government departments during the same period. Taking all factors into consideration we are probably fortunate that some information currently exists.

I have no doubt that certain individuals made their own personal notes relative to the various inquiries they made. These notes were probably retained by individuals until they retired, whereby they may have destroyed them or when they died, the notes were of no interest to descendants who then destroyed them. There was no obligation on any individual to retain their own personal notes or jottings. This same procedure applied to other participants involved in the investigation who were not police officers. I have sought answers to a number of general questions and specifically to the following questions:

Was the copy of the Rubaiyat found in the vehicle ever shown to the nurse?

Was the nurse re-interviewed after Boxall was located with his copy?

Did the nurse indicate to police that someone contacted her in Melbourne and was her mother interviewed?

Did the nurse state that someone made inquiries with her neighbours in Adelaide and were they interviewed?

Olive Neill nominated seeing a well-dressed gentleman wearing a dark suit and hat at the scene. Was he identified or interviewed?

Was the piece of paper containing the words 'Tamam Shud' and the copy of The Rubaiyat with the torn page deliberately placed in positions where they would be located and linked to the deceased, the nurse and the 'code'?

I have been unable to provide answers to these questions despite identifying the witnesses who may have been able to provide the answers. Every means available to the police and the media were made both nationally and internationally to identify the deceased.

THE UNKNOWN MAN

The sources of some of his clothing were identified but laundry marks and names written on other items of clothing were never identified to this country.

Taking into consideraton all of the circumstances, the facilities available in the late 1940s and the inquiries made to solve what appeared to be a suspicious death I believe the police investigations were of a high quality. A number of factors associated to the deceased, including the location of air-mail envelopes, the reference to a past 'sun tan' on his legs and the fact that he was never identified questions his country of origin. Without any evidence to the contrary I am of the opinion that if he was a resident of Australia he was a very recent arrival.

The final coronial inquisition

On 14 March 1958 the final inquisition was issued by Coroner Thomas Erskine Cleland under the Coroners Act, 1935:

> AND I, the said Justice of the Peace and Coroner, do say that I am unable to say who the deceased was. He died on the shore at Somerton on the 1st December, 1948. I am unable to say how he died or what was the cause of death.

Because the investigation of a suspicious death falls under the jurisdiction of the coroner, perhaps he should have at some stage subpoenaed the major witnesses who were eventually identified to give evidence.

Culling policies

In a newspaper article on 1 August 2009 the following information was printed.

> In a fit of spring cleaning in the late 1980's, police threw out the man's clothes and belongings, including a suitcase left in the locker at Adelaide Railway. Inside the case were personal items that included a dressing gown and slippers, thread, four ties and some stencilling equipment. The original copy of Rubaiyat of Omar Khayyan had been lost by police some time in the 1950's.

It is most unfortunate that these items are now not available. Hindsight is a wonderful thing but many 'culling' policies dictate in all organisations. If storage facilities are not available old exhibit items and hardcopy files must go. I have no idea what happened to The Rubaiyat in question.

Means of support

Many references have been made about the cleanliness of *the Unknown Man* and the neatness and quality of his clothing. This in itself would suggest that he was a man of some means. I have been advised that his two pairs of trousers were made from good quality cloth and were quite expensive for the times. Specific references and inquiries were made by the police to locate a hat and an overcoat because these items would be accepted attire for a man to possess during those times. Inquiries were made to locate an overcoat because it was thought that this item may contain the missing cloak room ticket or his means of support. Although a wallet was not a common item to possess in those times, a Cheque Book or a Bank Pass Book was.

I believe 'The Unknown Man' had access to a means of support other than that located in his possession. One can only speculate whether he donated it, gave it away, discarded it or it was stolen.

Body substitution

The witness who approached the police on 5 December 1959 and presented evidence of being with a group and sighting a man carrying another man along Somerton Beach at 10 p.m. on 30 November 1948 questions a number of theories.

The credibility of this witness is not in question. Whether or not the person sighted by witnesses at 7 p.m. on the foreshore was later substituted by the placement of the deceased I am at a loss to produce an acceptable explanation. The witness believed the two sisters moved interstate and may have married. Unfortunately the witness has since died. Despite extensive inquiries I cannot establish the original location of the 'dugouts'. I have only located one reference to the 'dugouts' made in 1931. The article made reference to bathing dress, women, police involvement and the customs adopted by some men and women of lolling about the sands too close together. An elderly gentleman advised me that prior to road development the area between Whyte Street and Bickford Street consisted of sand hills. He also advised that holes were dug into the sand hills by beach goers, and an area near Bickford Street was known as the 'bunkers'. In 1956 I was aware of many 'caves' dug into the sand hills on the foreshore between Somerton Beach and Glenelg. I am continuing my inquiries to identify and locate the other witnesses in this matter.

Current status

Over the years I have amassed a considerable amount of information in respect to this incident and the story is constructed from but a mere selection of those details. Wherever possible I have sought to protect the identities of people and their families who could be the subject of unwarranted attention.

I continue to analyse aspects of this incident. I have identified people who I thought may be able to assist me, only to find they have since died. I have inquiries in place and I am currently awaiting the results. There are also a substantial number of inquiries on my list that require interstate and overseas attention. Although time and financial restraints hamper my progress, my research and investigations will continue.

Ila ghairi 'n-nibayat

(Ad infinitum)

Fingerprints

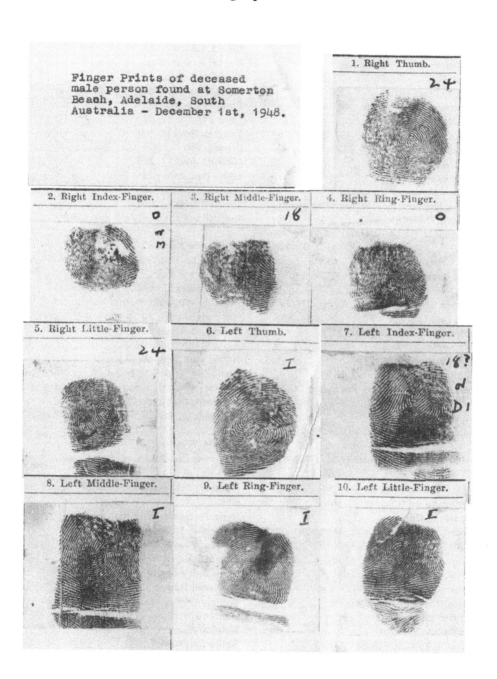

Finger Prints of deceased male person found at Somerton Beach, Adelaide, South Australia - December 1st, 1948.

1. Right Thumb.
2. Right Index-Finger.
3. Right Middle-Finger.
4. Right Ring-Finger.
5. Right Little-Finger.
6. Left Thumb.
7. Left Index-Finger.
8. Left Middle-Finger.
9. Left Ring-Finger.
10. Left Little-Finger.

Index

South Australia

Western Australia

THE UNKNOWN MAN